CROWNS

IN A CHANGING WORLD

ALSO BY JOHN VAN DER KISTE

Historical biography

Frederick III: German Emperor 1888 (Alan Sutton, 1981)
Queen Victoria's family: a select bibliography (Clover, 1982)
*Dearest Affie: Alfred, Duke of Edinburgh, Queen Victoria's second son,
1844–1900* [with Bee Jordaan] (Alan Sutton, 1984)
Queen Victoria's children (Alan Sutton, 1986; large print edition, ISIS, 1987)
Windsor and Habsburg: the British and Austrian reigning houses 1848–1922
(Alan Sutton, 1987)
Edward VII's children (Alan Sutton, 1989)
Princess Victoria Melita, Grand Duchess Cyril of Russia, 1876–1936
(Alan Sutton, 1991)
George V's children (Alan Sutton, 1991)
George III's children (Alan Sutton, 1992)

Music

Roxeventies: popular music in Britain 1970–79 (Kawabata, 1982)
The Roy Wood story (A & F, 1986)
Singles file: the story of the 45 r.p.m. record (A & F, 1987)
Beyond the summertime: the Mungo Jerry story [with Derek Wadeson]
(A & F, 1990)

CROWNS

IN A CHANGING WORLD

*The British and European
Monarchies 1901–36*

JOHN VAN DER KISTE

ALAN SUTTON

First published in the United Kingdom in 1993
Alan Sutton Publishing Ltd · Phoenix Mill · Far Thrupp · Stroud
Gloucestershire

First published in the United States of America in 1993
Alan Sutton Publishing Inc · 83 Washington Street · Dover · NH 03820

British Library Cataloguing in Publication Data

Van der Kiste, John
Crowns in a Changing World: Britain and the European Monarchies 1901–36
I. Title
940.5

ISBN 0 7509 0266 3

Library of Congress Cataloging in Publication Data applied for

Jacket picture: Coronation lunch for George V and Queen Mary *by J. Solomon,
Guildhall Art Gallery, Corporation of London (Bridgeman Art Library,
London).*

Typeset in Times 11/12.
Typesetting and origination by
Alan Sutton Publishing Limited.
Printed in Great Britain by
The Bath Press, Bath, Avon.

Contents

Illustrations

Nos. 20 and 61 appear by gracious permission of Her Majesty The Queen
(copyright reserved); Nos. 17, 24, 40, 47, 48 and 52 by kind permission of the
Commemorative Collectors' Society, 25 Farndale Close, Long Eaton,
Nottingham; No. 34 by kind permission of Huis Doorn. The remainder are from
private collections.

Foreword

The thirty-five years during which King Edward VII and King George V reigned over Great Britain saw a considerable change in the European monarchies. The British Crown and its standing with its subjects altered but little, while many of the thrones which seemed powerful or safe enough in the Europe of 1901 had gone by 1936. This book is an attempt to trace the personal relations between both Kings, and their royal and imperial contemporaries on the continent during that period which saw the last flowering of *l'ancien régime*, the Great War, and the rise of the dictators.

In accordance with usage generally employed by newspapers of the time, monarchs are referred to by their titles throughout, even after abdication. For example, the German Emperor William II is still 'the Emperor' and not 'the ex-Emperor' during his years of exile.

I wish to acknowledge the gracious permission of Her Majesty The Queen to publish material from the Royal Archives, Windsor. I am indebted to the following copyright holders for permission to quote from published sources: Collins Harvill (*Uncle of Europe*, by Gordon Brook-Shepherd); and Constable & Co. Ltd (*King George V*, by Harold Nicolson).

As ever, I am particularly grateful to my parents, Wing Commander Guy and Nancy Van der Kiste, for their constant encouragement, help, and advice throughout. I am also indebted to Charlotte Zeepvat, Theo Aronson, Steven Jackson of the Commemorative Collectors' Society, and John Wimbles, for their assistance and for providing invaluable sources of information which I would otherwise have missed; and to the staff of Kensington and Chelsea Public Libraries, for allowing me access to their excellent biography collection. Last but not least, my thanks to Stella Clifford, whose ideas were largely responsible for this book in the first place; and to Rosemary Aspinwall, for her work in helping to see this volume through to publication.

John Van der Kiste

Prologue

Throughout much of her reign Queen Victoria, the 'Grandmother of Europe', had connections through family ties with almost every other royal court in Europe. When she ascended the throne in 1837, her Uncle Leopold had been King of the Belgians for nearly six years. Her eldest daughter Victoria, Princess Royal, was married in 1858 to Prince Frederick William of Prussia, destined to reign all too briefly as German Emperor. Her eldest son Albert Edward, Prince of Wales, who succeeded her as King Edward VII, married Princess Alexandra of Denmark in 1863, thus becoming the son-in-law of the Prince destined to become King Christian IX before the end of the year. Her second son Alfred, Duke of Edinburgh, married Grand Duchess Marie, daughter of Alexander II, Tsar of Russia, in 1874. Three other daughters and one younger son also married German royalty, although less prestigiously; while in her latter years, two granddaughters married the heirs to the thrones of Greece and Roumania, and another the Tsar of Russia.

Inevitably, the consequent divisions in national loyalties involved them in heated arguments during several of the numerous albeit brief wars that took place in Europe during the second half of the nineteenth century. The Queen was entirely German by blood, with Hanoverian, Brunswick, Saxe-Coburg and Mecklenburg-Strelitz ancestry. Marriage to a first cousin from the house of Saxe-Coburg Gotha had merely reinforced the German element, and her sympathies always remained overwhelmingly German. If that nation's interests clashed with those of other countries, there was never any doubt which cause must always be upheld.

Early proof was given of this in 1864 when the Princess of Wales' father King Christian IX was embroiled in war with Bismarck's Prussia over the duchies of Schleswig and Holstein. The bellicose Otto von Bismarck, appointed Minister-President of Prussia in 1862, was determined to raise the standing of Prussia in Germany through a ruthless policy of 'blood and iron', and Denmark was his first victim.

The protests of Princess Alexandra, and her husband, that the duchies belonged to her father, carried no weight with the Queen. British public opinion sided firmly with the Prince and Princess, but while the government remained neutral during the short military campaign, Queen Victoria made no secret of her personal support for Germany and her eldest daughter and son-in-law. Family arguments at Windsor became so impassioned at one stage that the harassed matriarch firmly forbade any mention of Schleswig and Holstein in her presence.

Bismarck tested the Queen's Teutonic partisanship to its limits two years later when he turned on Austria, Prussia's ally in the Danish war, in order to drive her out of the North German confederation and establish Prussian supremacy in Germany. Among the German states taking Austria's side on the battlefield was the Grand Duchy of Hesse, whose heir presumptive, Louis, was married to Queen Victoria's second daughter Alice. Though the Queen was so angered by Bismarck's behaviour that she was tempted to express her support for Austria, Hesse and their allies, or at least help mediate between both factions, the swift, crushing Prussian triumph put paid to such hopes and ideas. Unpalatable as it was, Prussian hegemony had to be accepted.

In January 1871 the German Empire rose from the ashes of her conquest of the French Second Empire. Queen Victoria's son-in-law was now His Imperial Highness the German Crown Prince Frederick William, and her eldest daughter Crown Princess. It was a very different united Germany from the liberal nation fondly envisaged by the optimistic late Prince Consort when he had helped to arrange his favourite child's marriage in 1858, but still his widow did her utmost to show Germany preference even though it no longer retained her affection. It had long been her hope, as it had been that of the Prince Consort, that England would march together with a strong, united, friendly and liberal Germany. While the latter was ruled by Bismarck, now Imperial Chancellor, and reigned over by the ageing, ineffectual Emperor William I, such hopes were slim.

Yet she bided her time for the promise of a new era that would surely follow the accession of her son-in-law as Emperor. Though Crown Prince Frederick William had proved himself on the field of battle as a popular, conscientious leader, he detested the brutality of war and rejected the reactionary politics of Bismarck. Through his mother, born Princess Augusta of Saxe-Weimar, he had inherited liberal and artistic ideas which ran directly counter to those of the Prussian ruling class. During his reign Germany would surely be a very different nation from the warlike empire which his father and chief minister had made it; and his mother-in-law looked forward to that day almost as eagerly as he and the Crown Princess did.

Germany's march of conquest ceased for a time with the defeat of France in 1871. Yet she was not the only continental power which threatened the peaceful co-existence of European nations during Queen Victoria's reign. At the height of the Balkan crisis in 1878, there was the probability of war between Russia and England, and she threatened to abdicate rather than let the Tsar into Egypt. English public opinion relished the prospect of war with Russia, much to the alarm of the Duke and Duchess of Edinburgh, neither of whom were popular in England. The royal family were profoundly relieved when the Congress of Berlin found a solution to Balkan problems that satisfied the main powers of Europe for another generation.

The personal and political sympathies of the Prince of Wales did not run parallel to those of his mother. Despite his German ancestry he was less enamoured of the Teutonic element. The ponderous, earnest upbringing which he had endured at the hands of his father in league with the family mentor, Baron Christian von Stockmar, and a succession of unbending tutors, had been interrupted briefly by a visit to the Second Empire of Emperor Napoleon III and Empress Eugenie in August 1855, when he was a boy of thirteen. The charisma of the court at Versailles and the capital of Paris, added to the lavish hospitality of their genial hosts, had inspired a lifelong affection in him for France and everything French, very different from the tedium of life at home. These Francophile instincts survived the collapse of the French Empire. Though France became a Republic in 1870, the French way of life altered but little. Family loyalty to his mother and eldest sister did not prevent him from growing increasingly contemptuous of German militarism – as indeed did the reluctant German war hero Crown Prince Frederick William himself.

Their hopes of a brighter German dawn were sadly to be thwarted. As royalties, among them the Prince of Wales, flocked to Berlin for a dinner celebrating the Emperor William's ninetieth birthday in March 1887, the hoarseness in the Crown Prince's normally resonant voice was evident as he delivered a speech congratulating his father. Frequently unwell in winter, he was suffering from an unusually persistent heavy cold, which later proved to be an early symptom of throat cancer. When Emperor William died almost a year later, his son – now Emperor Frederick III – was in San Remo, where he had been sent to escape the rigours of the bitter German winter. Already his illness had taken such a turn for the worse that it was evident he could survive for only a few months at the most. Returning to Germany, he reigned for ninety-nine days before dying in June 1888.

He was succeeded by his eldest son, William, whose education and upbringing owed everything to the principles of Prussian autocracy and militarism, and nothing to the more enlightened ideals of his parents. The influence of Bismarck and his followers at the Berlin court had driven a wedge between Crown Prince and Princess Frederick William, whom they held in contempt, and their eldest son, whose differences with his parents had hardened into antipathy. Within weeks of his accession as Emperor William II, it was evident that any hopes for a liberal Germany had died with Frederick III.

By 1894 the major powers of Europe were divided into two armed camps. On one side was the Triple Alliance of Germany, Austria, and Italy; ranged against them was the Dual Alliance, signed that year by Russia and France. It was this balance of power on the continent with which Britain was confronted at the dawn of the twentieth century. British statesmen had to decide whether to remain aloof and maintain the traditional policy of 'splendid isolation', or throw in their lot with Germany or France. Lord Salisbury, who was three times Prime Minister between 1886 and 1902 and simultaneously held the office of Foreign Secretary for much of his tenure at 10 Downing Street, spoke of the dangers of being allied to one or other of the continental camps; Britain, he warned, would incur 'novel and most onerous obligations'.

Attempts to reach an understanding with Germany had been made regularly, if somewhat inconsistently, by senior politicians and the aristocracy over the preceding thirty years. The ill-feeling engendered by Emperor William's callous behaviour towards his widowed mother during the first few months of his reign had long since subsided. The Prince of Wales had been endlessly provoked by his nephew's behaviour, from public slights such as 'the Vienna incident' in September 1888 at which the Emperor insisted that a planned visit by the Prince of Wales to the Austrian capital should be cancelled as he himself was going to be there at the same time, to private arguments such as his passionate interest in yachting at the annual Cowes Regatta, his endless complaints about the British sporting rules, and his obsession with proving the superiority of German yachts and yachting prowess. Yet he appreciated, as did the more far-seeing members of the government, that

Royal family group at Coburg on the wedding day of the Grand Duke and Duchess of Hesse and the Rhine, 19 April 1894. Seated, left to right: William II, German Emperor; Queen Victoria; the Empress Frederick; with Princess Beatrice of Saxe-Coburg Gotha and Princess Feodora of Saxe-Meiningen in front. First standing row, left to right: Prince Alfred of Saxe-Coburg Gotha; Nicholas, Tsarevich of Russia; Princess Alix of Hesse and the Rhine; Princess Louis of Battenberg; Princess Henry of Prussia; Grand Duchess Vladimir of Russia; the Duchess of Saxe-Coburg Gotha. Second standing row, left to right: the Prince of Wales; Princess Henry of Battenberg; Princess Philip of Saxe-Coburg Kohary (facing her left); the Duchess of Saxe-Meiningen; Princess Aribert of Anhalt; the Duchess of Connaught. Two standing rows at back, left to right: Prince Louis of Battenberg; Grand Duke Paul of Russia; Prince Henry of Battenberg; Prince Philip of Saxe-Coburg Kohary; Count Mensdorff; Grand Duke Serge of Russia; Crown Princess and Crown Prince Ferdinand of Roumania; Grand Duchess Serge of Russia; Grand Duke Vladimir of Russia; the Duke of Connaught; the Duke of Saxe-Coburg Gotha

rapprochement with Europe was of major importance. And this should start with Germany, who was traditionally Britain's ally on the continent.

This necessity was reinforced in 1899 when long-simmering disputes in South Africa resulted in open conflict. The Boer War, in which the mighty British Empire was ranged against the small but unexpectedly tenacious Boer Republic of President Kruger, brought home to Britain on the outbreak of hostilities that she had no allies in Europe, let alone powerful sympathizers. As a result the pro-German faction in the government, headed by the Colonial Secretary, Joseph Chamberlain, took the initiative.

The German Emperor paid a brief private visit to Windsor and Sandringham in November 1899, and shortly after his departure Chamberlain made a speech at Leicester declaring that no far-seeing English statesman could be satisfied with England's permanent isolation; 'the natural alliance is between ourselves and the German Empire'. It was received coldly by Chancellor Prince Bernhard von Bülow, who commented in the Reichstag a fortnight later that 'the days of Germany's political and economic humility were over', and that in the new century the nation would 'either be the hammer or the anvil'. His remarks were soon followed by a German navy bill, which in effect doubled the navy programme of 1898 and amounted to the creation of a German High Seas Fleet. The threat was plain for the British Admiralty to see.

Bülow was particularly suspicious of the Prince of Wales, and feared the effect his accession would have on the balance of power in Europe. 'With his innate dislike of the German Empire and of everything German,' the Chancellor later noted in his *Memoirs*, 'with his strong predilection for France, Paris, and the French, would he, in the event of war, remain loyal and cheerfully true to the alliance with us?'[1]

None the less there were still regular attempts at bringing about a rapprochement between the two countries, at official and unofficial levels. The last one of the Victorian era was initiated by the Duke and Duchess of Devonshire, who invited Baron Eckardstein, First Secretary at the German Embassy in London, to talk politics with the Duke and Joseph Chamberlain. After dinner on 16 January 1901 the Baron had a long conversation with both men, and on his return to London reported that the Cabinet were evidently of the opinion that Britain's days of isolation were over. She intended to look for allies, either the Triple Alliance, or Russia and France. She evidently preferred the former to the latter, but if a permanent relationship with Germany proved beyond grasp, the Dual Alliance it had to be.

That same week – almost the very same day that British government and aristocracy were working behind the scenes – the final curtain began to fall on Queen Victoria's 63-year reign. The Duke of Connaught was in Berlin, representing his mother at celebrations for the bicentenary of the Prussian monarchy. On 17 January he received a telegram announcing that the Queen had suffered a mild stroke while at Osborne, and it was thought advisable to send for her surviving children. When told, the German Emperor proposed to return with him to England. The Duke, who was on better terms with his imperial nephew than anybody else in the family, tactfully suggested that he might not be welcome. But William insisted that his proper place was by his grandmother's side. Throughout the journey to England he seemed full of high spirits, explaining to his suite that 'Uncle Arthur is so downhearted we must cheer him up.'

The Prince of Wales came to Osborne on 19 January. Next day he returned to London to meet the Emperor, and both arrived on 21 January. They took their place at the hushed vigil with the Queen's other children (except the Dowager Empress Frederick, who was too ill to make the journey from Germany) and several grandchildren. By the time the Emperor arrived, her mind was wandering, and she mistook him for his long-dead father. She died at half-past six on the evening of 22 January.

Those who had known the new King, during his long apprenticeship as Prince of Wales, had little doubt that he would play a considerable role in ending British isolation from Europe. None of his ministers could rival his experience

The arrival of William II, German Emperor, at Charing Cross Station, and his reception by the Prince of Wales and the Duke of York, 20 January 1901. From a drawing by Richard Caton Woodville

Arthur, Duke of Connaught

and knowledge of European courts during the previous thirty years; and his close family relationship with many of the crowned heads of state on the continent gave him an immediate advantage over the politicians, which it was inevitable he would exploit to the full.

1 'What a fine position in the world'

Queen Victoria's death brought her children and her eldest grandson emotionally much closer than they had been for a long time. Among King Edward's first actions were to make Emperor William a Field-Marshal, his brother Prince Henry a Vice-Admiral of the Royal Navy, and to confer the Order of the Garter on Crown Prince William.

The German Emperor stayed in England for the funeral, which took place at Windsor two weeks later with a formidable galaxy of European royalties in attendance. As well as the Emperor and the new King, Edward VII, King Carlos of Portugal, King George of Greece, King Leopold II of the Belgians, the Austrian heir Archduke Francis Ferdinand representing the Emperor Francis Joseph, the Duke of Aosta representing King Victor Emmanuel III of Italy, and the Crown Princes of Denmark, Sweden and Roumania, all followed the coffin on its final journey. Afterwards King Edward's equerry, Sir Frederick Ponsonby, was shocked to see the German Emperor and two of the Kings standing by the fireplace at Windsor Castle puffing on their cigars. Nobody, he noted, had ever smoked there before.

King Edward was touched by his nephew's respectful and uncharacteristically subdued behaviour, writing to the Empress Frederick (7 February) that his 'touching and simple demeanour, up to the last, will never be forgotten by me or anyone'.[1]

On the last day of his stay in England, the Emperor attended a luncheon at Marlborough House given by the King. The latter proposed his nephew's health, and the Emperor replied:

> I believe there is a Providence which has decreed that two nations which have produced such men as Shakespeare, Schiller, Luther, and Goethe must have a great future before them; I believe that the two Teutonic nations will, bit by bit, learn to know each other better, and that they will stand together to help in keeping the peace of the world. We ought to form an Anglo-German alliance, you to keep the seas while we would be responsible for the land; with such an alliance, not a mouse would stir in Europe without our permission, and the nations would, in time, come to see the necessity of reducing their armaments.[2]

It was the kind of bombastic speech, combining sincerity and eloquence, in which he excelled. The King must have listened with mixed feelings. Yet shorn of its more fanciful embellishments, it expressed much of the idealism so close to the hearts of the Emperor's father and maternal grandfather.

For several days after his return to Germany, the Emperor remained under the spell of England, continuing to wear civilian clothes in the English fashion instead of the military uniforms in which his entourage were accustomed to seeing him. Even when officers from his local regiment at Frankfort came to dine, he continued to do so. Some of them felt that he was obsessed with 'Anglomania', and were disturbed by the sight of their Supreme War Lord spending so much time attired like an English country gentleman. It was the same Emperor who had irritated his military entourage while staying at Windsor in November 1899, pointing to the Tower every morning and exclaiming with admiration, 'From this tower the world is ruled.'

Later in February King Edward travelled abroad as sovereign for the first time. Court mourning ruled out any question of a state visit to foreign capitals for several months. This was purely a private journey to see his sister Vicky, the Empress Frederick, for what he realized might be the last time. He was not in the best of tempers after arriving to the sound of a 'hymn' being sung repeatedly, which on enquiry turned out to be the Boer national anthem. His irritation was compounded when, having requested an absence of formalities on this occasion, he was received at Frankfurt station by the Emperor in the uniform of a Prussian general.

The weather was unusually fine that February, with snow-clad pine forests around Friedrichshof glistening in the winter sun. Cheered by her brother's visit, the Empress ventured into the fresh air for the first time for several weeks, asking her attendants to wheel her in her bath-chair along the sheltered paths in the castle park as she and her three younger daughters talked to the King.

Among the King's entourage was Sir Francis Laking, his Physician-in-Ordinary for several years. The King hoped he might be able to persuade the German doctors to give the Empress morphia in larger doses than they had done so far. However, they viewed his presence with hostility. Ever since Morell Mackenzie had been summoned to take charge of the then Crown Prince Frederick at the onset of his final illness, Berlin had been deeply suspicious of British medical science. The previous autumn Queen Victoria had repeatedly offered, even begged, the Emperor to receive Laking, but he had refused; 'I won't have a repetition of the confounded Mackenzie business, as public feeling would be seriously affected here.'[3]

According to Ponsonby, dinner in the evening was hardly lively, though the Emperor kept small-talk going. His two youngest sisters, Sophie, Crown Princess of the Hellenes, and Princess Frederick Charles of Hesse-Cassel, would cut in tactfully 'if the conversation seemed to get into dangerous channels, and one always felt there was electricity in the air when the Emperor and King Edward talked'.[4]

One night the superstitious King was alarmed to find that thirteen people had sat down to dinner, but later he told Ponsonby it was all right as Princess Frederick Charles was *enceinte*. In fact time was to reveal that they had been

The Empress Frederick, 1900

safer than he thought, for in May the Princess gave birth to a second set of twins.

All the same, the atmosphere was gloomy. It would have taken more than the aftermath of one family bereavement and the imminent expectation of another to bridge the gap completely between uncle and nephew, in character and temperament so very different, both fellow-monarchs of two mutually suspicious nations.

One evening, Ponsonby was asked to go and see the Empress Frederick in her sitting-room. He found her propped up with cushions, looking 'as if she had just been taken off the rack after undergoing torture'. After she had asked him various questions about England, and the South African war, she said that she wanted him to take charge of her letters and take them back to England with him. She would send them to his room at one o'clock that same night. It was essential that nobody else – least of all the Emperor – should know where they were. Before she had time to explain any further, the nurse interrupted them and, seeing how tired the Empress looked, asked him to go.

Ponsonby had assumed that she meant a small packet of letters which he would have no difficulty in concealing. At the appointed hour, there was a knock on the door and, to his horror, four men came in carrying two enormous trunks, wrapped in black oilcloth and firmly fastened with cord. From their clothes, he suspected that the men were not trusted retainers but stable-men, quite unaware of the boxes' contents. At once, he guessed that the Empress wanted the letters published at some future date. Smuggling them away from

Friedrichshof would be easier said than done, as the place was probably full of secret police. Hoping for the best, he marked them 'China with care' and 'Books with care' respectively, and had them placed in the passage with his luggage later that morning. As a member of the King's suite, however, he was in little danger of having his luggage searched, and nobody queried anything as the soldiers carried them out of the castle later that week. The dying Empress' wish was fulfilled; her letters remained safely in English hands.*

With his other imperial nephew, Tsar Nicholas II, King Edward's relations were more harmonious. When Tsar Alexander III had died in November 1894, the Prince of Wales had impressed all fellow-guests as well as the inexperienced new Tsar by his tactful presence at the funeral. The Russian press had been loud in its praise of him, though, like the late Tsar and his family, they had never liked Queen Victoria herself. On his return to England the Prince was congratulated by the Prime Minister, Lord Rosebery, on his 'good and patriotic work in Russia', and for rendering 'a signal service to your country as well as to Russia and the peace of the world'.

Married to her granddaughter Princess Alix of Hesse, Tsar Nicholas had been almost unique among the Romanovs in his respect for and devotion to Queen Victoria. He and the heavily pregnant Tsarina were unable to attend the funeral in February, and they were represented by his brother, Grand Duke Michael ('Misha'). In his letter, the Tsar sent his condolences (29 January 1901):

> My thoughts are much with you & dear Aunt Alix now; I can so well understand how hard this change in your life must be, having undergone the same six years ago. I shall never forget your kindness & tender compassion you showed Mama & me during your stay here. It is difficult to realize that beloved Grandmama has been taken away from this world. She was so remarkably kind & touching towards me since the first time I ever saw her, when I came to England for George's & May's wedding.
>
> I felt quite like at home when I lived at Windsor and later in Scotland near her and I need not say that I shall for ever cherish her memory. I am quite sure that with your help, dear U(ncle) Bertie, the friendly relations between our two countries shall become still closer than in the past, notwithstanding occasional slight frictions in the Far East. May the new century bring England & Russia together for their mutual interests and for the general peace of the world.[5]

Even so, a few months later the Tsar did not hesitate to bring up the vexed subject of the Boer War (4 June):

> Pray forgive me for writing to you upon a very delicate subject, which I have been thinking over for months, but my conscience obliges me at last to speak openly. It is about the South African war and what I say is only said as by your loving nephew.

* See p. 167ff.

You remember of course at the time when the war broke out what a strong feeling of animosity against England arose throughout the world.

In Russia the indignation of the people was similar to that of the other countries. I received addresses, letters, telegrams, etc. in masses begging me to interfere, even by adopting strong measures. But my principle is not to meddle in other people's affairs; especially as it did not concern my country.

Nevertheless all this weighed morally upon me. I often wanted to write to dear Grandmama to ask her quite privately whether there was any possibility of stopping the war in South Africa. Yet I never wrote to her fearing to hurt her and always hoping that it would soon cease.

When Misha went to England this winter I thought of giving him a letter to you upon the same subject; but I found it better to wait and not to trouble you in those days of great sorrow.

In a few months it will be two years that fighting continues in South Africa – and with what results?

A small people are desperately defending their country, a part of their land is devastated, their families flocked together in camps, their farms burnt. Of course in war such things have always happened & will happen; but in their case, forgive the expression, it looks more like a war of extermination. So sad to think, that it is Christians fighting against each other!

How many thousands of gallant young Englishmen have already perished out there! Does not your kind heart yearn to put an end to this bloodshed?

Such an act would be universally hailed with joy.

I hope you won't mind my having broached such a delicate question, dear Uncle Bertie, but you may be quite sure that I was guided by a feeling of deep friendship & devotion in writing thus.[6]

Much as the King liked his nephew, family affection was tempered by a ready awareness of his shortcomings. 'Nicky', he felt privately, was 'as weak as water', surrounded by a determined wife and intimidating uncles with far stronger characters than his. Perhaps he suspected that the Tsar was voicing their opinions rather than his own; and he was naturally anxious to explain his country's position (19 June):

I can quite understand that it was in every respect repugnant to your feelings to write to me relative to the S. African war, though great pressure has been brought to bear upon you. I am also most grateful to you for the consideration you have shown during the incessant storm of obloquy & misrepresentation which has been directed against England, from every part of the Continent, during the last 18 months! In your letter you say that in the Transvaal 'A small people are desperately defending their country'! I do not know whether you are aware that the war was begun, and also elaborately prepared for many previous years by the Boers, & was unprovoked by any single act, on the part of England, of which the Boers, according to International Law, had any right to complain. It was preceded a few days before by an ultimatum from the Boers forbidding England to send a single soldier in to any part of the vast expanse of South Africa! If England had quietly submitted to this outrage, no portion of her Dominions throughout the world would have been safe. Would you have submitted to a similar treatment? Suppose that Sweden after spending years in the accumulation of enormous armaments & magazines had suddenly forbidden you to move a single Regt. in Finland, & on your refusing to obey had invaded Russia in *three* places, would you have abstained from defending yourself, & when war had once begun by that Swedish invasion would you not have felt bound both in prudence & honour to continue military operations until the enemy had submitted, & such terms had been accepted as would have made such outrages impossible?

If the S. African Campaign were to be stopped at this moment & England were to recall her troops, we should have no security whatever that the Boers would not commence anew the accumulation of armaments & magazines to prepare for another invasion of British territory. It is not extermination that we seek; it is security against a future attack, & against this, after our experience of the past we are bound to provide.[7]

With this forthright statement of facts there was no arguing, and although the war was to continue for another few months, the King did not hear again from his nephew on the subject.

South Africa was not the only territory outside Europe in which Britain, Germany and Russia had a particular interest at the turn of the century. For several years the Foreign Offices at St James and St Petersburg had regarded it as almost inevitable that both Empires would clash sooner or later over affairs in the Far East. Though the European powers were supposed to be acting in concert, Russia had for some time pursued an ambitious assault on northern China, in defiance of her European allies, and there seemed little hope of amicable relations being established between them.

His friendship for the Tsar did not prevent the King from suspecting the worst from hostile aims of Russian diplomacy, and he watched Russia's aggressive action in China with anxiety. The situation had been inflamed the previous year by the outbreak of the Boxer rebellion in China, a nationalist movement provoked largely by the way in which the European powers had been annexing territory. The threat to Europeans in the area intensified in June 1900 after the murder of the German minister in Peking, Baron Clemens von Ketteler. Emperor William inspected a German relief force before its departure for China, and in his speech his tongue ran away with him as he declared that 'as a thousand years ago, the Huns, under King Attila, gained for themselves a name which still stands for a terror in tradition and story, so may the name of German [*sic*] be impressed by you for a thousand years on China, so thoroughly that never again shall a Chinese dare so much as to look askance at a German'.[8]

The effect of the German effort, if not the speech (which would come back to haunt the Emperor a few years later), and of a declaration a few days later that 'no great decision would be made in the world in future without the German Emperor', was somewhat impaired by the appearance of an allied force under Russian command (without a German contingent), which relieved Peking in August, six weeks before the German relief force arrived. The Emperor was disappointed and furious with the Tsar for wanting to make peace. Despite an Anglo-German agreement in October 1900 preventing further territorial partition, to which Russia and Japan consented, by the time of King Edward's accession there was still a state of mutual suspicion. The King wrote to Lord Lansdowne (21 March 1901) of his fears 'that the Russians have got quite out of hand in China, and that the Emperor seems to have no power whatever, as I am sure the idea of war between our two countries would fill him with horror'.[9]

The German Emperor was impatient for a solution to the Chinese business, and equally suspicious of the other powers, writing to the King (10 April):

What a time the Powers are wasting over the Chinese Indemnity Question! Money must be paid by the 'Heathen Chinee' that is the rule of war all over the world, as he was the cause of the outlay, so the sooner we agree the better! I have already named my sum, & hope that if the British Government takes the same lines we will soon see clear. I am very grieved to hear from friends & private sources that the French & Russians are playing a violent game of intrigues at London, which has so far proved successful, that actually some members of the Government have given vent to the apprehension, that I was siding with the Russians against England! A most unworthy & ridiculous imputation.[10]

Yet the King's thoughts that spring and summer dwelt less on affairs in China, than on his sorely-tried elder sister whose sufferings would soon be over. He booked his usual suite of rooms at Homburg in mid-August, so as to be near Kronberg if she should suddenly take a turn for the worse, and the Emperor arranged to be in the area as well. Despite the severity of the Empress' illness, a rather inconsistent series of statements about her 'quite satisfactory' condition gave the impression that she would survive at least another six months.

The Emperor was taking part in Kiel week when he wrote to his uncle, from on board the yacht *Hohenzollern* (24 July 1901):

I hasten to answer the letter you so kindly sent me with enquiries about Mama's health as far as I am able from here. When I saw her last on the 15th she suffered much pain & was very low in spirits & downcast. She often grew quite despondent & sometimes gave way to despair. This however not so much from the pain she is suffering – so the doctor says – but on account of the utter helplessness in which she is placed by this horrid illness. The left arm is under ice in a sling & the whole position of her poor, very emaciated body is a bend forward. The right arm & hand is much freer than it was in February & she is able to write letters & notes again. She also says herself that she has more appetite than before, & the fine weather enables her to stay out for the greater part of the day. She takes interest in everything that is going on in the world, politics as well as literature & art, & even is taken up to the 'Burg' to superintend the details of the furnishing of the hall & rooms. But it takes a long time to move poor mother as the pain is awful for instance in settling her in her carriage, of course the same on her sofa or bed; & she frequently gives vent [to] most piteous cries which the violent spasms of pain wrench from her. The sight is most pitiful to me considering that one is utterly unable to give the slightest help. Morphia is being used in long intervals & larger doses & does her much good giving her rest for several hours. The vital organs up to this date are quite free & in no way attacked, so that there is nothing to inspire any momentary anxiety; if things go on like this at present the doctors think that it may go on for months even into the winter possibly. It is fearfully distressing![11]

Fortunately for the patient and her family, the doctors' estimates proved rather wide of the mark. On 4 August it was officially announced that her strength was 'fading fast', and her children were summoned to her bedside at

Friedrichshof. King Edward was on his yacht in the Solent, preparing for Cowes week, when the news reached him. He and Queen Alexandra made arrangements to leave immediately for Germany, but before they could depart they were told on 5 August that the Empress had died early that evening.*

They reached Germany four days later, Queen Alexandra taking a wreath of flowers from Windsor, the home which her dead sister-in-law had loved most of all. The Emperor saw fit to reproach his uncle for lack of feeling in having taken so long to arrive. Such an unwarranted rebuke was hardly calculated to improve the atmosphere.

When he arrived in Germany, the King had a memorandum containing confidential notes on Anglo-German relations from his Foreign Secretary, Lord Lansdowne. Meeting the Emperor at Homburg on 11 August, King Edward was still overwrought at his sister's death and anxious to avoid risk of any controversial talk at such a solemn time. He therefore handed the Emperor his minister's 'confidential' notes. Perhaps he did so on impulse; maybe it was done in a genuine moment of absent-mindedness. No harm was done, but Lansdowne was horrified. Thoroughly pro-German and, unlike Lord Salisbury, his predecessor at the Foreign Office, firmly in favour of ending British isolation, he resented his sovereign's somewhat unconstitutional insistence in taking foreign policy initiatives. As Ponsonby observed with masterly understatement, Lansdowne 'may have been a little jealous at the King being supposed to run the foreign policy of the country'.[12]

The Empress was buried on 13 August at Potsdam. Her son could not resist another chance to create a military display out of the occasion. The streets were lined with German troops, while King and Emperor both wore the blue uniform of the Prussian Dragoon Guards, marching at the head of the procession to the Friedenskirche. Perhaps the Emperor, who had treated his mother so callously, was making amends by trying to bury her like a reigning Empress; but King Edward found the constant jingle of Prussian spurs at such a solemn time distasteful.

He was relieved to escape next day for Homburg, where he was to take his annual cure, as well as indulge in other pastimes such as an automobile ride with another nephew Ernest, Grand Duke of Hesse. Ernest had nothing of the inflated dignity or military airs of the German Emperor, whom he loathed, and the King found him much more congenial company.

Ten days later King and Emperor met again at Wilhelmshohe for what were intended to be serious political talks. They got off to a bad start with the King uncomfortably squeezed into his Prussian Colonel-in-Chief uniform. Although the court was still in mourning for the Dowager Empress, and he had expected no pomp and ceremony, he was greeted with a parade of fifteen thousand

---

* After the Empress' death, it was rumoured that Friedrichshof was surrounded by troops, who searched and ransacked every room, presumably searching for the letters with which she had entrusted Ponsonby six months earlier. It has since been asserted that the only soldiers to arrive at the Schloss were twelve NCOs of her own regiment, the Royal Prussian Fusiliers, who were to act as bearers at her funeral, and that no search ever took place.

German troops. By 2 p.m., when the last salute on the march past was taken, he was starving.

The Emperor had been well briefed on Maltese affairs, and said how interested he was to hear that the British government was considering granting the Mediterranean island its independence. As the King had heard no such thing, he was most indignant with his ministers at home afterwards. That had been beyond the King's control; but the confusion over the Anglo-German discussions was not. The memorandum which he had carelessly handed to the Emperor had dealt with matters which could best be discussed between both sovereigns, such as the indemnities sought by Western governments from China after the Boxer revolt,* and relations with the ruler of Kuwait, where it was believed the Germans were planning to build a terminus for a trans-Caspian railway. The King was uninterested in such details, which were primarily the concern of his ministers and civil servants. In any case he was in no frame of mind to make concessions to his nephew. The talks achieved nothing, and the exhausted King arrived back at his hotel in Homburg, heartily thankful that this trying meeting was over.

After two weeks at Homburg, invigorated by his 'cure', he left for Copenhagen on 6 September. Here he joined a family party hosted by his widowed father-in-law, King Christian IX. Also present were Queen Alexandra, her sister the Dowager Tsarina of Russia, their brother King George of the Hellenes, and Tsar Nicholas II. At Copenhagen the King received a deputation congratulating him on his accession, and in reply to the address he alluded to his first visit to Denmark nearly forty years earlier, and to the great affection he had always had for her people.

On 19 December Count Metternich, the new German Ambassador in London, was officially informed by Lansdowne of the British government's decision to suspend Anglo-German talks. It was a step the British Cabinet took with some regret, but they had good reason to do so. The state of public opinion in Great Britain and Germany was not favourable to such a policy; the government had no wish to alienate France or Russia by involvement with the Triple Alliance; and it was necessary to avoid irritating the United States, displeased by the hostile and provocative attitude which Germany had adopted towards the Monroe Doctrine.

King Edward agreed wholeheartedly with this decision, though whether Crown or Cabinet was more determined to abandon their efforts at an alliance was hard to say. Although he regarded foreign policy as his own preserve to an extent, he was content to leave certain decisions to his ministers. Whereas Queen Victoria would have considered Anglo-German alliances paramount, and defended if not actively encouraged her ministers to this end until late in life, King Edward had no such sentimental attachment to their German ancestry. More than his mother, he appreciated the impossibility of trying to remain on friendly terms with the Second Reich. And even more than his mother,

---

* The Boxer Protocol was signed in September. Among the conditions was the payment of an indemnity of around $333 million to be paid over a period of thirty-nine years.

whenever he looked at Germany he was perpetually haunted by the ghost of 'Fritz'. Had Emperor Frederick III not been struck down by cancer, it would have all been so different.

Despite this formal end to negotiations, the Emperor would not give up hope. Although he seemed to be obsessed with trying to score off his uncle much of the time, he found it impossible to sever the emotional ties that bound him to Britain. When the King found the Highland suit that had belonged to Frederick III and had just been discovered while clearing out an accumulation of long-untouched possessions at Windsor Castle, he sent it to Emperor William as a Christmas present.

The latter was delighted, and his letter (30 December) from Berlin thanked his uncle for 'the most touching and splendid gift':

> . . . it was a most kind thought, and has given me great pleasure – I well remember having often stood as a Boy before the box in Papa's dressing Room, and enviously admiring the precious and glittering contents. How well it suited him, and what a fine figure he made in it. I always wondered where the things had gone to, as dear Mamma never said anything about them and I had quite lost sight of them. The last time I wore Highland dress at Balmoral was in 1878 in September when I visited dear Grandmamma and was able to go out deerstalking on Lochnagar . . .
>
> The vanishing year has been one of care & deep sorrow to us all, and the loss of two such eminent women as dear Grandmamma and poor Mother is a great blow, leaving for a long time a void which closes up very slowly. Thank God that I could be in time to see dear Grandmamma once more, and to be near you and Aunts to keep you in bearing the first effects of the awful blow.
>
> What a magnificent realm she has left you, and what a fine position in the world. In fact the first 'World Empire' since the Roman Empire. May it always throw in its weight in the side of peace and justice – I gladly reciprocate all you say about the relations of our two Countries and our personal ones; they are of the same blood, and they have the same creed, and they belong to the great Teutonic Race, which Heaven has entrusted with the culture of the world; for apart from the Eastern races, there is no other race left for God to work His will in and upon the world except ours; that is I think grounds enough to keep Peace and to foster *mutual* recognition and *reciprocity* in all that draws us together, and to banish everything which could part us. The Press is awful on both sides, but here it has nothing to say for I am the sole arbiter and master of German Foreign Policy and the Government and Country *must* follow me even if I have to 'face the music'. May your Government never forget this, and never place me in the jeopardy to have to choose a course which would be a misfortune to both them and us.[13]

The good wishes of such lofty phrases were greatly at variance with the speeches being made by both countries' statesmen. In October Chamberlain had spoken at Edinburgh, making an incidental if tactless reference to the behaviour of the German army in the Franco-Prussian war, leading to a renewed outburst of anti-British feeling in the German press and Reichstag. On 5 January 1902 he gave a totally harmless address, in which omission of any mention of Germany at all suggested to the Emperor that the British government regarded Germany as a negligible quantity. Bitter remarks were made in the Reichstag about the British Army in South Africa.

The Emperor thanked the King (6 January 1902) for planning to send the Prince of Wales to Berlin for his birthday, 'which is a most kind idea & gives me great pleasure – we shall do everything to make him like his stay'. In the same letter he announced that he was offering the King the rank of Honorary Admiral in the German Navy; 'it would be a great honour to our Navy though of course it cannot boast of any History or Tradition like the immense Fleet at your command. Still much work is done, and with God's will, & the officers & men have shown that their mettle is good, so that I may venture the proposal without transgressing too much on your leniency.'[14]

However, the King was so incensed by the constant attacks on himself and Britain from others in Germany that he threatened to cancel his son's visit to Berlin. The gesture had been meant 'as a personal mark of affection & friendship towards you', he explained to the Emperor (15 January), but after reading the violent anti-English speeches made in the Reichstag, 'I think that under the circumstances it would be better for him not to go where he is liable to be insulted, or to be treated by the Public in a manner which I feel sure no one would regret more than yourself.'[15]

Salisbury and Lansdowne both thought that this letter would cause a grave breach between the two countries, and would have preferred the King to take the easy way out by pleading a sudden diplomatic illness on his son's behalf. Too honest for his ministers' liking, the King brushed the suggestion aside; but the Emperor decided to ignore the letter, pretending it had been 'mislaid'. The King was therefore persuaded to reconsider, and agreed to let his son go after all.

On his arrival in Germany the Prince showed considerable tact. Harbouring none of his parents' prejudices against the Emperor, he found it easier to take the latter's mercurial, over-assertive behaviour in his stride. Among others, he met Bülow with whom, according to the terse account in his diary afterwards, he 'had a long talk'.

Bülow later recalled,* rather more expansively, that he gave His Royal Highness a brief summary of Anglo-German relations from the time of the Crimean War, alluded to the sympathy felt throughout Europe for the Boers, but insisted that the Emperor would never pursue an anti-English policy as long as England made it possible for him to pursue friendly relations. To this, the Prince of Wales replied that:

> My father asks me to tell you that he considers you as his friend, now as before. He is convinced that you are just as concerned about maintaining friendly relations with England as he is concerned about maintaining friendly relations with Germany. He only asks you to avoid future recriminations regarding the past and to

---

* Bülow's *Memoirs*, published in 1930–1, have to be treated with caution. The publishers of the English version emphasized that the work was 'presented solely as an historical document', and that they did not 'in any way associate themselves with the views or the criticisms expressed by the author as regards persons or events'. After reading them the Emperor William, by then an exile in Holland, remarked that it was the first instance he knew of a man committing suicide after he was dead.

see that the family letters written in connection with my visit here for the Kaiser's, my cousin's, birthday celebrations, are not made public. We must forget the past and strive only to be friends in the future.'[16]

It was with satisfaction that the Emperor could send a telegram to King Edward, the day after his birthday, that the Prince had left that morning, 'and we were very sorry to have to part so soon from such a merry and genial guest. I think he has amused himself well here.'[17]

Yet the whole business had merely reminded the King how necessary it was to treat his sensitive nephew's susceptibilities with the greatest care, and to avoid giving any offence. When an Anglo-Japanese alliance was formally signed in London on 30 January 1902, he suggested to Lansdowne that there should be no delay in informing the German government and Emperor officially. He knew that the Emperor liked to be the first man in Europe to be told about anything new and important, and he was keen to avoid the charge that his government was forging any secret alliances. His tact was rewarded by a delighted message of congratulation from his nephew.

This treaty was none of the King's making. It had been forged by the government, who were impatient to end British isolation, and saw in Japan a country which had mutual interests in blocking Russia's expansionist aims in Asia. It was not a direct and automatically binding military alliance, as the only circumstances under which English and Japanese soldiers would fight together would be in the case of a general war between the Great Powers fought in Asia. In the event of a Russo-Japanese conflict, England would remain strictly neutral.

King Edward regarded himself more as one of the European brotherhood of monarchs than a player on the world stage, and initially he had been unenthusiastic about the prospect of an alliance with a country so distant as Japan. However, he would shortly realize the dream of a lifetime by linking England with France, in a manner which would owe nothing to his ministers.

For the first few months of 1902 King Edward's main concern was with his forthcoming Coronation. Revelling in the trappings of monarchy, the pomp and ceremony, far more than his mother ever did, he could hardly wait. It was to take place as soon as conveniently possible after peace with the Boers in South Africa had been signed; shortly after the treaty was sealed in May, it was announced that the Coronation would be on 26 June.

Early in the year the German Crown Prince had visited England privately. While staying at Blenheim Palace, he allegedly fell in love with Gladys Deacon, an eighteen-year-old American. Soon after his return home, the liaison was eagerly seized on by the European press. One paper suggested that he had given her a valuable ring which was his confirmation present from Queen Victoria. The Emperor was outraged by his son's indiscreet behaviour, and as this English sojourn was the first time he had publicly strayed from the straight and narrow, his father decided that the example of his decadent Uncle Bertie was to blame. As a result he refused to allow the Crown Prince to represent him at the

William II, German Emperor, in the uniform of the Death's Head Hussars, c. 1903

Coronation in June, sending Prince and Princess Henry instead. They stayed at Wimborne House, and the ever-sensitive German press considered that they were not being treated with due importance as Prince Henry was not the eldest son of a sovereign. It was an 'affront' not shared by the Prince himself; in fact, he and his wife were welcomed most warmly by their British relatives, who found them far more genial than the touchy Emperor and sanctimonious Empress.

Within a few days of their arrival, the Prince and Princess were at the centre of a trifling argument over precedence in a carriage ride for a reception at Buckingham Palace. Prince Henry had arranged that he and his suite would take the first three carriages, while Field Marshal Count von Waldersee, who was representing the German Army, should have the fourth. Waldersee flatly refused to go last, and a heated quarrel between a handful of Prussian officers was only settled when the ever-diplomatic Sir Frederick Ponsonby promised to arrange the matter with Prince Henry. More easygoing than the rest of his countrymen, he replied that it did not matter to him in the least whose carriage went first.

Meanwhile the King had been taken seriously ill, yet he insisted that he would turn up at Westminster Abbey on the day even if he dropped dead as the crown was being placed on his head. Appendicitis was diagnosed by his worried doctors, who warned him firmly that, unless he was operated on at once, he would almost certainly die. The day after the reception at Buckingham Palace, the Coronation was postponed, and the foreign representatives returned home. Luckily the operation was successful, and a slimmer, fitter, more relaxed King was crowned at the Abbey on 9 August.

While he was convalescing, the German Emperor almost caused a diplomatic incident by allowing his tongue to run away with him. In July an American-owned yacht cruising in Norwegian waters put in at a harbour where the imperial yacht *Hohenzollern* was moored, with the Emperor on board. He was happy to pay the Americans a visit on their yacht. Barely had he been introduced to them by name before he began a political tirade, directed mainly against England. Lord Salisbury, who had recently resigned the premiership, was not a man, 'just a protoplasm'; and if he, the German Emperor, behaved like his Uncle Bertie, then the German people would soon get rid of him.

Unfortunately for him, one of the yachtsmen, a former attaché in the British Diplomatic Service, promptly reported the incident to the Foreign Office in London. As King Edward was still recovering from his operation at the time, he was not informed; had he been, it would probably not have surprised him. Yet it served to remind officials in London of the German Emperor's instability and fickleness as a potential ally who could barely be trusted.

The German Emperor's next visit to England was beset by complications which nearly resulted in its cancellation. Three of the leading Boer generals came to London in August to try and negotiate more favourable terms in the peace settlement signed at Pretoria in May. Having come and failed, they attempted to capitalize on Boer sympathies throughout the rest of Europe. At once the Emperor announced that he would receive them, although his advisers warned him that to do so would produce repercussions in London. The German government was still unwilling to risk jeopardizing any chances of an improvement in Anglo-German relations. King Edward wrote to the British Ambassador in Berlin, Sir Frank Lascelles, that for the Emperor to receive the Boer generals, so soon before his visit to England, would be very unpopular, though at this stage he wished 'no further comment'. The subtle warning was taken, and the Emperor cancelled the audience. Pro-Boer public feeling in Berlin made him hesitate, and he decided he would receive them after all, though he would have them presented by Lascelles. Further objections from his ministers, and from London, made him think better of it, and the generals returned to South Africa empty-handed.

Plans therefore went ahead for the Emperor's autumn visit, timed to coincide with the King's sixty-first birthday on 9 November. As discussions for an alliance between their countries had been placed in abeyance, King Edward was determined to keep the visit as much of an informal family business as possible. The Emperor would be invited to Sandringham, where the King traditionally celebrated his birthday, for a few days' shooting, and the King resolved that he would make no appearances at Windsor, London, or indeed outside his Norfolk estate for the duration of the German visit. Moreover, he expressed a wish that the Emperor should not bring too large a suite, and would he please wear civilian clothes.

The King took personal charge of all details. As a concession to his nephew's hopes of meeting some of the ministers, even though there was no question of any formal negotiations, the King invited Arthur Balfour, his Prime Minister, and other senior Cabinet members up to Sandringham at various times. This naturally gave rise to wild speculation in the press in London and Berlin, one English newspaper suspecting that an Anglo-German treaty was about to be negotiated secretly in Norfolk, and warning the King against 'subordinating the political interest of England to family affection'.

They need not have worried. The King and ministers took great care to keep politics at arm's length and be non-committal to the Emperor, even when the latter provocatively attempted to convince Balfour of Germany's need for a large fleet. Their days were largely occupied with shooting on the estate. Even here, though, the Emperor managed to irritate his host without really trying, as with his high leather boots, khaki-green cape and stiff dark hat, he always seemed to be in military uniform.

Moreover, he could never resist the temptation of showing his uncle how well-informed he was. When King Edward proudly showed him his latest motor car, of which he was very proud, the Emperor immediately asked whether it ran on petrol or any other fuel. The King had to admit that he had no idea, whereupon the Emperor held forth eloquently on the special merits of potato spirit for the internal combustion engine. A few days later he presented the King with a collection of glass bottles and chemical samples, which he had had despatched from Germany at top speed, to prove his point. How the King must have wished he had never mentioned his car in the first place.

When the Emperor departed on 20 November, he felt quite satisfied with his own treatment in England, but the King's reaction to his nephew's departure was summed up in the words he uttered as he saw him depart across the North Sea: 'Thank God he's gone!'

King Edward VII and Queen Alexandra

The signing of peace in South Africa had made the possibility of British rapprochement with France more likely. Disputes during the Boer War, and over other colonial areas during the closing years of Queen Victoria's reign, had not altered a belief among powerful French figures, notably at government and ambassador level, that an Anglo-French entente was advisable. The King was devoted to the Empress Eugenie, widow of Emperor Napoleon III, who had lived in exile at Farnborough since the fall of the Second Empire in 1871, and greatly respected her opinions. Yet he had remained on friendly relations with the French Republic, and despite her trials and tribulations she harboured no ill-will against her late husband's country. His quest for closer relations with France betokened no disloyalty towards her.

By the end of 1902 King Edward VII had started to plan an official visit to Paris. The idea owed everything to his own initiative, and it was devised with such secrecy that neither his ministers, nor Queen Alexandra, nor Sir Frederick Ponsonby, knew anything about it. He was anxious that his ministers should hear about it directly from him, when he felt it expedient to tell them; and he did not intend to alarm Emperor William II or Tsar Nicholas II by ill-timed disclosures. Earlier that year Sir Edmund Monson, British Ambassador in Paris, had been advised that the King planned to make an official visit to Paris, but the imminent Coronation and 'the many preoccupations which were descending upon him at this time' would lead him to postpone if not abandon the idea. That it was merely a postponement became obvious in January 1903, when Monson wrote to Lansdowne asking him if he could confirm any rumours regarding a royal visit to Paris. Lansdowne's reply has not survived, but as he knew nothing about it himself, it was unlikely that he could have answered any other way.

The first person to have any clear idea of what went on in the monarch's mind was his trusted confidant, Marquis Luis de Soveral, Portuguese Minister in London. Soveral was told in confidence that the King had been advised by his doctors to rest, and he intended to make a cruise in British waters. Political considerations, however, made it advisable for him to visit King Victor Emmanuel III in Rome and President Loubet in Paris. As relations between Britain and Portugal were so cordial, he planned to begin at Lisbon, to where he intended to sail directly.

King Carlos of Portugal was thoroughly flattered at the prospect of a visit from King Edward. There were only distant family ties between the Catholic house of Braganza and the Coburgs, but Portugal was traditionally Britain's oldest ally, notwithstanding fierce if short-lived colonial rivalry over South Africa in 1890. More recently, however, Germany had appeared as a new challenger to Portugal's declining imperial strength, and Portugal would welcome such a display of British solidarity. Moreover, the house of Braganza, unpopular at home, would gain in prestige from such a visit.

When advised of their monarch's plans, King Edward's ministers looked on the venture with some misgivings. They were naturally offended at not having been told beforehand; and they feared that he might be given a hostile reception in Paris. Lansdowne was particularly dismayed at the King's decision not to take a Minister of the Crown abroad with him. Technically this was in breach of the constitution. Even when Queen Victoria had paid private visits to Cannes or

Cimiez, a minister had invariably accompanied her. That King Edward should make an official visit to foreign capitals without making similar arrangements seemed an extraordinary use of the royal prerogative.

Undaunted, the King set sail from Portsmouth on board *Victoria and Albert* on 31 March 1903. Two days later he was rowed ashore at Lisbon in a state barge manned by eighty oarsmen, for a visit lasting five days. The first formal event of the programme was a reception in the Hall of the Geographical Society at which the King was presented with an address by both houses of the Cortes, and to which he gracefully replied alluding to the alliance which had bound their countries since the days of King Charles II. Later that week there was a pigeon-shooting match in the grounds of the Necessidades Palace, and a banquet followed by a gala performance at the San Carlos Opera House.

On 7 April the royal party set sail for Naples by way of Gibraltar and Malta. On arrival at Naples the King took a train to Rome, and thus became the first English sovereign to set foot there since King Ethelwulf in 855. He was met by King Victor Emmanuel III and a host of princes, nobles and notabilities.

As a Catholic monarchy, the Savoy dynasty had no connection with the British reigning house. While Prince of Naples and heir to the throne, Prince Victor Emmanuel had visited England in 1891 and shown some interest in the Prince of Wales' two unmarried daughters, though probably more out of duty and a desire to pacify his impatient parents, longing for him to provide the throne with a son and heir in the next generation, than out of any genuine feelings of affection. The Prince of Naples would have been no catch. He was taciturn, reticent, lacked self-assurance, and was barely five feet tall. Moreover, the newly-united kingdom of Italy was not regarded as a model of stability, and the idea never came to anything.

At a banquet given in his honour at the Quirinal Palace, King Edward made an improvised speech in which he referred to England and Italy as having 'often fought side by side'. Ponsonby, who was taking down his master's comments in shorthand, could only recall one such instance (when Sardinian troops assisted the British and French during the Crimean War), and prudently omitted the word 'often' in the text later handed to the press.

This was followed by a military review and several other formal events. The one gesture which, however, really set the seal on the success of his visit, came when the Kings were driving around the streets of Rome. They passed the Porte Pia, where Italian troops had entered the city in July 1870 as the climax to the campaign that had unified the Italian states into one kingdom. As they did so, King Edward had the carriage stopped, and then bared his head as a mark of respect. Greatly moved, King Victor Emmanuel came to the salute at his side.

The sun had literally shone on King Edward's visit to Italy. Shortly after, as the two Kings embraced on the platform of Rome railway station and King Edward departed, rain began to fall. Forty-eight hours later, when a somewhat jealous Emperor William greeted King Victor Emmanuel on the same platform, it was still raining. The street decorations, with British flags and coats of arms swiftly replaced by German ones, were drenched, and the Piazza where a military review was to take place was waterlogged and could not be used.

King Edward VII being received by King Victor Emmanuel III and Queen Eleanor at the Quirinal, 27 April 1903. From a drawing by Fred Pegram

Emperor William looked askance at his uncle's triumphal European progress. During the last two or three decades, Queen Victoria and Emperor Francis Joseph had only travelled abroad on private expeditions, while the Tsars rarely left Russia. The German Emperor had been accustomed to occupying the European stage himself. With the accession of his uncle, he had a rival. That King Edward had much more experience and knowledge of European courts, and was received so courteously wherever he went, showed the difference between the elderly but professional King and the brash, tactless Emperor.

The latter made a poor impression on the Italians. Even the German suite confessed to some embarrassment when they brought to Italy a troop of the imperial guard, all selected for their great height. To put the diminutive King Victor Emmanuel at such a disadvantage seemed unnecessarily offensive. So was the fact that, while King Edward had made a purely private call on the Pope, Emperor William paraded through the streets to the Vatican with a ceremonial escort of German soldiers, going out of his way to suggest that a papal audience was the chief aim of his visit, and the Italian alliance was of secondary importance.

King Edward's subsequent four-day visit to France was an even greater triumph. Disputes over Siam, Fashoda and South Africa had gravely damaged Anglo-French relations, but protests of *'Vivent les Boers!'* soon turned to *'Vive le Roi!'*. As Ponsonby pointed out later, any clerk at the Foreign Office could draw up a treaty, 'but there was no one else who could have succeeded in producing the right atmosphere for a rapprochement with France!'[18] A formal Anglo-French agreement was signed in April 1904, but few doubted that the King's visit to Paris had created the climate of trust and understanding between both nations which made it possible.

In Germany the significance was not properly appreciated. Bülow remarked to the German Emperor that he thought the King's wooing of the French might lead to a cooling of Franco-Russian relations and a drawing together of Russia and Germany. Baron Eckardstein was the first to suspect that it would more likely lead to a rival Triple Entente from which Germany would find herself excluded.

One month after the visit to France, Europe was shocked by a brutal palace coup in the Balkans. On the night of 10 June Serbian military leaders broke into the royal palace at Belgrade and murdered King Alexander and Queen Draga, as well as several ministers, army officers and others who had been loyal to them. The King and Queen, who had been deeply unpopular with their subjects, were butchered in a particularly revolting manner, their mutilated bodies thrown out on to the palace lawn below as if to prove beyond all possible doubt that they were dead. A hastily-convened provisional government in Belgrade elected Prince Peter Karageorgevitch, exiled in Geneva, as King. He was welcomed to his capital with rejoicing, which King Edward considered in poor taste.

At his insistence, diplomatic relations with Serbia were broken off, and the British Minister in Belgrade, Sir George Bonham, was recalled. While Austria and Russia were prepared to welcome the new regime, King Edward refused to

King Peter of Serbia

follow their example. As he pointed out, they were 'interested countries, and there was no need for England to recognise a government consisting of assassins'.[19]

On 25 June King Peter telegraphed the King of his election by the unanimous votes of the country's lawful representatives, and invited his recognition. Realizing that this placed him in a difficult position, King Edward's telegram of reply showed his ability to steer a middle course. While expressing his desire that the new reign would bring the people of Serbia the blessings of peace and prosperity, he hoped 'that Your Majesty will succeed in restoring the good repute of your country upon which recent events have left so regettable a stain'.[20]

He was adamant that diplomatic relations should not be resumed until all the regicide officers had been placed on the retired list. When the question of sending a diplomatic representative was raised the following year, he maintained that 'till they know how to behave themselves no British Minister should be sent to Serbia', and when King Peter's Coronation was held in September 1904, he made it clear that he did not wish to be represented in any way.

While King Peter feigned indifference to Britain's attitude, he secretly craved recognition, and both the Russian and Italian Ambassadors endeavoured to bring some influence to bear on King Edward. When they requested an audience at Windsor in June 1905, he remarked with regret that he could not comply with their suggestions. The assassination of King Alexander and Queen Draga, he insisted, had been so terrible that it had made a deep impression on British public opinion, which had not yet recovered from the shock, and would certainly not welcome a resumption of diplomatic relations with Serbia. Besides, there were personal reasons:

> Mon métier à Roi est d'être Roi. King Alexander was also by his métier 'un Roi'. As you see, we belonged to the same guild, as labourers or professional men. I cannot be indifferent to the assassination of a member of my profession, or, if you like, a member of my guild. We should be obliged to shut up our business if we, the kings, were to consider the assassinations of kings as of no consequence at all.[21]

The King kept to his word, and not until the principal regicides were placed on the retired list in May 1906 were diplomatic relations resumed.

2 'A *political* enfant terrible'

While King Edward VII's personal relations with Emperor William had never been easy, no such problems marked those between the King and the senior monarch of Europe, Emperor Francis Joseph of Austria-Hungary.

At the turn of the century there was no close affinity between the Protestant British court and its Catholic Austrian counterpart. As Prince of Wales, the King had been on excellent terms with the ill-fated Crown Prince Rudolf, and was deeply distressed after the Crown Prince had killed his mistress and committed suicide at his Mayerling hunting lodge in 1889. Though the personalities of both rulers had little in common, they respected each other as heads of state, and were justified in regarding themselves as the joint leading monarchs of their day. Although bound to the German Empire by time-honoured historical alliance as well as by monarchical solidarity, the Emperor privately had less respect for his headstrong young fellow-sovereign at Berlin. Moreover, King Edward had felt himself indebted to Emperor Francis Joseph since the latter had unexpectedly declared himself to be 'completely English' in his sympathies during the Boer War.

In September 1903, as a prelude to closer Anglo-Austrian relations, King Edward paid his first (and only) visit to Vienna as King. It was of personal rather than political importance, but still he could not resist doing things his way. At a banquet at the Hofburg on his first evening, he delighted the Emperor by announcing his appointment as Field-Marshal of the British Army. The gift itself was not unexpected, but the manner in which it was conferred startled everybody. Such appointments concerning foreign rulers were generally notified to their capitals and cleared with military authorities well in advance. King Edward, however, realized that it would be appreciated far more by its recipient if bestowed unexpectedly. He was right, for the Emperor was so astonished that he could talk about little else all the evening. The following morning, he sent personal telegrams of greeting to all fellow Field-Marshals in the British Army List.

'Nothing could have gone off better than my visit to Vienna', the King wrote to the Prince of Wales (5 September) on his return. 'The Emperor was as usual kindness itself – and I had an excellent reception from the people generally – who are not demonstrative but wonderfully orderly – No troops in the streets – as they are all at the manoeuvres.'[1]

Such close personal contact had been unknown in Queen Victoria's reign, and the King was determined to make it last. One way in which he felt this could be done was by consulting the Emperor on relatively uncontroversial topics of interest to him. When he asked the military attaché at the British Embassy in

King Edward VII and Francis Joseph, Emperor of Austria-Hungary, at the Opera, Vienna, 1 September 1903. From a drawing by Edward Cucuel

Vienna to enquire from the Emperor his views about arming cavalry with lances, the Emperor was flattered at his opinion being sought thus, and replied with a long letter. This paved the way for the regular interchange of ideas on other matters.

In the spring of 1904 the Prince and Princess of Wales visited Vienna. The Princess found the extreme formality of their reception at the Hofburg delightful though tiring, 'everyone so kind and the Emperor charming'. The Prince admitted afterwards succinctly that they had all been 'most kind and nice but my goodness this Court is stiff and they are frightened of the Emperor'.[2]

Like King Edward, King Victor Emmanuel of Italy understood the importance of personal contact between heads of state. Despite the Triple Alliance, he was keen to remind Berlin that it was not an exclusive contract where Italy was concerned. On a state visit to England, he had hoped to arrange matters so that his arrival would be in grand style on an Italian warship. None was available, but he was still given an appropriately grand reception.

On 17 November 1903 he and Queen Eleanor arrived at Portsmouth, staying for three days at Windsor Castle. While in England the King was awarded an honorary degree at Oxford University in recognition of his work as a numismatist. By the time of his accession to the throne in 1900, he already possessed one of the finest coin collections in Europe.

He and Queen Eleanor were also guests of honour at a grand banquet at St George's Hall, with the customary interchange of cordial toasts between both Kings. A command performance of *David Garrick* was staged at the castle theatre for their benefit, and King Edward took him shooting in the Great Park.

In the summer of 1904 the King planned a visit to Emperor William II, but announced that he would not travel to Berlin. Instead, he would take the royal yacht to Kiel and attend the regatta, and his entourage would include Captain Prince Louis of Battenberg.

Prince Louis, who was shortly to be promoted to Rear-Admiral, enjoyed a position vis-à-vis European royalty which put him on an even closer footing with his European contemporaries than the King. German by birth, he had served in the British Navy since the age of fourteen. Of his wife's three surviving sisters one, Irene, was married to Prince Henry of Prussia, the German Emperor's only surviving brother; another, Elizabeth, was married to Grand Duke Serge, uncle of Tsar Nicholas II; and the youngest, Alexandra ('Alicky'), was married to the Tsar himself. Louis was always willing to take part in, if not initiate, private discussions with his relatives on delicate subjects in which it would be less easy for the King to involve himself. On a public level, however, he hesitated to do so, as it demonstrated to his fellow officers and the world at large his special privileged links with the seats of power in Europe, and thus rendered his contacts less private.

When told in May that his presence at Kiel was requested during the summer, his initial reaction was to decline the invitation. To Lord Knollys, King Edward's secretary, he drew attention to the extreme inconvenience it would cause the navy for him to be absent in the middle of preparations for their manoeuvres, and also that it was 'very unpleasant' for him to visit Kiel in an official or semi-official position. His relationship to Prince Henry, his German name and origin, and his position at the Admiralty 'all combine to make it awkward for me. I very much doubt if the Emperor would appreciate meeting me there.'[3]

Such excuses were to no avail, and Louis reluctantly joined the entourage of naval figures accompanying His Majesty across the North Sea that June. The proceedings at Kiel witnessed the expected exchanges of decorations, dinners, speeches and meetings between both sovereigns. The Emperor good-humouredly chided Louis for having joined the British Navy instead of the German, and Louis reminded him that there had been no German Navy when he was fourteen years of age.

The Emperor was more prepared to confide in Louis than the King, and on the last night of their visit, Louis had a long private conversation with him. Both were anxious to preserve Anglo-German harmony, and Louis looked askance at the precarious position in which England was placed by the entente with France when the latter's ally, Russia, was being humbled by Japan in the Far East. He reported after returning to England that 'Now the clay feet of the Colossus over the Eastern border have been disclosed (the Emperor's actual statement to me) there will be no more coquetting with France.'[4]

The King never persuaded Emperor Francis Joseph to come to England. Such a visit for the latter was proposed early in 1904, but the Emperor had long since ceased to make state visits abroad as they were too much of a strain for a man of his age. In the spring Sir Francis Plunkett, British Ambassador in Vienna, informed the court at Buckingham Palace that His Imperial Majesty's doctors had advised against the 'fatigue and excitement of a visit to London'. Even his customary spring review at Vienna was not being held that year for similar reasons.

Unwritten rules of royal etiquette thus prevented King Edward from making a second visit to Vienna. A system of informal meetings between both sovereigns thus developed at the spas of Marienbad and Bad Ischl. The King preferred Marienbad to Homburg as the latter was part of the German Empire, and his presence there meant that the Emperor William was liable to pay sudden visits and arrange instant military parades. Homburg was therefore less relaxing, and the Emperor was so censorious about his uncle's morals and private friends that the King's August holidays there were ruined. At Marienbad, King Edward was left to his own devices. Although the spa dignitaries could not dream of letting His Majesty's arrival in their town go without some public reception, and although the public were sometimes too curious for comfort, Marienbad still proved more enjoyable than Homburg, and being out of the German Empire at least afforded him some protection.

The first of these Marienbad meetings took place in August 1904. Attired in his Austrian Field-Marshal's uniform, the King waited on the station platform with a small suite to greet the Emperor on his arrival. The city fathers had spared neither effort nor expense in decorating the town and hotel apartments for their distinguished guests, and both sovereigns drove to their respective quarters through triumphal arches festooned with Habsburg double-headed eagles and British lions and unicorns.

At dinner at the Hotel Weimar that night, informality was the key. There were no long tedious speeches, just short unrehearsed toasts between King and Emperor. Francis Joseph's entourage, who had always regarded him as formality personified, was impressed to see how relaxed their master appeared in the King's presence. The meeting was of no great historical significance, though courtiers and journalists tried to assume it was at the time. Rumours that the King took the opportunity to try and start weaning Austria away from her alliance with Germany were unfounded. Yet in the same way that he had helped to create a favourable political atmosphere with his very successful visit to France the year before, he was laying foundations for what could be harmonious relations between London and Vienna.

Among the other royalty who met King Edward there was 'Foxy' Ferdinand, Sovereign Prince of Bulgaria, a distant relation through another branch of the Coburgs. The smug, epicene ruler of Bulgaria was heartily disliked by most of his fellow sovereigns. Unpopularity did not bother him, if Crown Princess

Ferdinand, Prince of Bulgaria

Marie of Roumania was to be believed. As she told the author Hector Bolitho many years later, a few months before her death, Ferdinand was 'perhaps the only man you will meet who cherishes his enemies more than his friends. He is an actor. He enjoys each role that he plays – the benevolent uncle, the sinister old monarch, the scholar.'[5]

Prince Ferdinand had been low in King Edward's esteem since an unseemly incident at the beginning of the latter's reign. When told of Queen Victoria's death, he called at the British Legation in Sofia, to announce his intention of attending the funeral. First, though, he wanted to ensure that all precedence due to him as ruler of Bulgaria would be given. He had been treated, he felt, as a cadet member of the house of Coburg at her Diamond Jubilee festivities. A reply from London informed him tersely that this was not a fitting occasion to raise such questions, and no change could be made in the procedure already sanctioned. Taking it as a personal slight from King Edward, the touchy Ferdinand promptly cancelled all plans made for his journey to England, sent a deputation to represent him, and ostentatiously spent the day of the funeral celebrating the seventh birthday of his son Prince Boris, with a military review and gala luncheon to which the Russian envoy in Sofia was specially invited. King Edward was furious at this lack of respect.

Two years later Sir George Buchanan took up his post as Britain's new envoy in Sofia. He asked King Edward for a friendly message of greeting to pass to the Prince, but the King replied that, 'I have not forgotten the fact that he is my cousin, but that, as long as he continues his present two-faced policy, he cannot count on my support.'[6]

The King did not trust Prince Ferdinand, who was notorious for his constant changes in foreign policy. Bulgaria was technically under Turkish sovereignty, and the Prince set up pro-Russian or pro-Austrian administrations, depending on the prevailing attitude of Vienna and St Petersburg towards the Turkish Empire. Though it may have been astute politics, his perpetual playing off of one power against another was not calculated to gain him friends elsewhere in Europe, even if it helped him to keep his position. Moreover, he was suspected of encouraging discontent and rebellion by Macedonian subjects within the Empire under Turkish misrule; and his devious personality did nothing to dispel the impression.

In August 1904 King Edward and Prince Ferdinand came face to face at Marienbad, and a reconciliation of sorts was achieved. They enjoyed each other's company, and the King liked his witty conversation, though he found Ferdinand's 'unnecessary air of royal dignity' irksome. Ferdinand had his own private grievance; he did not forgive the King for helping himself one day to a dish of creamed mushrooms so liberally that very few were left for him.

Another small act of one-upmanship widened the gulf between both men. Ferdinand prided himself on being well-informed about events of the day, and was quite put out when the King told him about the Japanese naval victory over Russia, of which he had been informed by Henry Wickham Steed, *The Times* correspondent at Vienna.

By early 1904 European alliances were considerably strained as a result of the Russo-Japanese war, which had been caused largely by rivalry between the two powers in Manchuria. Japan had been a British ally since 1902, and King Edward was working towards better relations with Russia, which had been an ally of France for the last ten years. There was virtually no prospect of Britain sending her army to the Far East, but the war had put her and Russia on opposite sides politically.

In order to limit damage to international relations, King Edward despatched Count Benckendorff, Russian Ambassador in London, to St Petersburg. With him he took personal letters to the Tsar from the King, Queen Alexandra, and the Prince of Wales. The King was determined to assure his nephew that despite the Anglo-Japanese alliance, there was no intention of his country conspiring against Russia; British neutrality could be taken for granted. At the same time, the King appealed to President Loubet in Paris for understanding of Britain's delicate position.

In August 1904 there was Russian rejoicing at the long-awaited birth of an heir to the Tsar. After the Tsarina had presented him with four daughters, a son, Alexis, was born, and the Tsar asked his Uncle Bertie to be one of the godparents. The King was delighted to accept, and sent Prince Louis of Battenberg to attend the christening on his behalf.

After the ceremony Louis spoke privately to the Tsar about Anglo-Russian relations. He drew Nicholas' attention to certain individuals at the Russian court, notably his brother-in-law Grand Duke Alexander, who seemed determined to keep enmity between their countries alive by enforcing Russia's

Prince Louis of Battenberg

rights of a belligerent towards neutrals. The Tsar countered by complaining of Britain's refusal to allow the Russian reinforcing fleet coaling facilities. To this, Louis answered that it would be unjust to allow one belligerent any advantage over the other. Why, he asked, did Russia not come to terms with Japan at once. The Tsar replied that 'we must go on', deeming it inconceivable that 'the Russian Giant' could not in the end 'completely crush the impudent Japanese pygmy who had dared to attack Russia in so treacherous a manner'. He concluded with what Louis regarded as 'the extraordinary suspicion' that the Russian fleet at Kronstadt was in danger of attack from a flotilla of Japanese torpedo boats built, and their crews trained, in England.

Thanks to Louis' tact, they parted on the best of terms, and he was able to give King Edward a reassuring account of their conversations. The King was delighted with his work, writing to Princess Louis that there was '*no* one I could have chosen who would have fulfilled the Mission I entrusted *him* with – better than himself'.[7]

This timely Anglo-Russian mission helped to limit damage caused by the fiasco of the Dogger Bank incident later that year, which could have threatened severe repercussions.

On the night of 21 October 1904 the Russian Baltic Fleet, commanded by Admiral Rozhdestvensky, sailing from Reval on the Finnish coast through the North Sea en route to the Far East, opened fire on a group of small vessels which they assumed were Japanese torpedo boats operating from secret bases. Without stopping to see what they had hit, let alone trying to aid the survivors, the Admiral continued to lead his Fleet onwards. The victims, it turned out, had been British fishing trawlers. One vessel was sunk, others damaged, and several fishermen had been killed or injured.

Reaction in Britain was so violent that for several weeks war seemed imminent. No apology was received at first from Russia or the Admiral, and the Royal Navy was put on a war footing. Admiral Fisher had taken up his appointment as First Sea Lord only two days earlier, and was confined to his bed with influenza. Prince Louis was asked to act as his deputy, attending Cabinet meetings and conferences at the War Office as necessary, until Fisher was restored to health.

On the assumption that Britain would use force to prevent the Baltic Fleet from reaching the Far East, and also prevent Germany (still nominally considered a Russian ally) from assisting her, general mobilization of the navy was required, with every battleship in the North Sea on standby. The German Fleet would have to be shadowed, a prospect which Louis viewed with concern, as his brother-in-law Prince Henry was Commander-in-Chief of the Baltic station. None the less, he appreciated the importance of having an efficient fighting force on full alert as quickly as possible. He had never forgotten being told by his father, Prince Alexander of Hesse, how the unprepared Grand Duchy of Hesse had been overrun with such ease by Prussian forces in 1866.

The bellicose Lord Charles Beresford, Commander-in-Chief of the Channel Fleet, thirsted for action, and Louis knew he would have to bring some restraint to bear on him. Meanwhile both monarchs, who wanted war as little as did Prince Louis himself, took a temperate line in order to limit the damage. To Sir Charles Hardinge, British Ambassador in St Petersburg, the Tsar expressed his deep regret at the incident, and recognized that his Admiral had been guilty of unprofessional behaviour and an appalling blunder. He cabled his condolences to King Edward, regretting the loss of innocent lives while expressing a hope that the tragedy would cause no complications between their countries. In mitigation, if not very convincingly, he added that the Russian Fleet had received warnings that the Japanese were lurking among fishing smacks, and that the Admiral had suspected an ambush.

That the Admiral had not stopped to help the stricken trawlers was the most damning error of all, and at first King Edward and Lord Lansdowne were determined to press for the punishment of the Admiral and his officers. However, in the official Russian report, Rozhdestvensky insisted that he had been trying to hit a Japanese torpedo boat. While the British press called for Russian humiliation if not outright war, the King counselled caution.

An International Commission of Inquiry at The Hague conducted a full investigation into the incident, and four months later a settlement was concluded, with £65,000 damages being awarded against Russia. Yet ships of the China station kept a watchful eye when the Russian Fleet passed within sight of Singapore, in case of trouble. Many in Britain felt that justice had been done when the Russians reached Japanese waters in the spring of 1905, only to be virtually wiped out by the Japanese Navy at the battle of Tsushima.

With this, the threat posed to King Edward's Anglo-French policy in Europe by the war in the Far East receded. Before long, it came under renewed pressure as a result of an incident off the north coast of Africa.

For some months the Sultan of Morocco, Abdul Aziz, had shown increasing resentment of France on whose military, administrative and economic assistance he largely depended. The German Emperor was setting out on a Mediterranean cruise, and his senior ministers proposed that he should land at Tangier and promise the Sultan German support in maintaining his sovereignty. On 31 March the Emperor anchored off Tangier and went ashore, paraded through the streets on horseback, and delivered a theatrical speech in which he declared himself on the side of Moroccan independence, adding that his aim was, with the help of 'the brave pioneers of German commerce', to maintain and develop in a free Morocco, the interests of the German Fatherland. The German Empire, he said, had 'great and growing interests in Morocco'.

This speech was echoing round the world as he sailed for Gibraltar. While there he had a talk with Prince Louis of Battenberg, in which he alluded to his determination to prevent France swallowing Morocco as she had swallowed Tunisia.

In Europe it was tacitly accepted that Morocco was about to become a French protectorate, and the pact on North Africa featured prominently in the Anglo-French alliance. The King regarded the Emperor's conduct as a 'gratuitous insult' to Britain and France.

The German imperial family. Left to right: Princess and Prince Eitel Frederick; Prince Augustus William; Empress Augusta Victoria (seated); Crown Princess William; Prince Joachim; Crown Prince William; Emperor William II; Princess Victoria Louise; Prince Ethelbert; Prince Oscar. From a painting by Ferdinand Keller, 1906

The French Foreign Secretary, Theophile Delcassé, was 'positively cheerful'. He realized that this would put the new Anglo-French alliance to the test; 'nothing could have a more salutary effect on the English'. A German challenge, so close to the prized English possession of Gibraltar, would surely bring them closer still to France.

Complacency soon disappeared as pressure mounted in Berlin for a show of strength, and the threat of war hung in the air. Delcassé was criticized in the French Chamber for refusing to negotiate with Germany, and he resigned, although later he was persuaded to withdraw his resignation by the French President and Premier, Pierre Rouvier. King Edward had been distressed to hear of the impending resignation, and sent him a personal telegram begging him to reconsider. After being informed that he was staying on, he sent another, of congratulation – a quite unprecedented action for a monarch of another country to take. It was a tribute to his standing in Europe that no criticism was voiced in either Paris or London.

On the way back from his Mediterranean cruise, King Edward spent a week in Paris. It was an informal visit, and he did his 'traditional social round' as if no crisis existed. At the same time he did everything possible to demonstrate his support for the entente, and in a long private conversation with Delcassé assured him that the British government would give him every assistance in its power. Delcassé was thus convinced that if France was attacked by Germany, Britain would come to her aid.

The danger of war was not yet over. In June Prince Radolin, German Ambassador to Paris, told Rouvier that as long as Delcassé remained in office, there was no possibility of an improvement in Franco-German relations, and that unless France accepted a Moroccan conference she risked attack. Delcassé personally believed that the Germans were bluffing, but when he discovered that none of his colleagues agreed with him, and were afraid of war breaking out, he was obliged to resign once more, much to Emperor William's delight and King Edward's regret.

This incident, the King wrote to Lansdowne in April 1905, 'was the most mischievous and uncalled for event which the German Emperor has ever been engaged in since he came to the throne . . . . He is no more nor less than a political *enfant terrible* and one can have no faith in any of his assurances.'[8]

To Soveral, he was even more frank. The Tangier episode had confirmed any remaining doubts he had harboured about his nephew's emotional instability and the perils it might bring for Europe. It was dangerous for so vain a ruler to be constantly assured that he was the greatest sovereign on earth, believing he had a divine mission to make Germany the greatest power of all time. But the Emperor, the King went on, was 'even more cowardly than vain, and because of this he will tremble before all these sycophants when, urged on by the General Staff, they call on him to draw the sword in earnest. He won't have the courage to talk some sense into them, but will obey them cravenly instead. It is not by his will that he will unleash a war, but by his weakness.'[9]

When King Edward arrived at Marienbad for his annual cure on 17 August, his refusal to meet the Emperor at any stage of his journey led to hostile comment in Germany. Lascelles had thought that a meeting would help to ease tension between their respective countries, a suggestion which the King received sympathetically but deemed difficult to carry out at present. In Berlin there was pressure for the two sovereigns to get together, and Count von Senckendorff, one of the Emperor's courtiers, wrote to the King begging him to meet the Emperor 'in the interests of peace', and informing him that the latter would be at Homburg between 7 and 10 September for military manoeuvres.

The King thought this suggestion impertinent. He stressed that he had no quarrel with the Emperor, and was ready to resume direct personal contact as soon as Franco-German relations improved. In the meantime he was showing Germany all the courtesies which the situation allowed, such as inviting the Crown Prince and Princess to Windsor. Yet he could not appear to be 'running after the German Emperor'; it would be undignified, and not meet with the approval of his government or country. His main reason for being reluctant to meet the Emperor was mainly due to a desire to avoid any step which might indicate a want of sympathy with France, as he had deeply resented the German pressure with regard to Morocco. For this he found it impossible not to blame the Emperor, though he was discreet enough not to say so directly.

Relations between both monarchs were at a low ebb, and an invitation from the King to the German Crown Prince and Princess was vetoed by the Emperor on the grounds that King Alfonso of Spain was expected in Berlin at that time, and the Crown Prince's presence would be required at important functions. Attempts to bring about a rapprochement were made by the Emperor's youngest sister, Princess Frederick Charles of Hesse-Cassel, who invited the Emperor and Lascelles to lunch at Friedrichshof on 25 August. The meal passed pleasantly enough, but conversation was kept away from contentious subjects.

Earlier that month, the Admiralty in London had arranged for the Channel Squadron to visit the Baltic on one of its periodic cruises, calling at Copenhagen and two German ports. This proposal infuriated the Emperor, and he informed the Tsar that he had ordered the German Fleet to shadow the British, 'give them a dinner and make them as drunk as possible to find out what they are about'. The Fleet's itinerary went as planned, without any incidents (or drunken hospitality), and as arranged King Edward left Marienbad for England without having made any attempt to meet his nephew. The latter, now more angry still, complained to Lascelles that he had been grossly insulted. In desperation Lascelles threatened to resign, and at length the Emperor expressed regret at the strained relations between their countries, although he would not admit that any blame attached to him. He asked Lascelles to report the whole of their interview back to the King, which Lascelles did – after thinking it over carefully for nearly a week.

The King's answer was succinct. He had no quarrel whatsoever with the Emperor, and did not desire one, but 'the whole tone of the German Emperor's language to Lascelles is one of peevish complaint against me', and his points were 'almost too trivial to be taken notice of. I can only hope that next year some "rendezvous" may be arranged between us, but during the remainder of this year I do not think it will be possible.'[10]

Some of the Emperor's discomfort that summer had resulted from a piece of one-upmanship on the part of his uncle, culminating in another British princess becoming Queen in a different country of Europe.

Early in 1905 Norway declared her independence from Sweden, to whom she had been joined by an act of union since the Congress of Vienna in 1815. Both countries had one King, and Norway wanted her own sovereign. As a gesture of goodwill, the Storting in Norway invited King Oscar of Sweden to allow a prince from his family to become their independent sovereign. Declining to recognize Norwegian independence, King Oscar refused.

Political considerations appeared to rule out a candidate from the Great Powers. If a British or German prince was chosen, Anglo-German relations would be inflamed still further. Rumours that the German Emperor intended to nominate one of his own sons provoked alarm in the Foreign Office at London. Princes from Greece and Spain were suggested, but at length the Storting agreed that only someone from the ruling houses of Sweden or Denmark would be acceptable. King Oscar's refusal on behalf of his family meant that the candidate would have to come from the house of Glucksburg.

There were only two obvious princes. The first was Prince Waldemar, youngest son of King Christian IX. Aged forty-seven, he was placed at a disadvantage in that his wife was a Roman Catholic, and their children were adults. Though favoured by Emperor William, he had no enthusiasm for the throne. That left only Prince Charles, second son of Crown Prince Frederick of

Denmark. Aged thirty-two, and married to King Edward VII's youngest daughter Princess Maud, with an infant son, his claim could scarcely be bettered – except in the eyes of the German Emperor, who had no desire to see uncle Bertie increase his family's prestige in this way.

Charles' immediate reaction was to decline the offer, largely as he did not wish to relinquish his career in the Danish Navy. The shy retiring Maud, content with leading an unpretentious life divided between Copenhagen and Appleton, in the grounds of her childhood home at Sandringham, fully supported his decision. Yet it was difficult to refuse the call of duty. All Charles could do was stipulate that he would accept the crown if he could be of real service to Norway; if Sweden, Denmark and Great Britain fully endorsed his accession; and if the Norwegian people gave their wholehearted consent in a plebiscite.

Horrified at the apparent strength of Norwegian republicanism, the German Emperor begged King Oscar to recognize Norwegian independence and accept the crown for a member of the Bernadotte dynasty. Throughout the summer there was one delay after another. Charles refused to behave like an adventurer, going to claim the crown like some medieval baron. He would not go to Norway without permission from King Christian IX, but the latter would not grant such permission until King Oscar had formally renounced the crown, which he would not do until negotiations on the dissolution of the union had been amicably concluded.

King Edward found himself in an awkward position. Keen as he was to further his son-in-law's candidature, he was equally anxious to mollify the Swedish royal family, particularly as one of his nieces was about to marry the heir apparent. In order to help smooth matters over, he made King Oscar an Honorary Admiral of the British Fleet, and conferred the Order of the Garter on Crown Prince Gustav early in June, and the Grand Cross of the Bath on his son Prince Gustav Adolf. On 15 June, the day on which Prince Gustav Adolf married Princess Margaret of Connaught at St James's Chapel, the King of Sweden made King Edward an Admiral of the Swedish Navy.

With this exchange of courtesies, the latter now felt himself free to encourage Prince Charles of Denmark to act before Norway proclaimed herself an independent republic. 'I strongly urge that you should go to Norway as soon as possible to prevent some one else taking your place',[11] he telegraphed him on 30 July. The following month he voiced his opinion to Alan Johnstone, the British Minister at Copenhagen, suggesting that if a formal offer of the crown was made direct to Prince Charles, Sweden might be induced to give way and the King of Denmark and Crown Prince might allow him to accept even if Sweden did not yield, 'the only alternative apparently being a Republic. It seems absurd to King that affair should fall through owing to punctiliousness of Sweden.'[12]

Johnstone hoped to persuade the Danish government to let Prince Charles go and, if they refused, threatened to ask Baron Wedel, Norwegian Minister at Copenhagen, to march off with the Prince without the consent of the family, on condition that King Edward VII approved. As long as he was assured that Prince Charles would be recognized in these circumstances by the British government when he reached Christiania and was duly elected by the Storting, he was

Prince and Princess Gustav Adolf of Sweden on their wedding day, 15 June 1905

prepared to risk a reprimand from Lord Lansdowne and the displeasure of the Danish royal family. The scheme appealed to King Edward, but he felt such a move was too drastic even for him to sanction. That same day, 8 August, Johnstone telegraphed to the King, suggesting that His Majesty should write to the Crown Prince of Denmark, urging the necessity of sending Prince Charles at once, in order to avoid the declaration of a republic. Again the King hesitated to act on such advice, much as he approved in principle.

Matters had now reached deadlock. Sweden and Norway could not agree on the precise terms on which a separation of both countries should take place and, until those terms were settled, Sweden deemed it premature for Norway's provisional government to choose a new ruler. Yet leading members of the government still thought it best to choose a new ruler who could take part in the final settlement with Sweden.

'The time has now come for you to act or lose the Crown of Norway', King Edward VII informed his son-in-law bluntly on 11 August. 'On good authority I am informed your sister in Sweden* is intriguing against you. I urge you to go at once to Norway, with or without the consent of the Danish government, and help in the negotiations between the two countries.'[13]

Yet the Prince still declined to do anything which might hurt the feelings of his grandfather, King Christian IX, by acting without his consent. He had 'reason to believe' that Sweden would give a firm answer within a week, and was prepared to wait until then. This was not good enough for King Edward, who had heard rumours that the German Emperor was actively intriguing for the vacant throne to be filled by one of his sons. The King therefore wrote to Crown Prince Gustav of Sweden, impressing on him the view that Prince Charles' presence would hasten a final settlement. Reiterating the attitude of the Swedish government, the Crown Prince replied that the question of a candidature could not be discussed until the union of both countries had been formally dissolved. Having done all that he could, King Edward was now prepared to let matters take their own course.

In September a conference was called by both governments and, after some stormy exchanges, they reached an agreement which was ratified by the Storting on 9 October.

Prince Charles informed King Edward that he would not go to Norway unless summoned by a popular vote on a referendum. However, he might accept an invitation from the Storting, if the Danish Foreign Minister placed on formal record his own preference for a vote. On 25 October the Storting proposed the Prince as King of Norway, and on 18 November a plebiscite was held, with 260,000 votes cast in favour of a monarchy and only 70,000 against. The Storting endorsed this verdict by electing Charles as their King, and on 20 November he formally accepted the Crown at a ceremony held in the throne room of the Amalienborg Palace, Copenhagen, with Maud beside him. He took the name of King Haakon VII and conferred on their son, Prince Alexander, the name Crown Prince Olav. Four days later the family sailed into Christiania to a round of receptions and speeches.

* Princess Ingeborg, Duchess of Västergötland, daughter-in-law of King Oscar.

King Haakon VII and Queen Maud of Norway

Queen Maud and Crown Prince Olav of Norway

A few months later, after the King had returned to Spain, Princess Beatrice asked to speak to King Edward. She had been privately advised that King Alfonso was intent on marrying her daughter. King Edward was astonished that Princess Patricia was out of the running, but he was, none the less, very pleased. To have another niece as Queen of a foreign country was a gratifying prospect.

There were inevitably some objections in Spain. In particular Queen Maria Christina, King Alfonso's mother, was strongly opposed to the idea. She would have preferred him to marry an eligible princess from the ancient Catholic house of Habsburg and, like many other European royalty of the day, she regarded the morganatic Battenbergs as parvenus. Her views were shared by more conservative Spanish elements, who saw their King's choice of an English bride as a triumph for liberalism. The German Emperor was still keen to press the claims of Marie Antoinette of Mecklenburg-Schwerin to the young King. To have a German-born Queen of Spain would be some consolation for the German Empire, after seeing the crown of newly-independent Norway go to King Edward's son-in-law.

Yet the headstrong King Alfonso would not be swayed. He had set his heart on Ena. On 3 February 1906 he returned to Madrid, and later that same day Princess Beatrice notified King Edward that her daughter had officially accepted his proposal of marriage.

In Britain as well as in Spain, religion proved an obstacle. When leading churchmen voiced their disapproval at the prospect of an English princess forsaking her faith, King Edward side-stepped the issue by declaring that Ena was a Battenberg princess, not a British one.

In March 1906 Ena visited Spain to meet Queen Maria Christina, who had reluctantly accepted her son's decision, and she was received into the Catholic Church. On her return to England, King Edward insisted that she sign away her rights of succession to the British throne. As the likelihood of her becoming Queen Regnant was extremely remote, it was a mere formality. Rather bluntly, he advised her at the same time 'not to come whining back to England' if things went wrong.

The wedding took place on 31 May 1906, at the Church of San Jeronimo, Madrid. According to Spanish royal etiquette, so that pride of place could be given to the bridal pair, no other crowned head was invited to attend. This was convenient for King Edward, since it was deemed inappropriate for the head of the Church of England to attend a Catholic ceremony. He was represented by the Prince and Princess of Wales, at whose own wedding in 1893 the bride had been a bridesmaid. Less broadminded than his wife, the Prince had shared in his countrymen's misgivings about Ena changing her religion. According to Sir James Dunlop Smith, private secretary to the Viceroy of India, when confidentially asked his views on the subject, the Prince was '*very* angry', his language 'wasn't even Parliamentary and the Princess had to say "George!!!" more than once'.[1]

Other royalties who flocked to Madrid included Archduke Francis Ferdinand of Austria, the Duke of Aosta, the Count of Flanders (later King Albert of the Belgians), and Prince Henry of Prussia. The wedding ceremony lasted for

King Alfonso XIII of Spain and Princess Victoria Eugenia, shortly after their engagement, with their respective mothers, Princess Beatrice of Battenberg, and Queen Maria Christina of Spain, 1906

Fan commemorating the wedding of King Alfonso XIII and Princess Victoria Eugenia

almost three hours, and on the drive back to the palace afterwards the procession paused. Ena asked Alfonso why they had stopped, and he told her that there was possibly some delay caused by those ahead of them in the procession alighting ahead at the palace.

If so, the delay saved their lives. At this point, a large bouquet of flowers was thrown from the window of a house overlooking the procession to the other side of the road. It landed in front of the carriage to the right of the horses and exploded. Several soldiers and bystanders were killed, and many more wounded. Amid scenes of uproar and confusion, the King and Queen, shaken and splattered with blood and splinters from the bomb, scrambled down from their carriage and climbed into an empty one, which by tradition had been following immediately behind them. Back at the palace, all the horrified young Queen could say, over and over again, was 'I saw a man without any legs!'

Everyone was shocked at the attempt on the life of the young King and Queen at what should traditionally have been such a happy time; and it was rumoured that the would-be assassin, Mateo Morales, had attempted to gain admission to the church with his bomb concealed in the bouquet. The Dowager Duchess of Coburg, whose father, Tsar Alexander II, and brother, Grand Duke Serge of Russia, had both been assassinated in a similar manner, repeated, *'Moi, je suis tellement accoutumée à ces sortes de choses.'* If it was an attempt to cheer her fellow guests, it failed miserably.

'Nothing could have been braver than the young couple were, but what a beginning for her',[2] the Princess of Wales wrote to her aunt, Dowager Duchess Augusta of Mecklenburg-Strelitz.

The Prince of Wales was particularly angry about the poor security; 'I believe the Spanish police and detectives are about the worst in the world. No precautions whatever had been taken, they are most happy go lucky people here.' At the much-delayed lunch at the palace, he proposed the health of the bride and groom, 'not easy after the emotions caused by this terrible affair'.[3] The public were apparently permitted to roam at will around the colonnades of the palace, with no effort made to prevent them from wandering almost into the guests' apartments. Morales was arrested three days later, but as he was being taken into custody, he calmly shot his guard and then himself.

It put the Prince of Wales in no frame of mind to enjoy the ensuing festivities. A gala banquet at the palace on 1 June, followed by a reception attended by five thousand guests, was a 'very hot affair, & tiring; much talking, bowing & clicking of spurs'. The heat 'was awful & every window shut . . . Got to bed at 12.0 mightily pleased'.[4]

In his nonchalance, King Alfonso greatly underestimated the harm which the attempt on their lives had had on Spanish prestige abroad. Though no coward himself, and as one who had survived an attempt on his life in Brussels six years earlier, King Edward VII let it be known through his ambassadors that a reciprocal state visit to Madrid was quite out of the question.

Spain and Norway had just been added to the kingdoms closely connected to King Edward and Queen Alexandra by blood; but the family relationship with the Greek monarchy had been close for nearly half a century. In 1863, the year that the then Prince of Wales had married Princess Alexandra, her brother William had been elected King of the Hellenes. The Prince of Wales' brother, Prince Alfred, had been elected King by an overwhelming majority the previous year but, much to the family's relief, political considerations prevented him from accepting the crown. Though Greece was never as politically stable as the Great Powers, King George – the name by which Prince William had chosen to reign – seemed able to weather the internal storms better than some of his fellow Balkan monarchs. He had been shrewd enough to press for a guarantee from the Powers of £20,000 a year if he should ever be driven into exile.

In one crisis during his reign, King Edward did not hesitate to intervene directly. Since 1898 the island of Crete had been governed by Prince George, second son of King George, as High Commissioner. Despite the presence of British and other foreign troops and contingents, it was not an easy task. While the majority of representatives in the Cretan assembly were committed to union with Greece, a vociferous minority party aimed for complete independence for the island. It was led by Eleuthcrios Venizelos, who would shortly become a persistent thorn in the side of the Greek monarchy with devastating effect.

George I, King of the Hellenes

In June 1904 the British government raised the desirability of continuing with the presence of international troops in Crete. The King was insistent that British forces should not be withdrawn; 'Prince George leans on England more than any other country – and especially for advice.'[5] The Prime Minister, Arthur Balfour, took his sovereign's side, and British troops stayed on the island. However, by the end of the year, complaints against Prince George's rule had multiplied. In March 1906 Sir Charles Hardinge reported that it was difficult to maintain order on the island. The arbitrary rule of the High Commissioner was blamed, and King George thought that his son ought to resign.

King Edward and Queen Alexandra were cruising in the Mediterranean that spring, partly for family reasons. King Christian IX of Denmark, the father of the Queen and of the King of the Hellenes, had died in January, at the age of eighty-seven. Though his death at such an age was scarcely unexpected, the Queen longed to be with her brother at this time of bereavement.

The family gathering was joined early in April by the Prince and Princess of Wales, on their way home from India. The Princess made the most of her time in Athens, sightseeing; accompanied by the Crown Prince and Princess of the Hellenes, and her sister-in-law Princess Victoria, she saw the Parthenon, the Nike Temple, the Museum, and paid a visit to the Stadium where the Olympic Games were to be held. She noted that King Edward looked well, but Queen Alexandra seemed 'very sad & tired after her great sorrow'.[6]

While in Greece, King Edward agreed with his brother-in-law that the Prince should be asked to resign. Three months later, he did so, and the appointment of a former Prime Minister of the Hellenes helped restore tranquillity to the island. Though Prince George was disappointed by this setback to his career, King George was grateful to King Edward for his support in the problem. The latter continued to be held in high regard by the Greek royal family, and soon after the birth in December of Princess Marina,* daughter of the King's son Prince Nicholas, he was asked to be one of the child's godparents.

After the rupture caused to Anglo-German relations by the Tangier incident, dubbed by Winston Churchill with hindsight as 'the first milestone to Armageddon', the King and German Emperor were agreed as to the necessity of re-establishing better relations. In January 1906 the King wrote his nephew a conciliatory letter congratulating him on his birthday. Having expressed his hopes that the Algeciras Conference, which was just assembling, would serve the cause of peace and dissipate the threat of war in Europe, he went on to congratulate him on his forthcoming silver wedding and mentioned that his brother-in-law, Prince Christian of Schleswig-Holstein, would represent him at the festivities. 'Above all [wrote the King] I am most desirous that the feeling between our two countries may be on the best footing. We are – my dear William – such old friends and relations that I feel sure that the affectionate feelings which have always existed may invariably continue.'[7]

'The whole letter', the Emperor replied fulsomely on 1 February, 'breathed such an atmosphere of kindness and warm, sympathetic friendship that it constitutes the most cherished gift among my presents.

'There is no denying the fact that the political relations between the two countries had little by little become charged with electrical fluid to such an extent that its discharge might have created endless woe to both.'[8]

Prince Henry of Prussia, the Emperor's only surviving brother, was on excellent terms with his British relations, as was his wife, his cousin Princess Irene of Hesse, sister of Princess Louis of Battenberg. He was relieved at the apparent mending of relations between Britain and Germany after the Algeciras Conference. In February he called upon Lascelles at the British Embassy in Berlin, to express his delight with King Edward's friendly letter. The Prince, reported Lascelles, 'had been very unhappy last year on account of the strained relations between the King and the Emperor, but he hoped now that matters had really improved, and he could assure me most positively that nothing could give the Emperor greater pleasure than the re-establishment of the most friendly relations with the King'.[9]

It was not only the sovereigns and their families who were desperate for a friendly meeting. In May 1906 Count Metternich commented in a letter to Count Bülow on the unpopularity of Germans in English society, due mainly to the attitude of the English court and to personal relations between both

---

* Later Duchess of Kent.

Prince and Princess Henry of Prussia

sovereigns. 'If an amicable meeting could be arranged between them, this would change things greatly for the better.'[10]

To this end Viscount Haldane, War Minister in the new Liberal Cabinet, was invited to pay a visit to Berlin in August. He had been partly educated in Germany, spoke the language fluently, and was known to have strong pro-German sympathies. At the same time, the Foreign Secretary, Sir Edward Grey, was asked whether the King would be willing to meet the Emperor. A meeting was suggested at Friedrichshof, conveniently close to Marienbad.

The King was unenthusiastic, well aware that any sign of an Anglo-German rapprochement would disturb the French. How would France react if an Anglo-German agreement was to be signed? However, if the King was going to Marienbad that summer, he could hardly refuse a meeting with the Emperor. The previous year's crisis had been settled in April by the Algeciras Conference, by which Moroccan independence was affirmed, but the status of French control was unchanged, a solution which left affairs as they had been before, much to the German government's disappointment.

At the end of July 1906 the German Empress, the pious humourless Dona, who hated her husband's philandering uncle, tried to interfere; 'It seems to me after all the misunderstandings – not to give them any worse name – between the two sovereigns and their countries, King Edward ought to visit the Emperor, in one of his own Castles, at least, if not in his own capital . . . Why can't the fat old gentleman manage to get as far as Wilhelmshohe? Or couldn't the Emperor go to his Homburg Castle and meet his uncle there?'[11] Despite her objections, it was still at Friedrichshof, home of Prince and Princess Frederick Charles of Hesse-Cassel since the death of the Empress Frederick, that the meeting took place.

Everything passed off according to plan. Both sovereigns discussed conditions in Russia, King Edward being particularly concerned at the Tsar's refusal to grant liberal concessions to his increasingly restive people, and regarding it as an unfortunate state of affairs for twentieth-century monarchy elsewhere. The state of the Habsburg monarchy likewise disturbed him. Was Emperor Francis Joseph capable of standing up to 'subversive elements' in his vast sprawling empire? Moreover, in the next reign, what was to be done about the status of the wife of his heir, Archduke Francis Ferdinand, who was denied any rank higher than Princess? Would the court of Vienna swallow its pride and outdated sense of tradition, and recognize her as Empress?

On such matters they were in complete agreement, and the Emperor told his uncle how glad he was that they could act according to their 'common understanding' of such problems. King Edward also talked to von Tschirschky, of the German Foreign Office, deputizing for the indisposed Bülow. To von Tschirschky, and suggestions that England and Germany might conclude an entente similar to that already signed with France, he used the same arguments that the Foreign Office had used with German diplomats in London. An entente with France had been possible because there had previously been so many specific points of friction between both countries; but Anglo-German relations were different, as there was no friction, only rivalry. This was followed by a conversation between Hardinge and von Tschirschky on Anglo-German

King Edward VII's visit to Emperor William II at Homburg, August 1906. Group includes, left to right: Crown Prince Constantine of the Hellenes, Duke of Sparta (in white trousers); Crown Princess Sophie of the Hellenes; Prince and Princess Frederick Charles of Hesse-Cassel; an unknown lady (probably a lady-in-waiting); King Edward VII; and the German Emperor

relations, Hardinge stressing tactfully that any friendly relations between their two countries had to be compatible with the Anglo-French entente.

The meeting broke up the following day, and King Edward went to Marienbad. All parties agreed that it had been a great success. But the fragility of the entente was underlined a couple of weeks later when the French government was notified that Haldane, who had been a guest at Marienbad on his way to Berlin at the Emperor's invitation, had been invited to attend the 'Sedan review'. This was a spectacular military parade staged by the German Army each September, to commemorate its crushing defeat of the French in 1870.

M Paul Cambon, French Ambassador in London, warned the Foreign Secretary, Lord Grey, that if the British Minister of War associated himself publicly with a display so painful for France, then the following day articles inspired by German agents would appear in French newspapers attacking both Mr Haldane and the British government. The crisis was only averted when Haldane attended another review on the day before the anniversary of Sedan. Yet it proved how carefully national susceptibilities had to be treated, and if the German Emperor was serious about wooing Britain, he was going about it in the wrong way.

Nothing would ever persuade King Edward to set foot in Madrid, after the near-tragedy at his niece's marriage. All the same, the British Ministers considered it imperative for him to meet King Alfonso somewhere on Spanish territory, in order to put Spain herself beyond German political grasp. Germany was making friendly overtures to Spain, particularly by offering to construct a naval dockyard and arsenal at Ferrol, provided both were leased to the German Navy for use after completion.

A meeting afloat at Cartagena, off the south-east coast of Spain, was arranged to take place in April 1907, shortly after the King left Biarritz. Further complications were caused by an epidemic of typhoid raging in the port where the rendezvous took place on 8 April. Even the Military Governor of Cartagena, General Aldarve, had to remain on shore in quarantine as two of his daughters had gone down with the fever.

King Alfonso had risen to the occasion by transporting the treasures of his Madrid palace, including tapestries and oil paintings from the Escorial, to his yacht *Giralda*. In this floating palace, King Edward was created a Captain-General in the Spanish Army, and Hardinge, who accompanied the King as minister in attendance, worked with the Spanish premier, M Maura, on an exchange of notes by which England, France and Spain guaranteed each other's possessions throughout the Mediterranean. Every effort was made to prevent news of the transaction from reaching the German Foreign Office before it could be notified through official channels. None the less, the news leaked out prematurely, much to German discomfort.

Another country was now loosely allied to the entente, and Cambon reported that 'Spain has been snatched from German influence'. The Madrid paper *Correspondencia* noted that Germany wanted King Alfonso to ride two lengths behind the Emperor, 'whereas England put King Edward's horse right beside that of the King of Spain'.

From Cartagena, King Edward and Queen Alexandra visited Malta, before cruising to southern Italy and Sicily. The Mediterranean Fleet provided an escort when they met the King and Queen of Italy at Gaeta. Though it was a purely social visit, the German Emperor saw fit to denounce his uncle as a satanic encircler bent upon ringing Germany with enemies.

In London the Liberal administration, and particularly Lord Grey, felt that a formal state visit to Windsor by the German Emperor might have a soothing effect on Anglo-German relations after the Morocco crisis and the ever-closer rapport between England and Russia. A fresh spate of attacks in the Berlin press on Britain, and on King Edward in particular, put the scheme in some doubt, but after strongly-worded complaints to the German Ambassador in London, the atmosphere improved. By June the air had cleared sufficiently for the King to open negotiations at an informal level.

The Emperor suggested he should come and visit him later that summer at Wilhelmshohe, on his way to Marienbad. The King accordingly accepted, but true to form the Emperor greeted his uncle at the railway station at Kronberg with a full-scale military gala, with bands playing and a long programme of

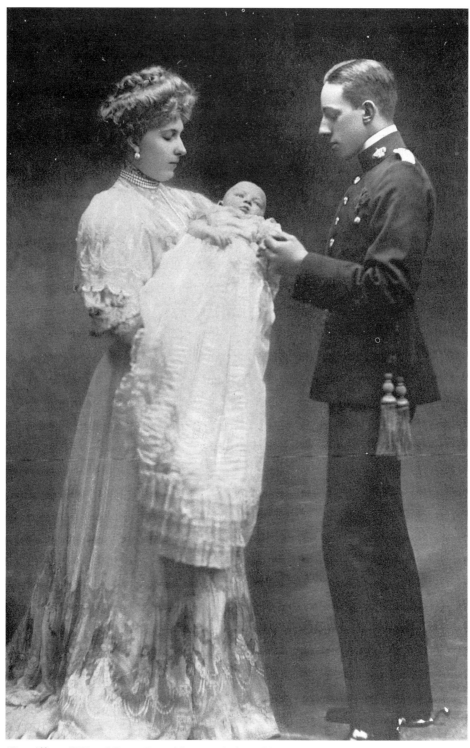

King Alfonso XIII and Queen Ena of Spain with their eldest son, Prince Alfonso, 1907

royal salutes. Instead of being given lunch on arrival at the palace, the hungry King then had to attend another parade, and was obliged to take the salute while half the German Army marched past. It was not calculated to put him in a receptive mood.

During this short visit, he avoided discussing politics with the Emperor, but honoured Bülow with a long conversation, assuring him of his and his government's fervent wish for Anglo-German peace and goodwill.

The following day King Edward arrived at Bad Ischl for a discussion with Emperor Francis Joseph and Baron von Aehrenthal, Austrian Foreign Minister. Despite later allegations by Baron Margutti, the Emperor's aide-de-camp, that King Edward was trying to detach his master from Germany, this was not the case. Anglo-German relations had improved as a result of the King's recent visit, and there was 'complete accord' between them, particularly with regard to Austria's policy towards the Balkans and Turkish ill-treatment of Christians in Macedonia.

Relations between the King and the Austrian Emperor, Hardinge reported to Sir Edward Grey, were 'of the most friendly and intimate character. They seemed to delight in each other's company and were practically inseparable.'[12] It was all so different from the apparent degree of tension which lurked behind the laughing and joking between King Edward and the Emperor William.

A long-overdue German state visit to Windsor Castle was arranged for November 1907. It was almost cancelled at the last minute, when the Emperor sent a telegram saying that he was suffering from the after-effects of influenza, leaving him unable to meet the strain of the programme. The King replied saying how disappointed he was, and begged him to reconsider. Bülow emphasized the damage that cancellation would do to relations between both countries, especially after the British Ambassador reported that he had seen the Emperor out riding down the Central Avenue in Berlin, apparently in the best of health. Privately, the Chancellor thought that the Emperor's trouble could be attributed to the fear of how he would be received in England as a result of the impending trial of his friend Count Eulenburg, then at the centre of a homosexual scandal in Berlin.

The Emperor and Empress arrived at Portsmouth on 11 November, and stayed a full week instead of the five days planned. It coincided with one of the greatest gatherings of royalty that Windsor Castle had ever witnessed. A cluster of former French royalty had gathered in England to celebrate the marriage of Prince Charles of Bourbon to Princess Louise of Orleans, and twenty-four royalties sat down to luncheon on 17 November. Apart from the German Emperor and Empress, they included King Alfonso and Queen Ena of Spain (paying a private visit), Queen Amelie of Portugal, Queen Maud of Norway, Grand Duke Vladimir of Russia, and others. It was a gentle reminder by the King, if any was needed, that for all the German Emperor's theatricality, Windsor was still the scene of the summit of royal prestige in Europe, if not the world.

During a state banquet in the Waterloo Chamber, held on the second evening of the visit, the King made a teasing reference in his toast speech to the fears

Royal group at Windsor Castle, 17 November 1907. Left to right: Queen Maud of Norway; King Alfonso XIII of Spain; William II, German Emperor; Augusta Victoria, German Empress; Queen Alexandra; Queen Amelia of Portugal; King Edward VII; Ena, Queen of Spain

that it was not to take place, 'owing to indisposition', but 'fortunately, Their Majesties are now both looking in such good health that I can only hope their stay in England, however short, will much benefit them'.[13]

On 13 November the Emperor was entertained to luncheon at the Guildhall, London, by the Lord Mayor, and presented with an address in a gold casket. In his speech afterwards, he reassured them that

> The main prop and base for the peace of the world is the maintenance of good relations between our two countries, and I shall further strengthen them as far as lies in my power. Blood is thicker than water. The German nation's wishes coincide with mine.[14]

Such fine words could not paper over Anglo-German tension for long. European politics were outgrowing family gatherings at Windsor, which could only act as a brake on international differences. Once the Windsor visit was over, the Empress returned to Germany, while her husband stayed with Colonel Stuart-Wortley at Highcliffe Castle in Hampshire. Here the Emperor could assume the role after which he secretly hankered, that of an English country gentleman. The weeks he spent at Highcliffe, however, were destined within the next twelve months to bear fruit of a particularly bitter nature.

4 'A mighty and victorious antagonist'

The year 1908 was to mark a turning point in Europe's march to Armageddon. Though he had but two years to live, King Edward was not slow to recognize the signs.

The year opened badly with tragedy in the Iberian peninsula. Portuguese republicanism had long been growing, fanned by financial crises and the government's escalating debts. Although the Braganzas lived modestly and without financial excess, they were accused of extravagance. In May 1907 the Prime Minister, Joao Franco, dissolved the Cortes, and announced that he would govern by decree, an act of despotism fully endorsed by King Carlos. A few months later Franco uncovered a republican plan for an uprising, but it was only one of many. On 1 February 1908, as the royal family returned to Lisbon, a group of revolutionaries opened fire on their carriage. King Carlos and his elder son, Crown Prince Luis Filipe, were killed instantly. Queen Amelie, who was unhurt, had stood up to shield their younger son, eighteen-year-old Prince Manuel, who was wounded in the arm. In these violent circumstances he succeeded his father as King.

King Edward and Queen Alexandra were deeply shocked, and the following day they and other members of the royal family attended a memorial service in St Paul's Cathedral. One week later, on 8 February, they were present at a Requiem Mass held in St James's Church, Spanish Place. It was the first time that an English sovereign had appeared at a Roman Catholic service in Britain since the Reformation. The Protestant Alliance 'viewed with astonishment and distress His Majesty's attendance at a Mass for the dead', a protest which he ignored.

His close friend the Marquis of Soveral, Portuguese Minister in London, was afraid that civil war would sweep his homeland and that the monarchy would be toppled. He begged the King and the Foreign Office to send a British naval squadron to Lisbon to quell a possible revolution. King Edward was keen to secure the position of King Manuel, who did not at first dare to leave the palace in Lisbon even to take the necessary oath before the Cortes. He agreed that British residents and commercial interests were entitled to protection, and that Britain could not stand idly by, allowing a state of anarchy to develop.

He was under no illusions as to the precarious standing of the Braganza dynasty, sadly advising Soveral that he knew how unfavourable the mood of the Portuguese people was towards their monarchy; 'I fear the country is rapidly

Manuel II, King of Portugal

drifting towards Republicanism!'[1] All the same, he thought that Britain should have ships ready at a moment's notice to proceed to Lisbon, 'tho' naturally we have no desire to interfere in their normal internal affairs, unless they become of an alarming nature!'[2] In the end, nothing was done. Practical considerations prevailed over monarchical solidarity.

While still wrestling with a crisis of conscience over the Portuguese throne, King Edward was embroiled in a new war of words over the Anglo-German arms race.

On 16 February the German Emperor wrote directly to the First Lord of the Admiralty in London, Lord Tweedmouth, about what he called the 'battle royal' being waged between the press of both countries over Germany's Third Naval Act, which provided for another 20 per cent increase in future German expenditure on her Fleet. This was being built, he said, solely to protect Germany's 'rapidly growing trade', and was directed against nobody, least of all Great Britain, whose navy he estimated to be about five times as great as that of Germany. Yet he stoutly defended the right of any nation to build as many warships as she felt she needed. As King Edward had from time to time sent personal messages directly to foreign statesmen, such as Delcassé, he could hardly object to his nephew's direct contact.

All would have been well had not Lord Tweedmouth, who had showed the letter to the King and to Grey, the Foreign Secretary, enclosed in his reply to the Emperor a draft of the paper he had prepared as his statement to be issued shortly to Parliament, with detailed estimates for the forthcoming year. In other words, the German Emperor was being given details of Britain's future naval programme before the House of Commons. Moves by the government and a sympathetic opposition to close ranks in order to prevent this embarrassing escapade from being leaked and made public were almost frustrated by Lord Tweedmouth's persistent gossiping in society about the exchange of letters. His behaviour was becoming ever more eccentric; unfortunately he was suffering from the onset of a brain disease to which he would succumb the following year.

That spring, King Edward and Queen Alexandra set out for a visit to the Scandinavian countries, delayed for several weeks by court mourning for King Carlos of Portugal. Hardinge advised him to treat his visit to Stockholm as official, thus ignoring the strict protocol which required King Gustav, who had succeeded his father King Oscar only the previous year, to visit England first.

The previous December, the German Ambassador in London had announced his government's intention of making an agreement with Russia as to the territorial status quo in the Baltic. There was also an intention to bring in Sweden, but none to include Denmark. King Edward protested firmly against the latter's exclusion, and on 23 April 1908 an agreement was signed in St Petersburg and Berlin between the four littoral Powers of the Baltic – Russia, Germany, Sweden and Denmark – recognizing in principle the maintenance of the territorial status quo in the Baltic.

The German government claimed that their signature on the agreement proved their country's innocence of any plans to annex the smaller Baltic states. At the same time as the Baltic Convention was signed, the North Sea agreement was signed between Great Britain, France, Germany, Denmark, Sweden and Holland, sanctioning a similar principle with regard to the North Sea. There was a general belief, in Germany and beyond, that these agreements satisfied German susceptibilities as a counterblast to the understanding between France, Spain, England and Italy as to the Mediterranean.

While the North Sea agreement was being drawn up, the British government decided that it would be right for the King to visit Copenhagen, Stockholm, and Christiania with a view to increasing international amity. Official visits to Denmark and Norway were postponed owing to the Portuguese tragedy, but Sir Rennell Rodd recommended strongly that a visit to Sweden was much looked for. The first visit paid by a British sovereign to that country would be 'a great event' in the history of that nation, and would help to heal the rupture in Anglo-Swedish relations caused by Norwegian independence.

While in Copenhagen, Queen Alexandra took her husband to see Hvidore. Since the death of her father King Christian IX in January 1906, Copenhagen had no longer seemed like home, so she purchased Hvidore as a retreat for her sister 'Minnie', the Dowager Tsarina of Russia, and herself. It was a summer holiday villa, with electric heating quite inadequate for any other time of year.

The King found it so cold that he kept his coat on all the time. The Queen fondly talked of converting the billiard-room into an extra bedroom for his benefit, hoping that she would thus persuade him to come and stay, but this first visit proved quite enough for him.

From Copenhagen they left for Stockholm, and were welcomed with a rapturous reception. A state banquet at the palace for 250 guests helped to restore cordiality. Any offence that might have been taken by the Bernadottes as a result of Britain's role in the Norwegian independence affair had evidently been short-lived, and now that Sweden had a British-born Crown Princess, the court was accordingly more sympathetic to Britain than it had been during the previous reign. King Gustav was so delighted with the presence of King Edward that he expressed a wish to pay a return state visit to England with his Queen at the earliest possible opportunity.

The King had worked hard to cement Anglo-French relations; but it still remained for him to try and bind the ties with Russia more tightly. The family relationship was extremely close, Tsar Nicholas being the son of Queen Alexandra's favourite sister, and the Tsarina daughter of the King's sister Alice, late Grand Duchess of Hesse and the Rhine. Alice had died of diphtheria at the early age of thirty-five, and Queen Victoria had taken such a keen interest in the

Tin tray commemorating the accession of King Gustav V and Queen Victoria of Sweden, 1907

upbringing of her Hessian grandchildren that they all regarded her with particular devotion. 'You have always been a second mother to me', Ernest, Grand Duke of Hesse, Alice's only surviving son, had told the Queen in 1893, and it was a sentiment his sisters eagerly shared.

Moreover it was the King's turn to visit Russia, especially as the Tsar and his family had paid a private visit to Balmoral in the autumn of 1896.

Nevertheless there were difficulties in their path. The King looked with no great favour on the oppressiveness of the Tsar's regime and the apparent weakness of the Tsar himself, who seemed to be little more than a mouthpiece for his reactionary ministers. The parlous state of Russia herself was a further obstacle. Violence and political turmoil throughout 1905 – the march upon the Tsar's palace, culminating in 'Bloody Sunday' and the shooting down of peaceful demonstrators, soon followed by the assassination of his uncle Grand Duke Serge – had made the King think again.

Moreover the Liberal government, which had won a landslide victory at Westminster in 1906, viewed Romanov autocracy in a far less favourable light than the King himself. In March 1906 he had been reluctant to entertain plans for an impending Russian visit on the grounds that there was little point in calling on the Tsar that year; 'the country is in a very unsettled state and will, I fear, not improve for some time to come'. In any case, he knew that his government would not approve of his going; a strange and not altogether convincing objection, in view of the way in which he had arranged his programme for 1903 with no ministerial consultation – and moreover he had 'no desire to play the part of the German Emperor who always meddles in other people's business'.[3]

That pressure would be continued for a Russian visit was never much in doubt. Ignoring the protests of his more radical government backbenchers, Sir Edward Grey argued that an entente with Russia remained a high priority in British foreign policy, and would strengthen the agreement with France. An Anglo-Russian convention was signed in September 1907. Although seen as uniting Britain, Russia and France in a Triple Alliance, its terms were limited to resolving outstanding disputes which had been a source of friction in Afghanistan, Persia and Tibet. Even so, it still offended left-wing opinion in Britain, which saw it as implicitly condoning Tsarist tyranny and pandering to Russian despotism 'for a very dubious and temporary advantage'. Yet a meeting between the monarchs could no longer be postponed indefinitely.

As Russia, like Spain, was still a place of considerable danger, any such reunion would have to be at sea. The sovereigns arranged to anchor off Reval in the Gulf of Finland in June 1908, where the Russian imperial yachts *Standart* and *Polar Star* were waiting, and the *Victoria and Albert* accordingly joined them there.

The meeting remained essentially an informal family affair. For two days, pinnace boats were kept busy as the royalties and their advisers were ferried to and fro between the three yachts. King Edward, attired in the uniform of the Kiev Dragoons, boarded *Standart* and delighted the guard of honour of Russian sailors by saying to them in Russian, 'Good morning, my children', to which they answered, 'God save the King'. This verbal exchange was followed by another Russian tradition, a snack of caviar sandwiches and kirsch, which Ponsonby thought tasted like boot polish.

Throughout the visit, the Tsar appeared contented and at ease, but not so the Tsarina. Perhaps she was particularly alarmed at the time over the health of the Tsarevich, who was a haemophiliac and had already once come close to death from a bleeding attack. One evening Hardinge, finding the festivities rather overpowering, wandered around on board *Standart* in search of peace and quiet. As he strolled along the deck, he heard the sound of a woman sobbing, and found the Tsarina in a deck chair, weeping uncontrollably. When he offered to help, she said that there was nothing anybody could do and she merely wished to be left alone.

There were three ethnic groups in Reval, the Estonians, the Russians and the Germans. Each had their own band and singers, and they all asked if they would be allowed to serenade Their Majesties. Security considerations forbade them access to any of the royal yachts, so they would have to perform on a special steamer hovering nearby. It would have to be extremely close, as their voices and actions would be meaningless from a distance. What, asked the Russian police, if any of the performers was concealing a bomb or a pistol? They proposed to strip and search all the entertainers, men and women alike, before allowing them aboard the steamer. Only the insistence of Ponsonby, visualizing angry newspaper headlines in England telling how the Tsar's despotic policemen had humiliated innocent women artists, persuaded them to exclude women from the body search.

Even so, the entertainment was not appreciated. After dinner, according to Ponsonby, the monarchs and their suites stood on deck while 'a steamer full of some choral society came and sang weird Russian songs'. The British Ambassador, Sir Arthur Nicolson, thought that King Edward was bored by the whole business.

Far more amusing were the antics of Admiral Fisher, who proved himself the life and soul of the party. After dinner on the second night, he asked the band on board *Victoria and Albert* to play the waltz from *The Merry Widow*, to which he proceeded to dance with the Tsar's sister Grand Duchess Olga, with his hands behind his head. 'How about Siberia for me?' he asked her jokingly in the middle of his performance. Even the Tsarina was seen to smile at his comic behaviour. Next he was asked to dance a hornpipe, and the others called for so many encores that at length he was too exhausted to continue.

Grand Duchess Olga was unhappily married to Prince Peter of Oldenburg, a hypochondriac who showed more interest in gambling than in the wife fourteen years his junior. Like her sister-in-law, she welcomed the diversion caused by the appearance of her British relations and Fisher, with whom she had made friends some time before, on a meeting at Carlsbad. It brought a ray of sunshine into their none too happy lives. Later, she recalled that he could tell the funniest stories, and when amused her laughter carried no mean distance. At a dinner on board the yacht, she laughed so heartily that the King was moved to ask Fisher to remember that they were not in the gunroom. Rather ashamed of herself, Olga waited until dinner was over, and confessed to Uncle Bertie that it was all her fault.[4]

The King had several conversations with Peter Stolypin, the Tsar's chief minister, who was impressed by His Majesty's grasp of European affairs. Stolypin was also struck by Kind Edward's detailed knowledge of Russian matters, particularly with regard to the gratifying collaboration between the government and the new Duma, and progress being made in the Russian railway system. Afterwards he told Hardinge that His Majesty had 'fascinated' him.

On the second day at Reval, there was the customary exchange of ranks. The King made the Tsar an Admiral of the Fleet, an honour which pleased the latter greatly. During dinner that night, the Tsar returned the compliment by inviting His Majesty to become an Admiral of the Russian Navy. It was left to later generations to point out that apart from one cruiser, the Russian Navy lay at the bottom of the Pacific; but it was the thought which counted.[5]

In personal terms at least, the visit was a great success. The Tsar's principal aide-de-camp, Prince Orloff, told Fisher that the King at Reval had changed the atmosphere of Russian feelings towards England from suspicion to cordial trust. In Berlin the German Emperor made no attempt to conceal his disgust at his uncle's meeting with the Tsar. Russia, France and England, he protested, were intent on encircling the Fatherland. That the hated Fisher, whom he suspected of poisoning King Edward's mind against Germany, had been among the party, gave him further cause for concern.*

Grand Duchess Olga thought the gathering 'a great historic event', which sealed the new Anglo-Russian entente. Relations with England, she believed, had almost reached breaking point during the war with Japan, and as the government and people of Britain did not conceal where their sympathies lay, so the King's arrival 'brought all the more pleasure to us all. We felt that at last the affection between the two reigning houses would work for a better understanding between the two countries.'[6]

King Edward's next meeting with Emperor Francis Joseph at Bad Ischl, in August 1908, took place amid a rather strained atmosphere. Grey and Baron Aehrenthal did not completely trust each other, and during friendly conversations with the Emperor King Edward took the opportunity to ask for some Austrian pressure on Germany to curb her shipbuilding programme. Tactfully the request may have been made, but the King received a polite refusal. The Austro-German alliance had been the main pillar of Francis Joseph's foreign policy for thirty years, and he was unlikely to do anything that might jeopardize this. Moreover, the unwritten code of imperial conduct would have dissuaded him from

---

* Earlier that year, Fisher had predicted that hostilities between Britain and Germany would begin in the late summer of 1914, as work on enlarging the Kiel canal would be completed by then; and with Tirpitz's shipbuilding programme, Germany would have enough vessels by that time to risk war. He attempted to convince King Edward that the Royal Navy should follow the precedent of Admiral Nelson in 1801, when he sank the Danish Fleet at Copenhagen, and launch a pre-emptive strike on the German Navy, but the horrified King refused to countenance the idea.

interfering by questioning a brother sovereign on his defence policy and armed forces. Yet King Edward was not discouraged. Crozier, the French Ambassador at Vienna, believed that he would certainly try again.

King Edward's faith in Emperor Francis Joseph was about to receive a heavy blow. Two days after his arrival in Marienbad, Wickham Steed informed him that Austria was about to annex the provinces of Bosnia and Herzegovina. The two states were nominally part of the Turkish Empire, though they had been occupied and administered by Austria since the Congress of Berlin in 1878. Austria, fearing Serbia planned to seize control of them, decided to absorb them into the Austro-Hungarian empire instead. It would, moreover, be some compensatory territorial expansion in the south-east, the only region where the empire could expand. This would counterbalance her loss of prestige in the earlier years of the Emperor's reign, when she had been expelled from Italy in the south, and removed from the German confederation in the north.

It was a bold step, and in terms of reputation it cost her dearly among the other monarchs. At first King Edward refused to believe Steed. Such a precipitate move, he declared, would upset the whole of Europe; and he was convinced that the Emperor would have mentioned it to him if it was true. In the eyes of every other European power, the Habsburg Empire was responsible for preventing the Balkan powder keg from igniting by maintaining the delicate balance. To annex the provinces would inflame Balkan relations, and could risk setting the whole of Europe alight.

The annexation was formally declared on 18 August, the Emperor's seventy-eighth birthday, but not made public for another six weeks. On 29 September he wrote personal letters to all his European fellow-monarchs and heads of state to inform them. King Edward received his on 5 October while staying at Balmoral, forty-eight hours after the President of France had received his. The King had been warned by Hardinge that Count Albert von Mensdorff, the Austrian Ambassador, who had seen him at the Foreign Office, was on his way to Balmoral with the letter. Aware of its contents, King Edward scanned it coldly as a formality. He regarded it as a gross breach of confidence, and discourtesy on the Emperor's part, for such a private letter to be dispatched through an ambassador.

He wondered whether Germany had put her ally up to it, in order to strengthen the Austro-German grip on the Balkans and humiliate Russia. As yet he did not know that Emperor William was just as angry at not having been taken into Francis Joseph's confidence.

Even worse was to come before the month was out. On 28 October 1908 an anonymous article headed 'The German Emperor and England – Personal Interview – Frank Statement of World Policy – Proofs of Friendship' appeared in the *Daily Telegraph*, virtually the only national newspaper then sympathetic to Germany. The article was based on the Emperor's relaxed but characteristically indiscreet table-talk with Colonel Stuart-Wortley, who had entertained him at Highcliffe Castle after his visit to Windsor in November 1907.

In his conversations the Emperor had recalled the Boer War when, so he said, Queen Victoria had appealed to him for advice, and in agreement with his general staff he consequently recommended a certain strategy which the British troops had successfully followed. He talked of the possibility of eventual war between the United States of America and Japan, and how he was building up the German Fleet partly in order to 'be ready to lend a helping hand' against the 'Yellow Peril' if necessary, and partly to protect German trade interests. Although he thought the First Sea Lord, Admiral Fisher, was 'a most dangerous and overrated man', he himself was Britain's greatest friend abroad, the only man capable of holding back the anti-British sentiments of his subjects in Germany. Yet he was cruelly misunderstood and regarded as an arch-enemy by the English, who were all 'as mad as March hares'.

In the autumn of 1908 Brigader-General Wortley, as he now was, was invited to attend army manoeuvres at Metz. On his return to England, after further conversations with the Emperor, he wrote up the remarks in the form of 'a supposed communiqué', and sent him a copy suggesting that it might be used in order to secure a 'fair hearing' for Germany in the British press.

Reaction to the *Daily Telegraph* article was the opposite of what had been intended. In Germany nobody thought that the Emperor had eased relations between both countries; on the contrary, they considered that he had made himself look foolish (or been made to look foolish by his conspiring ministers, who ought to have persuaded him to suppress the article), and that he had betrayed national interests by secretly siding with Britain in the Boer War. King Edward told Hardinge that 'of all the political gaffes which H.I.M. has made, this is the greatest'.[7]

The Emperor tried to make amends by giving a brief interview to an American reporter representing the *New York World*. The copy the journalist sent back afterwards was considered too inflammatory for publication, but a short synopsis was printed, informing its readers that the Emperor thought King Edward corrupt, his court rotten, and Anglo-German war inevitable.

The King was deeply affronted, and wrote to Francis Knollys in November that he knew the Emperor hated him, 'and never loses an opportunity of saying so (behind my back) whilst I have always been civil and nice to him'. The timing was unfortunate, as plans were under way for a state visit by the King to Berlin. In the same letter, he wrote that 'there is no hurry to settle anything at present. The Foreign Office, to gain their own object, will not care a pin what private humiliation I have to put up with.'[8]

A short but welcome diversion came when King Gustav and Queen Victoria of Sweden arrived at Windsor in November for a four-day visit to England. They were received at the station by King Edward and Queen Alexandra, and the Scandinavian monarch was amused at being given an address of greeting by the Mayor; 'A Mayor in England seems to be a far more magnificent and important personage than a King is in Sweden!'

Not only civic pomp and ceremony held surprises for King Gustav. He was astonished by the gargantuan appetites at the table of his host nation. 'My word, but these English *can* eat . . . !' he remarked in astonishment after a Mayoral banquet at the Guildhall, where he was presented with the usual address of welcome in a gold casket. His verdict after the royal dinner at Windsor was in similar vein. 'A thing that always impresses me about the English', he said afterwards, 'is that they talk so little and eat so much. And they seem to take their eating much more seriously than they do their conversation!'[9]

On the matter of the long-postponed state visit to Berlin, King Edward fully agreed with the Foreign Office staff. Unpalatable though it might be, it could not be deferred for long. It was unfortunate that the anti-German firebrand Lord Roberts should choose this time, just a month after the *Daily Telegraph* article, to deliver a much-reported speech proclaiming that Germany was a far greater danger to England than France had been in a previous age, and that she could easily concentrate a force of 150,000 or more at the Channel ports and launch a lightning invasion. Against such unpropitious circumstances was the visit prepared.

The Emperor's recovery from this crisis of personal self-confidence had been delayed by an episode of black farce. Horrified by reaction at home, he retired briefly with friends to a house in the country, where an after-dinner entertainment one evening ended in an elderly military aide donning a ballerina's tutu, executing a few dainty steps, and then succumbing to a heart attack. In order to lessen any subsequent scandal (for the Emperor was still nervous at repercussions from the Eulenburg affair), the late Count was hastily removed from his tutu and reattired in uniform, before being laid out for burial the next day. Soon after returning to Berlin the Emperor took to his bed with nervous prostration and told the family he was going to abdicate. The Empress talked him out of it, but something of his old panache had gone, never to return.

On 8 February 1909 King Edward and Queen Alexandra crossed the North Sea on their way to Berlin. The Queen, who had always hated Germany with a vengeance, steeled herself to act graciously towards her hosts, while the King was feeling unwell, pining for the bracing airs, the spring sun and a more relaxed way of life at Biarritz.

But the Emperor told the Tsar that he looked forward to receiving Uncle Bertie, not merely for family reasons but also 'because I expect the visit to have useful results for the peace of the world'.

The state visit was marred by one fiasco after another. As the royal train steamed into Berlin railway station on 9 February, the Emperor and Empress, Bülow and others were waiting on the platform to receive them. The ceremony had been meticulously rehearsed and the welcoming party was drawn up precisely where the King's carriage stopped. However, the King had decided to alight from the Queen's carriage with her. Their Imperial Majesties and the rest of the welcoming committee thus had to move with undignified haste more than a hundred yards down the platform in full regalia. During the state drive through Berlin, the coach in which the Empress and Queen were travelling suddenly came to a stop, the horses refusing to move. Both ladies had to transfer to a less ornate coach to complete the journey. Meanwhile Emperor and King waited apprehensively in the palace courtyard, fearing an assassination attempt. When the rest of the procession arrived, the Emperor was furious. He felt he had been made to look ridiculous in front of the English, who were masters of the perfectly-organized ceremony.

The Emperor had done his best to make everything a success. No detail was spared to make his uncle and aunt feel at home. In the study of the King's suite hung a portrait of Queen Victoria, and a coloured print of British naval victories. In the Queen's room were pictures of Copenhagen and Sandringham, the books included a selection of Danish classics, and a concert piano was thoughtfully provided for the Queen, whose premature deafness never prevented her from finding solace in her music.

Despite these homely touches, it was evident to observers that the King was unwell. He had a heavy cold and persistent cough, and looked tired. At the state banquet given in his honour on the first evening, in reply to the Emperor's formal speech of welcome, he read from a prepared text, contrary to his usual off-the-cuff speeches. By his standards, it was a lifeless performance.

At a reception at the Rathaus, the King had been uneasy, in view of the virulently anti-British reputation of Berlin's city fathers. Yet once he was there, he found the aldermen much more congenial company than the medal-jangling, heel-clicking princes and military officers at his nephew's court. There was one pleasant surprise in store for him. As the list of councillors for presentation was read out, the King caught the name of Dr Renvers, the kindly physician who had cared for the Empress Frederick during her last painful illness. He was called over, shaken warmly by the hand, and thanked with words that obviously came from the heart. Like the sceptical Parisians six years before, the astonished Germans were charmed, and suddenly saw the King in a much more favourable light than before.

From the Rathaus, he went to the British Embassy. A large luncheon given in his name for the diplomatic corps of the capital city passed smoothly enough, but it was almost followed by tragedy. Too tired afterwards to make formal conversation with any of the ambassadors, the King was chatting on a sofa with Daisy, Princess of Pless, a British-born society beauty who had always regarded him as a close personal friend. He was wearing a tight-fitting Prussian uniform, and smoking one of his usual huge cigars. Suddenly he coughed and fell back against the back of the sofa. The cigar slipped out of his fingers, he stared ahead and for a while was unable to breathe. The horrified Daisy thought he was dying; 'Oh! why not in his own country?' She tried to undo the collar of his uniform, then the Queen rushed up to help her, before he regained consciousness and did it himself. Everyone else tactfully withdrew and his physician, Sir James Reid, was fetched from an adjoining room. Within minutes, the King appeared to be his usual self, and lit another cigar as he stayed some time talking to the ambassador and guests. If anyone else guessed that the King was in the throes of chronic bronchitis and that his days were numbered, they kept it to themselves.

This was followed at the Opera by an incident of pure comedy. The programme included a ballet, *Sardanapalus*, devised by the Emperor. In the final act was a very realistic representation of the funeral pyre of Sardanapalus, beginning with small licking tongues of flame, spreading to a fierce blaze in which Sardanapalus and all his household perished. At the moment before the curtain fell, the whole stage had the glowing appearance of a furnace threaded with leaping flames and rolling billows of smoke. Bored and exhausted after the day's programme, the King had nodded off. On waking up to the staged conflagration he drew the understandable conclusion, and angrily demanded to know why the firemen in the wings were not putting it out. It took all the Empress' powers of persuasion to assure him that they were in no danger.

Nobody had ever expected this state visit to give an opportunity for serious discussions. From London, Count Metternich had warned that any attempt at high-level political talks at this stage would be highly inappropriate. Nevertheless, King Edward saw fit to raise the increasingly explosive issue of Germany's shipbuilding programme with his nephew. He chose the end of the visit, either on the drive to the station or perhaps even on the railway platform itself. It was apparently a politely defensive, conciliatory conversation of which the only written report was one produced afterwards by the Emperor.[10]

Perhaps realizing that he was seeing his nephew for the last time, and feeling there was nothing to be lost, the King felt obliged to make one final effort. Still far from well, he was probably too tired to care whether his efforts would bring any success or not. As a sovereign who had travelled several hundred miles every year during his reign, partly in the cause of promoting peace on behalf of his country, he had done his best, often against overwhelming odds. A few friendly words with the Emperor might fall on stony ground, but not for want of trying on his part.

Five weeks later, writing to his friend Sir Ernest Cassel from the bracing air of Biarritz, the King referred to his Berlin visit as 'in every respect a great success'. Even overlooking the mishaps which marred it, few others can have shared this optimistic verdict. It had done nothing to alleviate the tension caused by Anglo-German naval rivalry. Moreover, anti-English elements in Berlin still felt insulted that despite the close family ties between Windsor and Berlin, state visits had been paid to virtually every other capital in Europe first. It was conveniently overlooked that the King had offered to come to Berlin in 1904, but been put off by the Emperor; and it also took no account of the fact that uncle and nephew had met several times elsewhere during the previous few years. That His Majesty attended the state opening of a new session of Parliament a few days after returning to England, and that an increase of nearly £3 million on naval expenditure was agreed, did not pass unnoticed in Berlin either.

It still remained for the Tsar to pay an official state visit to England, and arrangements were made for him to do so after a meeting with the French President at Cherbourg in July 1909.

Once again, radical members of Parliament at Westminster protested, saying that King Edward's reception of the Tsar was an insult to the good name of the nation, especially when 'his personal approval of the criminal agents had been placed beyond question', and that the Reval meeting of the previous year had made the Russian domestic situation worse than before. To these objections, Sir Edward Grey replied that it was a grave offence to criticize the internal administration of foreign countries, and he urged that efforts were being made to establish constitutional government in Russia. Moreover, the Tsar was the head of a great state with whom England desired to be on friendly terms. Even so, on 2 August, the day of the Tsar's arrival, newspapers carried a letter to the Foreign Secretary protesting against the official welcome to the Tsar, signed by seventy Liberal and Labour MPs, three peers, two bishops, and many Free Church Ministers.

The arrival of *Standart* at Spithead was heralded by a flotilla of twenty-four battleships, sixteen armoured cruisers, and forty-eight destroyers. The Prince of Wales's three elder children were to act as companions for the Grand Duchesses and the Tsarevich. However, Albert, the Prince of Wales' second son, had developed whooping-cough and had to be kept in quarantine until after the imperial guests had departed, as the risk of the haemophiliac Tsarevich catching the infection and rupturing a blood vessel from prolonged bouts of coughing was too great. It was left to Edward to show his 'Uncle Nicky' around Osborne, and for Mary to be a playmate to the Grand Duchesses, of whom one, Tatiana, was her exact contemporary in age.

Even in England, the Russian government would not risk the Tsar's presence at London or Windsor, for fear of assassination plots. Only Cowes was deemed safe enough from anyone whose business might be remotely suspicious. Some forty years later Prince Edward, by then Duke of Windsor, noted that he did not recall the Tsar 'as a man of marked personality; but I do remember being

The Russian imperial family's visit to Osborne, 1909. Seated, from left: the Princess of Wales; Tsar Nicholas II; Tsarevich Alexis (on ground); King Edward VII; Grand Duchess Anastasia (on ground); Tsarina Alexandra; Prince of Wales; Grand Duchess Marie. Standing, from left: Prince Edward; Queen Alexandra; Princess Victoria; Grand Duchesses Olga and Tatiana

astonished at the elaborate police guard thrown around his every movement when I showed him through Osborne. This certainly made me glad I was not a Russian prince [*sic*].'[11]

Despite such restrictions, the visit was still a friendly occasion. For three days, breakfast was the only meal which the families did not share. Everyone was impressed by the good looks and charming behaviour of the Grand Duchesses, and the Tsarevich captivated his English hosts, though he shyly rebuffed the friendly advances of his regal great-uncle. In the evening there were firework displays and more of the dancing that had enlivened the previous summer's visit off Reval, with Admiral Fisher, who insisted on partnering each of the Grand Duchesses and their mother in turn, once again the life and soul of the party.

The Tsarina always seemed to associate the sunshine of England with her happy memories as a young girl under the affectionately watchful eye of Queen Victoria, which had provided one of the few really joyful interludes in the life of that most tragic of women. Not only did it revive childhood days, but it also reminded her of the summer at Osborne twenty-five years before, when she and Nicky, just betrothed, had spent a carefree holiday on the Isle of Wight, blissfully unaware of the overwhelming responsibilities which would be theirs by the end of that year. To see their children playing on the beach, spending their pocket money on postcards and rock which they eagerly shared with their parents, transported them briefly into another world, far away from the shadows of their life in Russia.

At least one of their young British cousins always remembered the Tsarina, as well as her children, with lasting affection. In 1913 the thirteen-year-old Prince Louis of Battenberg, later Earl Mountbatten of Burma, was thrilled to be allowed to indulge his passion for model aeroplanes by requesting that his Christmas present from his aunt in Russia, a generous £5, should be spent on a new model which worked with compressed air like a tornado, capable of flying up to a mile.[12]

By autumn 1909 King Edward had only one more royal guest to entertain on his own soil. The disturbed state of Portugal had precluded any immediate visit by the young King Manuel, but the King was determined to show sympathy towards the young monarch. In November he invited King Manuel to Windsor, where he was invested with the Order of the Garter, and saluted at the state banquet as 'the heir of our oldest ally in history'.

Already there was talk of an English Queen for Portugal. King Edward suggested to Louise, younger daughter of Prince and Princess Louis of Battenberg, that she could do well to consider marriage with the visiting King. He was highly indignant at her refusal to hear anything of it, rebuking her for not having a 'more patriotic approach to marriage, as it would be a great thing'[13] if Portugal, like Spain and Norway, was to have a British Queen.

On 23 January 1910 King Edward wrote his customary congratulations to the Emperor William on his birthday, sending him a walking-stick as a present, and

King Edward VII, shortly before his death

reiterating 'that it is essential for the peace of the world that we walk shoulder to shoulder for the good of civilisation and the prosperity of the world',[14] and expressed his regret that the press of both countries was still stirring things up.

The Emperor's reply (31 January 1910) struck an appropriately valedictory chord:

> Your remark: 'That it is essential for the Peace of the world that we should walk shoulder to shoulder for the good of civilisation & the prosperity of the world' strikes a familiar note in my heart. This wish has always been the leading maxim of my policy & the goal which I have ardently striven to reach. It is a firm part of my political creed that the future of the world would be assured & safeguarded if the Anglo-Saxon & the Teutonic Races worked together. They are the powerful guardians of the Ideals of Christian Faith & Christian Civilisation & it is their common duty to proclaim & disseminate them over the world.[15]

The following month, Prince Henry of Prussia came to stay at Buckingham Palace. One evening he had a conversation with Ponsonby in which he expressed his concern that their countries seemed so far apart. He was not satisfied by Ponsonby's tactful references to the press being responsible for bad feeling, and commercial rivalry. Pressed further, the equerry said that it was not surprising a feeling of mistrust and suspicion had arisen when Germany insisted on building a Fleet. It was assumed that the new navy did not intend to fight France or Russia, or any other Power, except Britain.

Prince Henry assured him that nothing was further from German thoughts than war with Britain. With forty years' peace behind them, the Germans had formed themselves into a nation which had nothing to gain by going to war, which would cripple them and probably cost them their trade. All they wanted to do was defend their commerce. As Britain had a Fleet, why should Germany not as well? When Ponsonby mentioned the increased taxation being felt and resented by all classes in both countries, the Prince said there was no feeling of suspicion and distrust in Germany; so why did Britain continue to mass her Fleet at Dover? Told that Britain regarded it as commonsense to keep her Fleet at a point where it was most likely they would want it, Prince Henry laughed, saying, 'You are the first that has dared to tell me that.'[16]

The bronchitis which had alarmed everyone on the King's visit to Berlin attacked him again that winter, and the family and doctors were particularly concerned at his violent fits of coughing. His regular winter journeys to Biarritz, attributed by the cynical to a love of pleasure, were increasingly vital for health reasons. Though he was reluctant to leave his kingdom at a time of political crisis, caused by virtual stalemate between the Liberal government and the House of Lords, the doctors were anxious to get him away from the fogs of London.

Health problems followed him across the Channel that March. In Paris he had a violent attack of acute indigestion, and a heavy cold exacerbated his bronchitis by the time he reached Biarritz. For a few critical days Sir James Reid hesitated as to whether to reveal to the public just how ill his royal patient was.

Fortunately he recovered sufficiently to receive Queen Amelie of Portugal a few days later. Their meeting gave rise to a fresh spate of rumours that King Manuel was to marry Louise of Battenberg, or failing her, another niece of the King. It was reported that he would readily give his approval to the marriage, dependent on the internal conditions of the country and an inquiry into the circumstances of the assassination of King Carlos and the Crown Prince. The Portuguese Foreign Minister deprecated any such discussion as an affront to national dignity. That Louise had made her lack of enthusiasm plain, however, rendered the question largely hypothetical. Four or five years earlier, the King would have surely pursued any such matchmaking with vigour; but he was all too aware of the Braganzas' precarious hold on their crown, and he knew that his life's work was done by now. It no longer mattered quite so much.

On 27 April he returned to London, apparently in good spirits and all the better for his holiday. However, after spending several hours on a bitterly cold wet day inspecting the gardens and farms at Sandringham, bronchitis set in once more, and by the time he returned to Buckingham Palace on 2 May he was feeling very unwell. Despite entreaties from his doctors to rest, he continued to see people and receive official audiences, though they all noticed the change in him. Begged by one visitor to rest after he had recovered from one of his choking fits, he brushed the idea aside, retorting that he would work to the end; 'Of what use is it to be alive if one cannot work?'

The family were warned, and Queen Alexandra and Princess Victoria were summoned home urgently from their Mediterranean cruise. Only when the Prince of Wales went to meet them at Victoria station on the evening of 5 May did the British public realize just how ill their sovereign was. Not till the following morning would he himself admit to feeling 'miserably ill'. That afternoon he was told that his horse, Witch of the Air, had won a race at Kempton Park. 'Yes, I have heard of it', the King said when the Prince of Wales told him. 'I am very glad.' They were the last coherent words he spoke. At fifteen minutes before midnight, he died. He was in his sixty-ninth year.

Reaction throughout Europe was almost as respectful as at home in England. In Vienna the press regretted the passing of 'the most influential man of the present day', a King who 'had been his own Foreign Minister'. In St Petersburg it was observed that the King had 'not only reigned but also moulded the destinies of his realm', and that Bismarck had created an overlordship for Germany in Europe, for which King Edward substituted 'the hegemony of England'. Somewhat acidly, but not without admiration, the German press remarked that the nation stood 'at his bier as that of a mighty and victorious antagonist'.[17]

Several kindly tributes of a personal nature were paid in the form of letters of condolence to his son and successor. Prince Henry of Prussia wrote to his cousin (7 May):

Needless to say, you know how I feel for all of you & especially for you during this period of grief & sorrow, which at the same time puts a heavy weight of responsibility on yr shoulders!

None of you hardly guessed how much yr dear Papa was to me – how devoted I was to him! His memory will ever be dear & sacred to me, never can I forget how much friendship & kindness he showed me & how much I owe him!

I telegraphed to William, asking him for leave to attend the coming ceremonies. From his answer to the affirmative, I gather and hope, that I shall not be sent in any official capacity as I much prefer coming privately! No doubt numbers of foreign relations & Princes will want to come, or be sent, & I earnestly entreat you not to bother about putting me up at Buckingham Palace, which under the circumstances would even be *painful* to me, in remembrance of the last happy days spent there with yr dear father![18]

Tsar Nicholas wrote (8 May) in similar vein:

It is difficult to realize that your beloved Father has been taken away. The awful rapidity with which it all happened! How I would have liked to have come now & be near you!

I beg you dearest Georgie to continue our old friendship and to show my country the same interest as your dear Father did from the day he came to the throne.

No one did so much in trying to bring our two countries closer together than him. The first steps have brought good results. Let us strive and work in the same direction.[19]

The Tsarina commiserated likewise with her cousin:

Only a few words to tell you how very much we think of you in your great grief. Besides your heart being full of sorrow after the great loss you have entertained, now come the new & heavy responsibilities crowding upon you. From all my heart

'Royal mourners at King Edward's funeral', from a contemporary postcard

I pray that God may give you strength & wisdom to govern your country. It is a new life with many a serious task awaiting you, that you have now begun. May God's blessing be upon you dear. Your sweet May, whom I kiss, will be a great help to you I am sure in every way. I think so much of you, as Nicky & I began our married life under similar trying circumstances.

Thank God we saw yr. dear Papa still last summer – one cannot realise that he is gone.[20]

From Portugal, Dowager Queen Amelie wrote: 'you know what your beloved father was to us, in our Family and in our Country, and the consternation is general. Never shall I forget all the friendship, all the kindness always showed to me, and I can hardly realize I saw your dear father in Biarritz for the last time!'[21]

'What a difficult moment it is for you to take up the reign of old England and especially after uncle Bertie, who not only in his own country was esteemed but too admired by the whole world', wrote King Frederick VIII of Denmark (7 May). 'But thanks to him I believe peace was kept here in Europe, and I had that particular feeling that no harm would happen to us and that is the reason, why I only beg you not to forget our Country, and I believe you understand what I mean.'[22]

During his nine years as King, Edward had sought to improve friendly relations with all the European powers. The Entente Cordiale with France, nobody could

Frederick VIII, King of Denmark

deny, was largely his doing. Relations had been severely strained during the last years of Queen Victoria's reign; without his triumphant visit to sweep the bitterness away, it could not have been achieved. Likewise, relations with Russia had been put under severe pressure by the Dogger Bank incident, and the Anglo-Japanese alliance. Indeed, his contribution towards bringing about a new climate of friendship with France and Russia perhaps gave him more satisfaction than any other achievements during his reign.

Although he lacked formal negotiating skills, his charm and friendly manner, his reasonable attitude and persuasiveness, and his sound judgement of character, added to the weight and dignity of his rank, were indispensable as a prelude to the detailed negotiations which resulted in the signing of alliances between foreign powers. The only other two monarchs of commensurate prestige were the excitable, thoroughly undependable Emperor William, and the little-travelled, impossibly remote Emperor Francis Joseph. Beside the doomed Hohenzollerns and Habsburgs, the head of the house of Saxe-Coburg Gotha cut a far superior figure.

The effect of King Edward's personality was felt more in conversations with others, as unlike his mother, he preferred meeting people to writing letters. Yet he personified those in Britain who were determined to put an end to their country's nineteenth-century isolationism, understanding that Britain must have allies, and recognize the threat confronting her. He preached vigilance, demanded battleships, and promoted the Triple Entente. In much of this he was facilitated by the royal relationships which bound so many of the European courts to that at Windsor.

According to the diarist Wilfrid Scawen Blunt, his foreign policy was consistent with his easy-going nature: 'he liked to be well-received wherever he went, and to be on good terms with all the world. He was essentially a cosmopolitan, and without racial prejudice, and he cared for popularity abroad as at home. This made him anxious to compose international quarrels. He wanted an easy life, and that everybody should be friends with everybody.'[23]

It was his tragedy – indeed Europe's tragedy – that Frederick III was not German Emperor at the same time. King Edward failed with his nephew merely because the latter was so unstable, and provoked his neighbours to unite against Germany. The King had been under no illusions. On his way home from Biarritz for the last time, he had stopped in Paris, where he told an old friend, the Comtesse de Greffuhle: 'I have not long to live. And then my nephew will make war.'[24]

The King's funeral took place at Windsor on the hot sultry day of 20 May. It provided the occasion for an international pageant of royalty, as glittering and splendid as any he had witnessed in life. Even Windsor Castle had rarely, if ever, seen such an assembly of crowned heads within its confines.

Nine monarchs led the main body of the procession. Immediately behind the coffin marched the new King, George V, in Admiral's uniform. On his right was Emperor William II, and on the left their last surviving uncle, the Duke of Connaught. Behind them, after a line of aides and equerries, came King Haakon

The funeral procession of King Edward VII, 20 May 1910. Princes Edward and Albert, in naval uniform, follow behind the German Emperor, King George V, and the Duke of Connaught

of Norway, King Alfonso of Spain, and King George of Greece. The next rows included Tsar Ferdinand of Bulgaria, King Frederick VIII of Denmark, King Manuel of Portugal, and King Albert of the Belgians. All these monarchs were either related by marriage to the late King, or through the Coburg line.

A procession of carriages followed the Kings and Princes, containing the Queen Mother and her sister, the Dowager Empress of Russia, Queen Mary, the King's daughters, and republican representatives, including the former President of the United States, Theodore Roosevelt. The procession also included many royal, grand ducal, and serene highnesses from Prussia, Saxony, Hesse, Teck and Saxe-Coburg, nearly all related in various ways. The Archduke Francis Ferdinand, heir to the throne of Austria-Hungary, and the Hereditary Prince of the Ottoman Empire, were almost alone in not being part of the family.

It was a cavalcade of European royalty and imperial power at its height which King Edward, who had been one of the most widely-travelled of them all, would have relished.

5 'A thorough Englishman'

King George V knew that he could never hope to compete with his father as a personality on the European stage. As heir to the throne, he had not attempted to make a name for himself as a figure of international standing, in the way King Edward VII had as Prince of Wales during the nineteenth century. As far as the rest of Europe was concerned, the new King was a somewhat shadowy figure. 'It is curious how little May and George are known in general', wrote his cousin Grand Duchess Cyril of Russia to her sister Marie, Crown Princess of Roumania. 'No Crown Prince and Princess have ever mounted a throne so entirely unknown to people abroad.'[1]

Mensdorff considered him to be 'through and through an Englishman, with all the prejudices and insular limitations of the typical John Bull'.[2] The Austrian Ambassador reported to his government that the King had no special affection for, or prejudice against, any foreign country, although his personal sympathies appeared to incline to the side of his mother's relations rather than to those of his father. However, his contemporaries thought Mensdorff tended to attribute exaggerated importance to dynastic affiliations.

King George was particularly attached to his cousins in Denmark, Norway, Greece, and to Tsar Nicholas II of Russia, to whom he bore such a marked physical resemblance. On his first meeting with the King in June 1913, President Poincaré of France was immediately struck by his resemblance to the Tsar; 'yet his colour was not so pale, his expression less dreamy, his smile less melancholy & his gestures less timid'.[3]

King and Tsar had been close friends ever since, as Duke of York and Tsarevich respectively, they had joined in at Fredensborg family reunions with 'Apapa' and 'Amama', their grandparents King Christian IX and Queen Louise of Denmark. The resemblance, recalled Grand Duchess Olga, was more than physical; 'both were honest, shy, and modest'. The Duke of York had taken a great liking to her and her elder sister Xenia. He would mischievously ask Olga to come and roll with him on the ottoman, and it became a secret joke between them. Later, when they were adults, attending tedious official functions, his blue eyes would twinkle as he whispered the same age-old invitation in her ear. Every time, she would blush as she looked around to make sure nobody had heard the future King of England making such an improper suggestion in public.[4] As for Xenia, she had particularly large, striking eyes, and he nicknamed her 'Owl'.

The King's relations with the German Emperor were perfectly amicable. As Sir Harold Nicolson remarked many years later, he displayed a shrewder understanding of Emperor William's nervous and impulsive temperament than any sympathy that King Edward had been able to acquire.[5] King Edward and Queen Alexandra had had good reasons for disliking their German nephew, and during their son's upbringing, they made no effort to help him see any great merit in Germany.

Yet he had no desire to pursue the long-standing family feud. On a personal level, on sporting expeditions at Sandringham he had particularly admired the way in which his cousin had overcome the handicap of his withered left arm and become such an accomplished shot. In 1900, when Britain's stock had fallen in Europe as a result of the Boer War, he had invited the Emperor to be one of the godparents to his third son Prince Henry, later Duke of Gloucester. Politically, he appreciated the importance of good personal relations, and on his visit to the court of Berlin in January 1902 he had impressed everyone with his tactful demeanour.

In turn the Emperor had always liked and respected his cousin George, of whom he spoke to Theodore Roosevelt as 'a thorough Englishman', who hated all foreigners, 'but I do not mind that as long as he does not hate Germans more than other foreigners'.

'Let me thank you for the kind thought of sending me the photo of the 9 Sovereigns at Windsor', he wrote to King George (8 July 1910). 'A souvenir of a sad but ever to be remembered day of mourning, which never can be effaced from my memory. That I was permitted to come over to stay with you through all those hours has created a link between us which I always shall cherish.'[6]

The King's personal character, so very different from that of his father, dictated much of his personal attitude towards his fellow-sovereigns at the start of his reign. Firstly, he disliked travelling to the continent, and his distaste hardened into aversion with the conservatism of increasing years. Abroad, in his memorable phrase, was 'awful – I know, because I've been there', although he made an exception in the case of India, the Empire always appealing to the romantic strain in him. Lord Esher, a much-respected royal confidant, was struck by his enthusiasm for attending the Indian durbar the following year, and his intention of visiting every dominion. Following a conversation with him three months after his accession, he noted that the King 'means to do for the Empire what King Edward did for the peace of Europe'.

Much to Queen Mary's dismay, he found no pleasure in travel, expressed no curiosity in the history, arts and general culture of other lands, and he was a lamentably poor linguist. A brief career in the Royal Navy failed to help him overcome his basic shyness and a dread of public occasions; and poor digestion made him dread rich, unfamiliar food.

Secondly, he had little of his father's confidence. While he was just as well-informed on foreign and international affairs, and never hesitated to express his own opinions, he was not tempted to follow King Edward's example in pursuing a foreign policy independent of his ministers. He understood equally well the limited powers of a constitutional sovereign, and unlike his predecessors he was generally content to subordinate his personal prejudices to the dictates of his government.

King George V and Queen Mary

To this, there could be exceptions. There were differences between King and Cabinet about the importance of state visits to the capitals of Europe. He recognized that he had a constitutional duty to make such visits, notwithstanding personal inconvenience. Adamant on preserving the entente, Grey tried to insist that a state visit should be made to Paris before St Petersburg, Vienna, and Berlin. To this the King answered that France, 'being only a republic', must yield pride of place to the three continental imperial powers. Close friendship with Mensdorff, and the advanced age of Emperor Francis Joseph (eighty in August 1910) led him to argue that Austria must have priority. He told Sir Francis Bertie, British Ambassador in Paris, that in such revolutionary times the sovereigns should stand together; 'we make too much of the French'. The coolness of Lord Stamfordham, his private secretary, towards France and his desire for an understanding with Germany, sharpened his antipathy to Francis Knollys, King Edward VII's secretary, who had shared his late master's Francophile inclinations.

In the event, the question was hypothetical. The protracted political crisis between Lords and Commons which had overshadowed King Edward's last months, followed by a Home Rule crisis, the King's Coronation and visit to India for the durbar ceremony, and industrial unrest at home, conspired between them to distract him from any immediate plans for state visits to the capitals on the continent. After that, Europe rapidly became a very different entity from the one with which they were faced in 1910.

Though King George and Queen Mary saw their cousins who had married abroad but rarely, several of them were prolific correspondents. One to whom the King had once been very close was Marie, Crown Princess of Roumania. At one time it was suspected that he was about to become betrothed to his lively, fair-haired cousin, eldest daughter of the Duke and Duchess of Edinburgh. That she was soon engaged and married rather hastily, at the tender age of seventeen, to Crown Prince Ferdinand was due in no small measure to the designs of the Anglophobe Duchess of Edinburgh. Yet the cousins always maintained a deep affection for each other. Bitterly homesick, she missed England greatly, and was always grateful for a friendly word from her old home. Her early married life had been unhappy, particularly as she was too young and too innocent to avoid getting caught up in what seemed to her harmless flirtations but, at one point, resulted in a scandal at the court of Bucharest which was only ended when she and her suitor were sent abroad separately in disgrace.

'How dear of you to say that you still take interest in me – My life is so changed and I am so far off down here that I expect everyone to forget me', she had written in one particularly depressed mood to the then Prince of Wales (26 November 1901):

Yes, I have been through hard moments, partly through my own fault I know, but also because many things have been very difficult, and above all because I have been dreadfully lonely – I know one must not expect too much of life . . . I very soon found out that down here one has to be very strong, to stand the loneliness of it all, & I was not always strong, and expected too much – and wanted to be happy – and of course I had to learn by bitter experience all that one cannot have, and may not expect! – You will try and understand me, won't you – and when one speaks unkindly about me – will you sometimes take my part, just because I have suffered a great deal – The brightest times I ever had were those Malta days, and you used to be so kind to us three sisters – God bless you for it still now! – Now I have grown quieter in many things, and don't struggle for what cannot be – I mean also to try hard & like it all – and do my duty, the thought, that I am not quite forgotten down here – will help me on! – We have seen much sadness lately, and I am no more quite the bright Missy of happier days – but my heart is the same in spite of all – and I never forget those who I care for, nor those who are kind to me. When you think of me, let it be of a very lonely creature who tries to do her best – but who has failed often.[7]

The King's first experience of the necessity of subordinating personal affections to requirements of state policy came five months after his accession. Soveral's gloomy forebodings about the future of the Portuguese monarchy were realized when revolution broke out that autumn. On 4 October regiments mutinied, murdered their officers, and advanced towards the centre of Lisbon. King Manuel immediately drove to his capital and established himself in the Necessidades Palace, determined to make a stand against the rebels. By midnight republican forces had secured complete control of the capital, and warships in the Tagus were starting to bombard the palace. The heavily-outnumbered King was persuaded to escape by the garden gate, and drove to Mafra, where he was joined by other members of the royal family. The revolution had evidently triumphed, and there was nothing for the King and his family to do but embark on their yacht and sail for Gibraltar, with no possessions but the clothes they were wearing. On reaching their destination, they accepted hospitality from the Governor, Sir Archibald Hunter.

In London Soveral asked King George to send a British warship to Gibraltar to bring the royal family to England. Grey felt that such a gesture was excessive. As a compromise, the King insisted on sending the royal yacht, and Grey reluctantly agreed. He was anxious to forestall any criticism such action might arouse by immediately according official recognition to the new republican government at Lisbon. Keenly aware of monarchical solidarity, King George viewed with concern the prospect of Great Britain being the first of the Great Powers to accept and thereby fortify the revolution, but against Grey's insistence he was powerless. King Manuel and his mother were transferred from Gibraltar to Southampton in the royal yacht. They settled for a while at Woodnorton, Evesham, as guests of King Manuel's maternal uncle the Duke of Orleans, where King George visited them at the end of the month.

Still not quite twenty-one at the time of his abdication, King Manuel was a lively personality. Prince Christopher, youngest son of King George of the Hellenes, became a firm friend after meeting him for the first time in 1912, in Harrogate. King Manuel's changed fortunes, he related, 'had not affected his sense of humour. His gaiety was infectious; he had a schoolboy's love of fun.' Their first meeting, after dinner one evening, ended up with both under the table squirting siphons of soda water at each other and the King's elderly equerry getting soaked through.[8]

As expected by statesmen in both countries, King Edward VII's death seemed to herald an improvement in Anglo-German relations. During the lying-in-state at Westminster Hall, spectators had been moved at the sight of King George and Emperor William clasping hands at the head of the coffin, and Mensdorff contrasted the Emperor's sympathetic, dignified self-effacement with what he saw as the noisy merriment of the Greek family mourners. Ominously, but less publicly, during the luncheon which followed in St George's Hall, the Emperor took Cambon aside and made a sinister suggestion as to the possibility of a Franco-German pact in the event of Germany challenging England.

William II was the first monarch to be received at court by George V after the funeral ceremonies were over. Early in 1911 he invited the Emperor to attend the unveiling of the Queen Victoria Memorial outside Buckingham Palace. As the eldest of her grandchildren, King George thought that the Emperor and his wife should have a special place at the ceremony. His letter of invitation brought forth an effusive reply (15 February):

> You cannot imagine how overjoyed I am at the prospect of seeing you so soon & making a nice stay with you. You are perfectly right in alluding to my devotion & reverence for my beloved Grandmother, with whom I was on such excellent terms. I shall never forget how kindly this great lady always was to me & the relations she kept up with me, though I was so far her junior, she having carried me about in her arms! Never in my life shall I forget the solemn hours in Osborne near her deathbed when she breathed her last in my arms! These sacred hours have riveted my heart firmly to your house & family, of which I am proud to feel myself a member. And the fact that for the last hours I held the sacred burden of her – the creator of the greatness of modern Britain – in my arms, in my mind created an invisible special link between her country & its People & me, which I fondly nurse in my heart.[9]

The Emperor hoped that his presence at the unveiling might help to improve relations between England and Germany, and was disappointed when his Chancellor, Bethmann-Hollweg, and Grey both insisted that the visit should be regarded as a purely family gathering, with no political conversations taking place. They had evidently had quite enough during the reign of King Edward with their sovereigns attempting to take the political initiative, without reference to their respective governments.

All the same, the three days which the Emperor spent in London passed happily. Crowds in the streets greeted him with marked enthusiasm, and all the festivities laid on were as well organized as ever. He assured his Chancellor that he had never found the atmosphere at the Palace so open or friendly before.

At a ball held in the imperial family's honour, the King danced with the Emperor's daughter, the striking-looking nineteen-year-old Princess Victoria Louise. Over-zealous observers suggested that an engagement would be announced between her and Prince Edward, shortly to become Prince of Wales. 'Certainly her marriage would be one of the most important events imaginable, fraught with tremendous consequences for the whole of Europe', commented the *Daily Express*. 'The Kaiser's daughter has taken London by storm, and everywhere is reaping golden opinions by her winning smile and abounding interest in everything and everybody with whom she comes into contact.'[10] The German Empress lost no time in denying any such idea.

The Emperor saw Prince Louis of Battenberg several times while in England, but only once alone, on the afternoon of 20 May. Louis reported to King George V afterwards that he found the Emperor quite determined to cultivate friendly relations with England, but warning that 'you must not *differentiate* in the way you have been doing of late. You must not preface every conversation with the condition that you cannot come to an agreement with us on this or that subject if it were to affect the interests of France or Russia.' When Louis pointed out that England's understanding with both countries was the natural and necessary counterpoise to the Triple Alliance, the Emperor insisted angrily that Germany was the sole arbiter of peace or war on the continent. 'If we wish to fight we will do so without your leave.' The continental powers had armies amounting to millions, he stated, and it would be ridiculous of Britain to send a force numbering merely 50,000 men anywhere. As for the French, Germany had beaten them once and would beat them again. 'You know you can't mount your Dreadnoughts on wheels & come to your dear friends' assistance.'

The Emperor became ever more impassioned, declaring that Britain must not interfere with Germany's friendly relations with Russia. Their nations were old allies, and had fought side by side against the yoke of Napoleon. If revolution endangered the Russian throne, the Emperor insisted, both he and the Emperor of Austria 'would instantly march in shoulder to shoulder, and re-instate the Emperor Nicholas'.[11]

Louis was not given the opportunity to reply. Perhaps intentionally, the conversation was broken up by the Empress calling out to them that tea was ready.

King George sent a confidential report of the conversation to Churchill, who promised not to speak of it to anyone but Grey. It was his view that the German Emperor had long since ceased to have any settled policy, and was taken less seriously by his own subjects every year. One was tempted to discern in some of his statements the workings of a disordered mind.

Up to the outbreak of war, Louis' opinions and knowledge on German and Russian affairs were highly respected at the Foreign and War Offices as well as the Admiralty. He was the first to appreciate that Emperor William was much more disturbed at British friendship with Russia than with France.

The Emperor could not avoid making one serious diplomatic gaffe. Just before leaving for the railway station, he brought up the question of Morocco with King George. To quell an insurrection in Fez, France, responsible for maintaining peace in the North African country, had sent troops to restore order. Such action was bitterly resented by Germany.

The only record of this conversation was one written by the Emperor himself. Asking the King whether he considered that French methods were in accordance with the Algeciras agreement, the King replied that the agreement 'was no longer in force, that the best thing to do was to forget it'.[12] According to a note by Bethman-Hollweg on the Emperor's return to Berlin, the latter assured King George that he would 'never wage a war for the sake of Morocco', but that Germany might claim compensation elsewhere in Africa. To this suggestion, the report continued, King George made no reply.

Emperor William II and King George V

This was not what the Emperor meant. He insisted later that he had warned the King of his intention to take this action, and His Majesty had agreed. The Emperor, therefore, was convinced that Britain would stand aside and take no action.

Four weeks later King George and Queen Mary were crowned at Westminster Abbey. The German Emperor was represented by his eldest son, the Crown Prince, and Princess. Shortly after they had arrived in England, Crown Prince William presented King George with the baton of Field-Marshal of the German Army.

In his *Memoirs*, the Crown Prince recalled with irony that during the Coronation festivities in London, 'the reception accorded to me and my wife by all classes of the population was exceptionally cordial'. As the foreign princes moved down the aisle of the Abbey, and as he and the Crown Princess reached the middle of the nave, 'the same spontaneous cheers that had greeted the King and Queen were accorded to us. Afterwards I was told by English people that I might be "proud of myself"; for never before in the history of England had a foreign princely couple received such an ovation in Westminster Abbey.'[13]

Ten days later, on 1 July, the German Ambassador in London, Count Metternich, handed the Foreign Office a note stating that the government in

Berlin had despatched a gunboat to Agadir, on the Moroccan coast, in order to protect the lives and properties of Hamburg merchants on the coast. As Agadir was not a trading port, and as there were not thought to be any German merchants in the area, the Foreign Office was suspicious. On his return to London three days later, Grey told the Ambassador that the despatch of a German gunboat had created 'a new, highly important and delicate situation'. British commercial interests in Morocco were far more important than any which Germany might have. The British government must insist on taking part in any discussions that might ensue, and would not recognize any arrangement made without her knowledge and consent. To this the German government gave no answer for seventeen days.

By playing for time, ministers in Berlin hoped to isolate France from Britain, and force the French to pay generous compensation in return for a free hand in Morocco. They were encouraged by the recent elevation of M Caillaux as French Prime Minister. He was known to be an advocate of a new deal with Germany, and an uncompromising critic of the Anglo-French entente. Negotiations between France and Germany began with Germany demanding as their price the whole of the French Congo. If her demands were disregarded, Germany might be forced to adopt 'extreme measures'. The British government, thoroughly alarmed, insisted that she should be admitted to the discussions. A fiery speech by Lloyd George (Chancellor of the Exchequer, and regarded throughout Europe as spokesman for the pacifists of the British Cabinet) in which he declared that peace at the price of surrendering her interests would be an intolerable humiliation for Britain to endure, filled Germany with indignation. For a while Grey feared that it would end in war. Not till the conclusion of an agreement between France and Germany, by which the former obtained a free hand to establish a Protectorate in Morocco for the price of part of the Congo, was the crisis regarded as over.

When King George V was told of the Emperor's version of their conversation on Morocco, he was surprised. To Count Mensdorff, he explained that the Emperor had indeed raised the Morocco question, although he recalled nothing being said about warships; 'And I absolutely did not express to him my own, or my Government's consent to any such action.'[14]

It was evident that Emperor William had either deliberately or carelessly misquoted the King, and for one reason or another misinterpreted his words. In apparently hearing only what he wished to hear, he had supposed that Britain would stand by and do nothing in the face of German aggression. Such foolishness had come perilously close to bringing Europe to the brink of war; and the episode would have its parallel, with far greater consequences, three years later.

The following year was marked by two very different royal visits to England. First came the Dowager Tsarina with her daughter Grand Duchess Olga, still chafing at the refusal of her apathetic husband to honour a promise he had made several years earlier to set her free. A long stay by mother and daughter at Sandringham did nothing to lift their spirits. Mourning her son-in-law the Duke of Fife, who had succumbed to pneumonia in January after his family were shipwrecked off the coast of North Africa, Queen Alexandra had aged greatly and was by now almost stone deaf. She and her sister did nothing but sit around indoors and talk about the past. Olga and the Queen's unmarried daughter Princess Victoria spent as much time as they could outside, riding and driving. When the four of them sat down to meals, said Olga, 'I had a feeling that we were all shelved.'

Matters did not improve when they left Norfolk to stay at Buckingham Palace with the King and Queen. Though London had its share of entertainments and diversions, the Grand Duchess was in no fit state to enjoy them to the full. Attending the theatre with Lady Astor one evening, she was 'taken ill', suffering from the onset of a nervous breakdown. For months after her return to Russia, she was on the verge of collapse.

In the first week of December 1912, Prince Henry of Prussia visited King George at York Cottage. After his departure the King informed Grey of their conversation. Henry had asked him point blank whether, in the event of Germany and Austria going to war with Russia and France, Britain would come to the assistance of the two latter powers. The King answered, 'undoubtedly, yes – under certain circumstances.' Henry expressed surprise and regret, but did not ask what these circumstances were, and said he would tell the Emperor. 'Of course,' the King commented to Grey, 'Germany must know that we would not allow either of our friends to be crippled.'

To Mensdorff, the King said that Prince Henry had been 'horrified' by the statement that England would not allow France or Russia to be crushed. To this the King said, 'Do you believe that we have less sense of honour than you? You possess signed alliances: we unsigned Ententes. We cannot allow either France or Russia to be overthrown.' Mensdorff duly reported this conversation to Vienna.

Replying to the King, Grey said he thought it would be dangerous and misleading to let the German government be under the impression that under no circumstances would England come to the assistance of France and Russia, if Germany and Austria went to war with them, and he thought it very fortunate that the King was able to give an answer that would prevent Prince Henry from giving that impression at Berlin. The British government, he added, was not committed in the event of war, and public opinion in Britain – as far as Grey could judge – was adverse to war arising from differences over Serbia. But if Austria attacked Serbia aggressively, Germany attacked Russia if she came to the assistance of Serbia, and France subsequently became involved, it might become necessary for Britain to fight for the defence of her position in Europe, and for the protection of her own future and security.

Grey optimistically supposed that Prince Henry would pass on, or the Emperor would somehow derive, a correct impression of the conversation at York Cottage. What the Prince actually reported was that Great Britain was peace-loving, and if war broke out Germany would have to reckon 'perhaps on English neutrality, certainly not on her taking the part of Germany, and probably on her throwing her weight on the weaker side'. As so often before, the Emperor noticed only the words he wanted to hear, and concluded that he could count on

British neutrality. On the margin of his brother's letter, he scribbled a note to the effect that 'we can now go ahead with France'.

To King George, Prince Henry wrote (14 December 1912):

> The day after my return to Kiel I wrote a letter to William, in which I carried out your instructions to the letter, carefully hereby omitting the one sore point, which I put down, as my personal impressions, gathered from conversations with friends, during my recent stay in England, to the effect, that I thought, if Germany were drawn into a war with Russia & may be, as a result of this, with France, England *might* be neutral, but that I feared, she *might* also, *under circumstances*, side with our foes; William sent me a reply, in which he said, that my impressions were, he was sorry to say, correct, in as much as Haldane had, in a conversation with our Ambassador, on the 6th of December, the day I was kindly received by you at Sandringham, stated the fact point blanc officially from the part of Sir E. Grey.– W[illiam] further mentioned, that though this was felt as rather a blow, he would have to take the consequences.
>
> We all feel, that England is hereby adhering to her old principle, not allowing any nation to predominate on the continent. You will I hope be aware of the fact, that the responsibility which England herewith takes, as regards the world peace is very great.
>
> Germany has not, believe me, the least intention of going to war with any one, and never had, this she has proved in more than one case, during 43 years! We always were – & I am still – in hopes that England & Germany might go together, for the sake of the world's peace! Mind you Georgie, we are not afraid, but we mean no harm to anyone! Please consider the situation once more, before it is too late! If England & Germany were united, even mutually, who on earth would dare stir? Haldane's statement of the 6th however leaves alas no doubt & you will not be astonished, if we, in future, do all we can to be prepared against any blow, which may, or may not be dealt, with an object to ruin our existence.
>
> England, I take it, has got it in her hands, to keep, or to maintain the world's peace!
>
> You will, I hope, understand, that my 'impressions' have not created any bitter feeling, but that it was Haldane's statements of the 6th inst. which have.
>
> You know me well enough by now & you know, that my feelings on the subject are absolutely sincere. I always have & always shall consider it my duty to avoid misunderstandings & try & smooth difficulties between both our countries. Your dear Father trusted me & I hope you will do the same! You also know, that I am a loyal German subject & that my duty lies first with my sovereign, who, I am thankful to say, believes in me. Might I once more suggest, that under the circumstances, you should consider the question of your visiting Germany, i.e. William first, next year? Please think about it seriously – it might do a world of good![15]

When Herbert Asquith, the Prime Minister, recalled Prince Henry's conversations after war had broken out, he wondered whether His Imperial Highness was a fool or a knave. Had he been made a fool of by Admiral Tirpitz, who had sent him to England to allay suspicion, or did he know the true facts and was he merely posing as a candid friend to conceal his country's genuine warlike intentions? Asquith believed him to be the latter; but Sir Frederick Ponsonby, who knew him better, thought that the Prince was a friend of Britain,

Sophie, Crown Princess of the Hellenes

and was doing his best to smooth matters out between his brother and his cousin, King George V; 'he was a perfectly straightforward man and never gave the impression of having any Machiavellian cunning'.[16]

Prince Henry's fervent admiration for England was shared by his sisters. One of them, the Crown Princess of the Hellenes, had braved the opposition of her father-in-law, by her insistence on letting her children have an English education. His own children, including her husband, had been educated in Greece, and he saw no reason why matters should be any different for his grandchildren, especially as at least one of them was certain to succeed to the Greek throne some day.*

A compromise was reached by which the two younger sons, Princes Alexander and Paul, and the Princesses, would attend preparatory or boarding schools in England, but only during the summer term each year, when their mother was visiting relatives in England. Princesses Helen and Irene attended the Links, and the Princes St Christopher's Preparatory School, at Eastbourne. The Crown Princess generally visited them on Sundays, travelling down from Windsor and staying the night at the Grand Hotel. Sometimes her youngest

---

* In fact, all three sons were destined to become King of the Hellenes in turn.

Constantine, Crown Prince of the Hellenes, later King Constantine I

sister, Princess Frederick Charles of Hesse-Cassel, would come over from Frankfurt with her young sons, and both families would stay at a rented house in Seaford.

The Crown Princess's brother-in-law, Prince Christopher, was also devoted to England, and nearly ended up marrying a niece of King George V. While he was staying in England in the summer and autumn of 1911, the King's spinster sister Princess Victoria dropped thinly-veiled hints that an engagement between him and Princess Alexandra of Fife would meet with general approval. She persuaded the young Princess's parents, the Duke and Duchess of Fife, to invite him to stay at Mar Lodge. What she omitted to tell him was that this invitation had been reluctantly wrung from them on the condition that he was not to propose to their daughter. He went to stay, the young couple appeared to fall in love, and he proposed to her.

When the Duke found out, he was furious, and a stormy interview took place. A chastened Prince Christopher left Mar Lodge early that morning, and went to explain his behaviour to King George and Queen Mary, both of whom rocked with laughter. They advised him to write a letter of apology to the Duke, and as a result he was invited back to Mar Lodge, but on the strict understanding that the betrothal was cancelled, and the still simmering Duke of Fife made certain that the two young people should not be left alone with each other for a moment while the Prince was under their roof. Neither he nor the Princess were remotely heartbroken by the episode. As he recalled, 'the scars were not very deep with either of us, for we had been more in love with love than with one another.'[17] Both went on to make happy marriages soon afterwards.

6 'A terrible catastrophe but not our fault'

As the new year of 1913 dawned, King George and Queen Mary hoped that they might at last be able to pay what seemed a long-overdue state visit to their cousins in Berlin. But the unsettled state of European politics led Grey to urge that this was not the time to alarm France and Russia by such a formal affirmation of friendship with Germany. War was raging in the Balkans, with Bulgaria, Greece, Serbia and Montenegro on one side, Turkey on the other. Within a few weeks of the outbreak of hostilities in October 1912, the Bulgarians were close to capturing Constantinople.

Russia viewed the possibility with alarm, and the territorial ambitions of Tsar Ferdinand of Bulgaria provoked one of King George's very rare criticisms of his contemporary European crowned heads. Thanks to the Tsar of Bulgaria's 'sense of history, vanity and theatricality', and his irresistible desire to ride into the city in triumph and celebrate Mass in St Sophia, he would probably place his cross on the dome of St Sophia, the Moslems would be certain to blow it up, there would be massacres of Christians in Asia Minor, and Moslems all over the world would start agitating in protest. All countries with Moslem subjects would suffer, the King feared, including France and Russia, but above all England, in India and the Sudan. The King himself had good reason to fear; 'I have 80 million Mohammedan subjects.'[1]

Before peace was formally signed in May 1913, the shadow of assassination had fallen across Europe again. One evening in March, King George of Greece was taking an evening stroll in the streets of Salonika, when a vagrant opened fire, killing him instantly and turning the gun on himself after arrest. The King had been Queen Alexandra's favourite brother, and she was particularly distressed to lose him in such a violent manner.

Much as they distrusted Germany's intentions throughout Europe, the King and Queen were pleased to be invited to the wedding of Emperor William's only daughter, Princess Victoria Louise, to their cousin Ernest Augustus, Duke of Brunswick-Luneburg, a grandson of the last King of Hanover, and son of Princess Thyra of Denmark, youngest sister of Queen Alexandra. The Duke was known in Germany as the 'vanishing Duke', as he was inclined to disappear if the Emperor was in the neighbourhood of Hanover and there was a chance of meeting him. Ever since Hanover had been overrun and absorbed by Prussia in

1866, there had been a perpetual feud between the Hohenzollerns and the descendants of King Ernest Augustus, Queen Victoria's uncle. Now this family antipathy was to be wiped out by marriage between their houses.

'We intend to invite your dear mother, as a near relation to our future son in law & it would give us great pleasure if you & May would do us the honour of being present also', the Emperor wrote to King George on 15 March. 'I do heartily hope that you may find it possible to get away from London at that date & to accept our invitation. Of course we shall miss our daughter with her sunny temperament very much. But we are quite confident that she will be happy.'[2] The reaction of Queen Alexandra, who hated her nephew in Berlin, was not recorded; but her son and daughter-in-law were happy to accept.

At Grey's insistence, any royal visit to Berlin still had to be regarded as strictly private, and no minister accompanied the King and Queen. What Queen Mary described as 'a purely family gathering' began nevertheless with a stately reception at Berlin station. The wedding itself took place on 24 May 1913, a symbolic date in the royal calendar; it had been the birthday of Queen Victoria, ninety-four years earlier. The banquets and gala operas, military parades and other trappings of imperial German splendour, which preceded it, saw the last great congregation of family and European royalty. King George and Queen Mary could not have imagined that this was the final time they would meet the German Emperor and Empress, the Tsar and Tsarina, or indeed nearly all the other European royals to whom they were so closely related.

'I cannot tell you how very much we enjoyed our visit to Berlin or how touched we were at the kindness shown us by William & Victoria & indeed by everybody', Queen Mary wrote to her Aunt Augusta afterwards. 'It was a most interesting time & so beautifully arranged in every way, nothing could have gone off better.'[3]

Yet there was unease behind the splendour. As Sir Frederick Ponsonby observed, 'on these occasions everyone goes out of their way to be civil, and one hardly has an opportunity of judging the real feeling. On the whole, I am inclined to think that the visit helped towards establishing good feeling between the two countries, but, of course, one can never get over the fact that we were practically rivals.'[4]

Even King George, who was not suspicious by nature, never forgot how Emperor William seemed almost childish in his jealousy of the close friendship between him and Nicholas, trying to ensure that they were never left alone, neurotically imagining that they were plotting behind his back. Whenever they managed a private talk, thought the King, he suspected that 'William's ear was glued to the keyhole.'[5] The German Emperor avoided contentious subjects with the King, venting his feelings instead on Lord Stamfordham at an officers' luncheon, taking him fiercely to task for 'making alliances with a decadent nation like France and a semi-barbarous nation like Russia and opposing us, the true uplifters of progress and liberty'.[6]

However, the family were so used to the Emperor's outbursts that they did not read anything sinister into his words. At any rate, no change was made in the King's plans to send the Prince of Wales to the court of Germany that summer. The Emperor had acknowledged his letter in March, 'informing me of your

Guests at the wedding feast of Princess Victoria of Prussia and the Duke of Brunswick-Luneburg, 24 May 1913, after a watercolour by Fortunino Mascania

boy's intended visit to Germany', and hoping that he would 'be able to spare the time necessary for improving his German & for the study of this country'.[7]

For six weeks the Prince was based at 'the sleepy little town of Neu Strelitz', with his host Adolphus, the Grand Duke, where the dominating personality was his mother, the old Grand Duchess Augusta. Now aged ninety-one, she could still just recall her childhood and a pat on the head from King George IV.

The atmosphere at the court of Neu Strelitz was distinctly elderly, and the Prince of Wales eagerly took advantage of invitations elsewhere. The first came from Prince Henry and his family, living at his estate of Hemmelmark, near Kiel. Whether it was his naval training or the more flexible and sympathetic approach to life that had made him the man he was, the Prince of Wales felt ill-qualified to judge, but of all his German relatives, Prince Henry impressed him the most.

In the navy yard at Kiel, where he took me aboard some of the latest German warships, there was no mistaking his authority as a *Grossadmiral*. But back at the Herrenhaus, which he had built for himself, he preferred working about his property or in his garage to the more pompous pastimes of those days. Uncle Henry sponsored modern ideas and inventions with vigour and enthusiasm. In fact his great interest in the development of the still comparatively primitive motor-car brought him often to Great Britain, where he competed in automobile endurance tests. He had a great way with people and looked you straight in the eye. His unquestioned popularity and his pro-British leanings brought him, so I was told, into conflict with his Imperial brother, who jealously denied him the top Navy posts, for which he was pre-eminently qualified.[8]

A similar invitation came from another second cousin, Charles, Duke of Saxe-Coburg Gotha. The Duke, the posthumous son of Queen Victoria's haemophiliac son Leopold, Duke of Albany, had succeeded to the German Duchy at the age of sixteen. With his thoroughly British upbringing, he was unhappy with his 'enforced exile' in Germany, and pleased to have a guest from England who was only a few years his junior. Both men spent several happy hours shooting deer on the wooded estates in the Thuringian Forest.

Before leaving Germany, the Prince of Wales paid a courtesy call on the Emperor. Taken to meet him in his study at the Schloss in Berlin, he was astonished to find the Emperor in uniform sitting behind an extraordinarily high desk. In greeting, the Emperor 'rose in a most curious manner, as if dismounting from a horse'. The seat at his desk was a wooden block shaped like the body of a horse, to which was attached a saddle, complete with stirrups. Noticing his young guest's startled expression, the Emperor smiled as he explained condescendingly that he was so used to being mounted on horseback that he found a saddle more conducive to clear, concise thinking than an ordinary desk chair.

That night the Prince dined with the Emperor and his family, and was taken to the opera for a performance of *Aida*. They swept through the streets of Berlin, the Prince recalled, in a gleaming limousine, with a *Jager* in green uniform and plumed hat riding in front, while distinctive notes on the horn warned the police to hold the traffic for His Imperial Majesty.

Charles, Duke of Saxe-Coburg Gotha, c. 1913

The nineteen-year-old Prince was thoroughly impressed with the undoubted charm of the Emperor. Before taking his leave the next afternoon, the Emperor expressed the hope that Prince Edward had learned something of the German people, and that 'despite all the terrible things my country thought about them, he and they really were not so difficult to get along with'. He came away with the impression of a ruler who was 'impatient, haughty, equally eager to please, to frighten, or to astonish; paradoxically stubborn-minded and weak-minded, and, above all, truly humourless. He did little in foreign affairs – or in anything else – that he did not shout from the housetops.'[9]

In the early years of his reign, King George managed to forge a useful and potentially powerful connection with the one European court which had eluded his father – that of the Habsburgs. The Emperor Francis Joseph's nephew and heir, Archduke Francis Ferdinand, had long coveted an invitation to the court of St James, to set the seal of European social acceptance on his morganatic wife Sophie, Princess of Hohenberg.

The Archduke, a brusque, humourless, touchy man, was almost unique among the Habsburgs in having made a happy marriage. It did not, however, meet with the court's approval, for Sophie was a mere countess, and the marriage could only be morganatic. Yet when the Archduke succeeded his uncle, it was assumed that he would insist on his wife being accorded the full honours due to an Empress.

The Archduke had represented his uncle at the funeral of Queen Victoria, the Coronation and in due course the funeral of King Edward VII, albeit under duress, having been informed that his wife could not accompany him. At the last occasion he found fault with almost everything and everyone, returning to Austria full of venom against the 'arrogant English'.

His next visit to England was in happier circumstances. In May 1912 the English Horticultural Society was planning to stage its first international flower show. The Archduke had a passion for flowers and gardening, and an invitation was accordingly extended to him. As it was not an occasion of state, there were no difficulties about his wife being openly included in the invitation. While in London, they were invited to lunch at Buckingham Palace with King George, Queen Mary, and Queen Alexandra. The Archduke and Princess, noted the King, were 'charming and made themselves very pleasant'. The shy King and Archduke had much in common; they were happiest in their family and domestic circle, fond of shooting, and interested in the navy.

When Mensdorff mentioned in July 1913 that the Archduke was going to stay with the Duke of Portland at Welbeck Abbey, Northamptonshire, the King suggested that he should be invited to Windsor as well. The Archduke accepted most fulsomely, asking Mensdorff to tell His Majesty how 'quite exceptionally enchanted' he was at the prospect. It did not matter that their sojourn would be a private affair; on the contrary, he looked forward to avoiding 'terrible banquets and toasts'. The equally retiring King would not have been out of sympathy with such sentiments.

Francis Ferdinand, Archduke of Austria-Hungary, with his wife Sophie, Princess of Hohenberg, and their children Ernest, Maximilian and Sophie, 1913

Despite his request for formalities to be kept to a minimum, Francis Ferdinand and Sophie were honoured on the weekend of their arrival in November 1913 with a dinner party at the Embassy in London. At last the Archduke and his wife were being treated with the dignity which he felt was their due, and which had been denied them by hidebound court functionaries at Vienna. The Princess of Hohenberg may not have been an archduchess, but she was being granted full honours as befitted the next Habsburg Empress. On the following Monday they went by train to Windsor, where King George was awaiting them on the platform. Malicious tongues commented on Queen Mary's absence, but no slight was intended as it was her customary practice to await royal guests, other than crowned heads, at the castle.

At Windsor, King and Archduke made the most of the shooting, though there was a political twist to the conversation when guests such as Grey and Rosebery joined them. But the main aim of the visit, from Francis Ferdinand's point of view, was to set the British seal of appoval on Sophie's equal rights. His wishes could not have been fulfilled more adequately.

On 27 November Queen Mary wrote to her Aunt Augusta that the Archduke had formerly been 'very anti-English but that it quite changed now, and her influence has been and is good, they say, in every way. All the people staying with us who had known him before said how much he had changed for the better and that he was most enthusiastic over his visit to us and to England.'[10]

Much was read into the political implications of this visit. As it was private, the assertions of the Archduke's secretary that he sought to play the role of mediator between the mutually suspicious England and Germany were undoubtedly exaggerated. However, Archduchess Zita, who saw much of her uncle at this time, was certain that he hoped to see a revival of the 'Three Emperors League' between Germany, Austria and Russia, and as an additional safeguard sought 'the greatest possible participation of England' in this new alignment of the powers. The personal antagonism between Emperor William and King Edward had made such a possibility remote during the latter's lifetime, but with King George V on the British throne, it was surely a probability. Archduke Francis Ferdinand, who had his political enemies at home and in the Balkans, was accused of many faults, but stupidity was not one of them. He was intelligent and energetic enough, and as heir to the imperial throne well placed, to be able to help bring about such a move.

In March 1914 the Duke of Portland accepted a return invitation to the Archduke's estates at Konopischt. While there, they discussed the possibility of King George and Queen Mary coming to stay at the Archduke's autumn retreat, Blühnbach, in September. Emperor William, it was suggested, could join them all for shooting that same month. What could not be achieved informally through a friendly meeting between the English and German sovereigns on Austrian territory? Emperor Francis Joseph had recently suffered a bout of his regular enemy, bronchitis, and at the age of eighty-three he was not expected to live much longer. By September 1914, Emperor Francis Ferdinand might be on the throne, and it would fall to him and Empress Sophie to welcome the sovereigns.

Rather reluctantly, King George and Queen Mary paid a state visit to Paris in April 1914. It was to follow a visit President Poincaré had made to London the previous summer. 'Of course I wanted to go to Vienna first,' Queen Mary admitted privately, 'but Sir Edward Grey will not hear of it!'[11] The dynast in her was all too aware that she and her husband were making their first state visit as sovereigns to a foreign republic. Some of her mother's greatest friends had been the princes and princesses of the exiled house of Orleans, and the Queen herself had always liked the Empress Eugenie. All this weighed on her conscience. As France was the only great European country without a court, there were no royal cousins, and thus no family, with whom visiting royalties could relax. It would thus be the very opposite of their visit to Berlin.

Nevertheless it was a great success, and their reception in Paris was even favourably commented upon in the German press. It was evident King George V did not attract the same distrust in Berlin that his father had.

The exchanges of visits between crowned heads, their heirs and heads of state during the spring and early summer of 1914 – King George V to Paris, Emperor William to Archduke Francis Ferdinand at Konopischt, and President Poincaré

Marie Feodorovna, Dowager Tsarina of Russia

to the Tsar at St Petersburg – partially masked but could not completely conceal the undercurrents of armed conflict. Chiefs of state brought diplomats and generals who conferred secretly with their opposite numbers to compare plans and confirm understandings in the event of attack by a third power, while reviews of troops and fleets provided an opportunity to assess how ready their country was for war.

On 8 May, Prince Henry of Prussia came to breakfast with King George V. During the Prince's visit, both had discussed their anxieties over the European situation. Although the King still held an exaggerated view of the Emperor William's power to stem the current, it was a diplomatic channel which had often proved effective in the past.

In June, Admiral David Beatty led the First Battle Cruiser Squadron of the Royal Navy up the Baltic on a visit to Russia, as if to demonstrate that Britain indeed wished to provide a display of naval might to counter the ever-increasing strength of Germany's High Seas Fleet. The Tsar and his family went aboard Beatty's flagship *Lion* for lunch, and the British Ambassador, Sir George Buchanan, considered that he had never seen happier faces than those of the four young Grand Duchesses, aged between eighteen and thirteen, than on that day. In view of the gathering storm, and even more particularly in the light of the imperial family's eventual fate, it seemed ironic.

Earlier that week, King George V had written to the Tsar, asking him to dissuade his government from actions in Persia which could only put a strain on Anglo-Russian co-operation. Yet the time was coming when such minor issues would be swept away by infinitely more pressing affairs.

The Russian imperial family, c. 1914. Seated, left to right: Grand Duchess Olga; Tsar Nicholas II; Grand Duchess Anastasia; Tsarevich Alexis; Grand Duchess Tatiana. Standing: Grand Duchess Marie; Tsarina Alexandra

How prepared the sovereigns were for war has ever since been, and continues to be, a matter for inconclusive debate. Writing eight years later in his *Memoirs*, Emperor William II recalled that he had been told (in November 1918) that Tsar Nicholas II was asked by his officials at court in the spring of 1914 as to his plans for the next few months, and was told, 'I shall stay at home this year, because we shall have war.' This, William noted with emphasis, was the same Tsar who had given him his word of honour as a sovereign that he would never draw his sword against the German Emperor, least of all as an ally of England, in the event of war in Europe. He was eternally grateful for the German Emperor's personal support in the Russo-Japanese war, 'in which Russia was involved solely by England. He added that he hated England, because of the great wrong she had done him and Russia by inciting Japan against them.'[12]

On 28 June Archduke Francis Ferdinand and Sophie paid their fateful visit to Sarajevo. Warned that his life was in danger from underground Serbian revolutionary elements, perhaps even with the complicity of Serbian army officers, the imperial heir was reluctant to make the journey. All the same, it was the first opportunity he had to travel officially within the Austro-Hungarian empire with his wife, and as it was their fourteenth wedding anniversary, he thought it a propitious day to take the woman whom he confidently expected to reign with him as his Empress.

Shortly before eleven o'clock that morning, Gavrilo Princip, one of the revolutionary Bosnian students swept along by the tide of anti-Habsburg, pan-Slav feeling in Serbia, watching the motorcade passing through the city streets, fired his revolver at the Archduke and his wife. Within a few minutes, both were dead, the Archduke muttering feebly, 'It is nothing', as he expired. In retrospect it was one of the classic understatements of all time, for the assassination would shortly prove to be the catalyst for the fiercest war ever to engulf the nations of Europe.

The crowned heads of state reacted with varying degrees of indignation and sorrow. King George V, who had been the dead couple's host at Windsor only seven months earlier, ordered a week of court mourning, and as a personal gesture cancelled his annual attendance at the Newmarket midsummer race meeting due to take place the following week. 'It will be a terrible shock to the dear old Emperor and is most regrettable and sad', he noted sincerely if somewhat woodenly in his diary.

While Austria sent Serbia her punitive ultimatum, while Emperor William II waxed indignant against the Serbian fanatics who had struck down his friends, and while German Chancellor Bethmann-Hollweg and Chief of Staff General von Moltke braced themselves for an all-out war, in England the government's attention was distracted by the Ulster Home Rule crisis. Not until 25 July, almost a month after the assassination, did the King note in his diary that it looked 'as if we were on the verge of a general European war'.[13]

On the following morning, Prince Henry of Prussia came to Buckingham Palace to say goodbye on his return to Germany from sailing at Cowes. Asking the King if there were any developments in the international situation, the King replied that the news was very bad; 'it looked like a European war & that he better go back to Germany at once'. After saying that he would go to Eastbourne to see his sister, Queen Sophie of Greece, and leave for Germany in the evening, he asked what Britain would do if there was an European war. The King admitted he did not know; Britain had no quarrel with anyone, and he hoped they would remain neutral; 'but if Germany declared war on Russia, & France joins Russia, then I am afraid we shall be dragged into it. But you can be sure that I & my Government will do all we can to prevent a European war!'[14] The Prince said that if their two countries were fighting on opposite sides, he trusted it would not affect their personal friendship. They shook hands and he left.

In later years, Prince Henry admitted that in the excitement of the moment, he may have misinterpreted King George's expressions of hope as a definite assurance of neutrality. It did not, however, matter what Prince Henry reported back to the Emperor, for events were already moving beyond their control. The Hohenzollerns were always inclined to overestimate the British sovereign's influence on his or her government, and the Emperor almost certainly believed that Britain would remain neutral. When Tirpitz expressed his doubts that she would stay out of any forthcoming war, the Emperor retorted that he had the word of her King, 'and that is enough for me'.

On 25 July Queen Mary wrote to her Aunt Augusta, 'God grant we may not have a European War thrust upon us, & for such a stupid reason too, no I don't mean stupid, but to have to go to war on account of tiresome Servia beggars belief!'[15] It was a sentiment echoed by most of her husband's subjects, who doubtless agreed with the late Archduke Francis Ferdinand that Serbia was 'a country of rascals, fools and prune trees'.

Messages pursued each other around Europe with increasing urgency. On 29 July the Tsar telegraphed to King George V:

> I am writing to you at a most serious moment. I do not know what may happen in a few days. Austria has gone off upon a reckless war, which can easily end in a general conflagration. It is awful! My country is confident of its strength & of the right cause it has taken up. We have been patient and have tried to quieten Austria – but of no avail.
>
> Now we are compelled to take strong measures in case of emergency – for our own defence. Of course that will be explained by our two neighbours as a recall to arms. If a general war broke out I know that we shall have France's and England's full support.
>
> As a last resort I have written to William to ask him to bear a strong pressure upon Austria so as to enable us to discuss matters with her. He has promised to be mediator between us, though he continues looking upon Austria's behaviour in a wrong light. I do hope this may still save matters, as a war at the present moment would be a dreadful calamity.[16]

On the following day, after consulting the German Emperor, Prince Henry telegraphed the King from Berlin:

> Am here since yesterday have informed William of what you kindly told me at Buckingham Palace last Sunday who gracefully received your message. William

much preoccupied is trying his utmost to fulfill Nicky's appeal to him to work for maintenance of peace and is in constant telegraphic communication with Nicky who today confirms news that military measures have been ordered by him equal to mobilisation measures which have been taken already five days ago. We are furthermore informed that France is making military preparations whereas we have taken no measures but may be forced to do so any moment should our neighbours continue which then would mean a European war. If you really and earnestly wish to prevent this terrible disaster may I suggest you using your influence on France and also Russia to keep neutral which seems to me would be most useful. This I consider a very good perhaps the only chance to maintain the peace of Europe. I may add that now more than ever Germany & England should lend each other mutual help to prevent a terrible catastrophe which otherwise seems unavoidable. Believe me that William is most sincere in his endeavours to maintain peace but the military preparations of his two neighbours may at last force him to follow their example for the safety of his own country which otherwise would remain defenceless. I have informed William of my telegram to you and hope you will receive my informations in the same spirit of friendship which suggested them.[17]

As the King replied, he was doing all that he could, but the last chance of holding Russia back was for Germany to persuade her Austrian ally to be satisfied with the occupation of Belgrade and neighbouring Serbian territory as a hostage for the satisfactory settlement of her demands in the ultimatum. The aged Emperor Francis Joseph was too isolated from reality, too much at the mercy of his war party, to bring any personal pressure to bear; the German and Russian Emperors no longer trusted each other, or at least their governments; and matters had passed the bounds of monarchical diplomacy.

Whether King Edward VII, who would have been seventy-two years old in August 1914, would have had the personal power to call his fellow-sovereigns to account, is debatable. Yet he would have had the warmongering politicians and military leaders in Europe to contend with as well. The Emperors were no longer in control; and as he had foreseen in the aftermath of the Tangier incident, the German Emperor would unleash a war not by his will, but by his weakness.

To his sister Grand Duchess Olga, the Tsar remarked that 'Willy was a bore and an exhibitionist, but he would never start a war'. She was anxious that her brother was not strong enough to inspire fear in his contemporaries. The German Emperor had been afraid of Tsar Alexander III and of his Uncle Bertie, but she doubted whether he feared 'Nicky and Georgie'.

Shortly after midnight on Friday, 31 July, King George was woken by his equerry, Rear-Admiral Sir Colin Keppel, with a draft of a telegram which Mr Asquith wanted him to send to Tsar Nicholas II. From Westminster, the view of the rapidly deteriorating European situation was that Russian mobilization was impeding mediation efforts between the other powers, particularly Germany who was more concerned than any other state. Although the telegram was sent, it was too late.

That same day, the German Emperor acknowledged King George V's last message:

Your proposals coincide with my ideas and with the statements I got this night from Vienna which I have had forwarded to London. I just received news from Chancellor that official notification has just reached him that this night Nicky has ordered the mobilization of his whole army and that he has not even awaited the results of the mediation I am working at and left me without any news. I am off for Berlin to take measures for ensuring safety of my eastern frontiers where strong Russian troops are already posted.[18]

On the following day, 1 August, general mobilization was ordered almost simultaneously in Germany and France. A final desperate telegram went from Emperor William to King George:

I just received the communication from your government offering French neutrality under guarantee of Great Britain added to this offer is the Enquiry whether under these conditions Germany would refrain from attacking France. On technical grounds my mobilisation which had all ready been proclaimed this afternoon must proceed against two fronts East & West as prepared. This cannot be countermanded because I am sorry the telegram of your cabinet came so late. But if France offers me neutrality which must be guaranteed by the British Fleet & army I shall of course refrain from attacking France & employ my troops elsewhere. I hope that France will not become nervous the troops on my frontiers are in the act of being stopped by telegraph & telephone from crossing into France.[19]

On 2 August, Tsar Nicholas telegraphed to King George:

I would gladly have accepted your proposals had not German Ambassador this afternoon presented a note to my Government declaring war. Ever since presentation of the ultimatum at Belgrade, Russia has devoted all her efforts to finding some pacific solution of the question raised by Austria's action. Object of that action was to crush Servia and make her a vassal of Austria. Effect of this would have been to upset balance of power in Balkans which is of such a vital interest to my Empire as well as to those Powers who desire maintenance of balance of power in Europe. Every proposal, including that of your Government, was rejected by Germany and Austria, and it was only when favourable moment for bringing pressure to bear on Austria had passed that Germany showed any disposition to mediate. Even then she did not put forward any precise proposal. Austria's declaration of war on Servia forced me to order a partial mobilisation, though, in view of threatening situation, my military advisers strongly advised a general mobilisation owing to quickness with which Germany can mobilise in comparison with Russia. I was eventually compelled to take this course in consequence of complete Austrian mobilisation, of the bombardment of Belgrade, of concentration of Austrian troops in Galicia, and of secret military preparations being made by Germany. That I was justified in doing so is proved by Germany's sudden declaration of war, which was quite unexpected by me as I had given most categorical assurances to the Emperor William that my troops would not move so long as mediation negotiations continued.

In this solemn hour I wish to assure you once more that I have done all in my power to avert war. Now that it has been forced on me, I trust your country will not fail to support France and Russia in fighting to maintain balance of power in Europe.[20]

That same day, Germany informed Belgium that she would be obliged to invade her territory in order to execute war plans in the west, but would leave again after victory, having paid all her war dues and debts, provided the Belgians stayed 'benevolently neutral'. Belgium, given twelve hours to reply, announced that she would fight to repel all invaders. King Albert sent King George an appeal for his personal intervention 'for the safeguarding of German neutrality'.

King George replied that Sir Edward Grey's statement in Parliament that same afternoon, 3 August, would prove England's 'desire and intention' in this respect. The speech fell short of announcing war against Germany, but left the Commons in no doubt that this was the only choice. If Belgium fell, Holland and Denmark would surely follow; if France was overrun, crushed and eliminated as a major European power, England would be threatened by the 'unmeasured aggrandizement' of Germany.

On the following day, 4 August, German troops crossed the Belgian frontier. At 2 p.m. Grey issued a ten-hour ultimatum to Berlin to withdraw. It was taken by Goschen to Bethmann-Hollweg, who remarked with derision that 'just for a scrap of paper', Britain was going to declare war on 'a kindred nation who desired nothing better than to be friends with her'. The 'scrap of paper' was the treaty of 1830 guaranteeing Britain's upholding of Belgian neutrality, in effect a promise that Britain would stand by France in the face of invasion by Germany.

At 10.45, as King George noted laconically in his diary, he held a Council to declare war officially; 'it is a terrible catastrophe but not our fault'. Large crowds collected outside Buckingham Palace; 'it was a never to be forgotten sight when May & I with David went on to the balcony, the cheering was terrific'.[21]

Watching from the window of Marlborough House, where he was staying with Queen Alexandra, Prince Christopher of Greece looked at the crowds in The Mall, 'waiting in a silence that could almost be felt while the last moments of the ultimatum to Germany expired; and when at length the clock boomed out the hour, one deep breath was drawn by all those thousands like a mighty sigh. Then the tension relaxed and a second later everyone was laughing, singing patriotic songs and shouting for the King and Queen.' The King himself was white and drawn, listening to his subjects with tears in his eyes; 'he had grown years older in the last week'.[22]

The Tsar had despatched a telegram to the King, entreating him to support France and Russia in fighting to maintain the balance of power in Europe. Although it never reached its destination, it proved unnecessary. Simultaneously, the German Emperor had appealed to the Tsar to stand his army down. The telegram, preserved in the Russian archives, was marked, 'Received after war had been declared.'

At midnight on 4 August the ultimatum expired. Next morning in Berlin, just before Goschen and the staff of the British Embassy left for England, the Emperor sent a message to the ambassador by an aide-de-camp. It was to tell King George that 'in consequence of what had occurred', he must resign his posts as Field-Marshal in the British Army and Admiral of the British Navy, and return his insigniae with the departing ambassador. This was the thanks, he said bitterly, for Prussia's help to the British at the battle of Waterloo.

To the end of her life, Grand Duchess Olga maintained that the British government was responsible for the outbreak of war. Had ministers made it clear from the start that England would join Russia and France if Germany 'made trouble', she believed, Emperor William would never have dared to make a single move. His ambassador, Count Pourtales, had personally informed the Romanovs 'that he was convinced Britain would never enter the war'.[23]

'To think that Georgie and Nicky should have played me false', Emperor William commented. 'If my grandmother had been alive, she would never have allowed it.'[24] Yet the arch-culprit in his eyes was his late uncle, who had 'slowly and subtly set in motion' a sinister plan between England, France and Russia to encircle and bring about the destruction of Germany. 'Edward VII is stronger after his death, than I, who am still alive.'

King George V's personal verdict on the cousin who had technically become his country's greatest enemy was more temperate. He told the departing German Ambassador that he did not believe the Emperor wanted war, but he dreaded being thought a coward by his people and was afraid of the Crown Prince's popularity; 'his son and his party made the war'.

7 'We are all going through anxious times'

Monarchs no longer led their armies into battle during the Great War. The exception was King Albert of the Belgians, who by virtue of his country's constitution was Commander-in-Chief of the Belgian Army in practice as well as rank. Otherwise, leadership at the front was left to the generals, while sovereigns remained supreme commanders only in theory. Not since the battle of Solferino in 1859, when the Emperors of Austria and the French and their armies faced the King of Sardinia and his forces, had a monarch of one of the great European powers commanded his troops on the battlefield; while the battle of Dettingen in 1745 marked the last occasion on which a British King, George II, had done so. Kings and Emperors now remained firmly in their places, paying occasional, morale-boosting visits to their forces, or else established in country houses safely behind the front line, where they would be kept informed on progress as to the conduct of the war.

The Infanta Eulalia of Spain, King Alfonso's aunt, remarked with astonishment on the British monarchy's 'faculty of honest self-deception which makes the Englishman so insoluble a puzzle to the foreigner'. The English royal family, she noted in 1915, was 'the most popularly revered in Europe, even though it has, of all the Royal families, the least governmental power to compel awe, and has no English blood in it to endear it to the nation, and is allowed not even a pretence of leadership in peace or war to make it picturesque'.[1]

If people in Germany thought he was the Supreme Commander, remarked Emperor William bitterly, they were mistaken; his General Staff told him nothing and never asked his advice. 'I drink tea, go for walks and saw wood.' Meanwhile Prince Henry of Prussia was appointed Commander-in-Chief of the Baltic Station in the German Navy. It was largely a nominal post, with the fighting at sea left to other commanders and officers. Of all the Hohenzollerns, he would have been the most reluctant to take up arms against his cousins and in-laws in England.

King George V also understood perfectly the unobtrusive role which he was required to assume. It was to leave the business of fighting to generals and the armed forces; and he found it easier to accept this role in his own country than his imperial cousins did in theirs. It was his duty to carry on the business of a constitutional monarch, knowing yet relinquishing ultimate responsibility, easing the path of his government while safeguarding prerogatives which could be lost forever. He paid occasional visits to the front and to the Fleet, but for most of the time he identified himself with his people at home, visiting air-raid victims, touring munitions factories, living strictly on rations and voluntarily giving up alcohol for the duration of the war.

Balmoral was closed, and York Cottage, Sandringham, provided them with the only home where they could really relax. Buckingham Palace was put on an austerity footing; many members of the household and domestic staff had volunteered for active service, carriage horses were sent from the stables to do ambulance work, and royal carriages were used to bring wounded men from the railway stations. A plan to turn the palace into a hospital was only rejected when it was found that the building was too old-fashioned and inconvenient for such a purpose. When the German submarine campaign created a serious food shortage in Britain, the King and Queen planted potatoes in the gardens at Frogmore, near Windsor.

Had Emperor William similarly remained in or near his capital as the focal point of authority and met the need for a visible leader in victory and defeat, it has since been suggested, the subsequent fate of the Hohenzollern dynasty might have been different.

When it came to encouraging his troops, King George lacked his father's personal touch. After a visit to the Grenadier Guards in France, Raymond Asquith, son of the Prime Minister, found him 'looking as glum and dyspeptic as ever'. It was the kind of criticism to which the King would have responded unashamedly that he was not 'an advertising sort of fellow'.

As later historians would readily observe, British public opinion in 1914 was less temperate than in an even fiercer world conflict a quarter of a century later. Anti-German feeling verged on hysteria; but although his patriotism was not initially to be doubted, King George V refused to abandon reason and regard Germans as having suddenly ceased overnight to be human, simply because his subjects were at war with them.

While government departments did not necessarily concur with such strong feeling, they felt honour bound to heed public opinion. Five days after the outbreak of hostilities, the King was astonished to receive from the War Office a proposal that the German Emperor and Crown Prince William should be publicly deprived of their honorary commands of British regiments. To this, he answered that their names should remain in the Army List until they chose to resign. Lord Roberts was then prevailed upon to persuade him to reconsider his decision. At length he agreed with reluctance that their names should be dropped quietly from the next edition of the Army List, but he refused to issue any public notice to this effect.

There was a further demand that the Garter banners in St George's Chapel, Windsor, of enemy emperors, kings and princes should be removed. The King ruled that these banners, which were symbols of past history, should remain above the stalls until after the war, 'when there may be other developments'. Queen Alexandra added her voice to public indignation, writing to her son (12 May 1915) that it was 'but right and proper for you to have down those hateful German banners in our sacred Church'. On the advice of Asquith, a notice was issued on 13 May to the effect that the names of the eight enemy Knights of the Garter had been struck off the roll of the Order, and that same

'To fight for the right', a contemporary postcard of allied heads of state

German plate with portraits of Emperor William II and Francis Joseph, Emperor of Austria, 1914/15

day the banners were quietly removed. The King insisted that the brass plates bearing the names and titles of these foreign potentates should remain affixed to their stalls, as historical records. Queen Alexandra was not satisfied, complaining that he had not merely removed 'those vile Prussian banners', but also those of other Garter knights fighting on the German side, mostly relations of hers, who were 'simply *soldiers* or *vassals* under that brutal German Emperor's orders'.[2]

Among them was Charles, Duke of Saxe-Coburg Gotha, who had succeeded his Uncle Alfred in 1900. As the son of Queen Victoria's short-lived haemophiliac son Leopold, Duke of Albany, he was denounced in Germany for being English, and in England for being German. The war, claimed his sister Alice, later Countess of Athlone, quite shattered her brother's life. Had it not been for his wife and family, he would have returned to England. As an officer, he had no choice but to serve in the German Army, but his refusal to fight against England was respected, and he was posted to the Russian front.

The German-born Duchess of Connaught, whose health was visibly declining, was spared any personal attacks in her husband's country. Yet the divided national loyalties which had caused Queen Victoria's children to quarrel so bitterly between each other half a century earlier were to find an echo in family barriers erected by the Great War.

Just as distressing on a personal level was the campaign of vilification waged against Prince Louis of Battenberg, Admiral of the Fleet and First Sea Lord. He had carried out mobilization of the Fleet at the end of July 1914 when war looked imminent. Yet his German birth, name and accent inevitably made him the object of suspicion. His younger son Louis, a schoolboy of fourteen, was bitterly upset by rumours that 'Papa' had turned out to be a German spy and was in the Tower. Losses at sea made the Prince a scapegoat, and rising press hysteria forced the government and Winston Churchill, First Lord of the Admiralty, to ask with a heavy heart for his resignation. On 28 October he resigned, acknowledging that his birth and parentage had 'the effect of impairing in some respects my usefulness on the Board of Admiralty'.[3] As Queen Alexandra wrote, he had 'sacrificed himself to the country he has served so well and who has now treated him so abominably'.[4]

King George felt for him deeply; 'there is no more loyal man in the country'. Louis retired into private life, consoled by the somewhat empty distinction of a Privy Councillorship.

His resignation had taken place, ironically, within a few hours of receiving news that his nephew, Prince Maurice of Battenberg, had died of wounds sustained in the retreat from Mons. This death occurred the same week as that of a first cousin on the German side, Prince Max of Hesse-Cassel, eldest son of the German Emperor's youngest sister. Lord Kitchener offered to have Prince Maurice's body brought back to England, but his mother Princess Beatrice requested that he should be permitted to lie with his comrades.

King George V at the Front, c. 1915

As Queen Ena of Spain despatched her wreath to Ypres, she received a telegram from the German Emperor offering his condolences. He received the stiffest of stiff replies. Evidently his cousin's death weighed heavily on the Emperor William's conscience, for he later sent word to the village priest who had buried Prince Maurice, asking to know where the grave was. To this, the priest allegedly replied, 'Tell the Kaiser that I will let him know the prince's burial-place when there are no more German soldiers in Belgium, and when restitution is made for the crimes committed against our people.'[5]

At the time of his death Prince Max had been wearing a chain, on which hung a locket containing his mother's photograph. It was sent to Queen Mary, who returned it to his parents via the Crown Princess of Sweden.

The Crown Princess, living in a neutral country, was a useful go-between between relations on opposite sides, as well as a valued observer on how Germany was viewed in neutral territories. To Queen Mary, she wrote (24 January 1915):

> I will send on the things for Mossy as soon as there is a courier going to Germany. I will also write to her about it & give your messages. The courier goes to Berlin & there letters are posted, so if I might be allowed to suggest, don't put Germany on your envelope for Aunt Augusta as it might make them suspicious about it coming from abroad! The Germans, though, are obviously getting less careful, hardly anyone's letters are now opened by the Censor & my mother in law tells me she writes letters to some of her own relations out there, like Max Baden, all in English (which seems funny!) & though it is not correct they don't bother about it any more! I wish I could think or devize some way of helping the prisoners in Germany, they seem badly in need of help & it is so impossible to get at them!
>
> I have heard of several cases here where things for them have actually been personally handed over to the German officer in command & yet have never reached the prisoners! It makes one quite desperate & if they really get short of food what will happen!
>
> I met the minister for foreign affairs here the other day, he happened to sit next to me at dinner & he was about as much against Germany & the Germans as any neutral could be.[6]

For Queen Ena, in a similar position, the war provided many a trying moment, apart from the loss of a brother. She thanked Queen Mary (21 February 1915) for sending her a photograph taken by the Prince of Wales of Maurice's grave:

> It was very dear of David to have thought of doing this for us & I have written to thank him. Would you mind sending my letter to him as I do not know his address. What a terrible winter this has been for everyone & I so often think of you all in these sad anxious times. I feel for you more than I can say at having had to part with Bertie. God grant that the dear boy may keep safe & well. It is very hard to be away from my old home at such a time as this and especially so since Maurice's death when I know that Mama is so sad and needs me so much. I would give anything to be able to go to her but that I fear will not be possible for a long time to come.

It is really awful to think of the suffering this war brings to nearly everyone. Daisy* & I keep up a pretty regular correspondence because as she says it is curious that we are in exactly the same position, both living in neutral countries & with our mothers-in-law on the German side![7]

Like Sweden, Spain was neutral throughout the conflict, but the country and royal family were deeply divided. Sympathies of the upper and professional classes were openly on the side of the central powers. There was widespread unease that if the Allies won, the cause of traditional monarchy in Europe would suffer an irreparable blow. Yet the Spanish working classes, Liberals and Socialists, all favoured an entente victory. 'The aristocracy were pro-German, the middle classes anti-French', according to Winston Churchill. 'As the King (Alfonso XIII) said, "Only I and the mob are for the Allies."'[8]

The passionately pro-German Queen Mother made no secret of her feelings. In 1916, when the death of Lord Kitchener at sea was announced, she did not attempt to conceal her delight. The Spanish royal family were dining at the time, and a visibly shaken Queen Ena was observed digging her fingernails fiercely into the upholstery of her armchair.

Queen Alexandra kept up a private correspondence with her nephew King Christian X of Denmark who had succeeded his father, King Frederick VIII, in 1912. Many of her letters to him were carried by Hans Andersen, a Danish ship-owner, who enjoyed the friendship of the English, Danish and Russian royal and imperial families, and also the German Emperor. The Scandinavian monarchs remained neutral throughout the war, though King Gustav V of Sweden was broadly sympathetic to the central powers. He was married to Princess Victoria, daughter of the Grand Duke and Duchess of Baden. Sweden had traditionally close links with Germany, yet she resisted pressure to enter the war on the German side, much to the relief of Crown Prince and Princess Gustav Adolf.

The Kings of Denmark and Norway, closely related by marriage to King George, were always pro-entente. In the spring of 1915 King Christian suggested that Copenhagen would be an ideal place for a peace conference. Queen Alexandra thought it an excellent idea, though it was still too soon to think of peace – 'We must thrash them first of all.'[9] King George replied in more measured terms (16 April 1915):

[Mr Andersen] gave me your message with regard to your offer to mediate between the belligerents whenever the right moment comes and that Copenhagen should be chosen as the place where the terms of peace should be considered and settled. This I think an excellent idea and I am grateful to you for having proposed what I understand has since been agreed to by Nicky and the German Emperor. But I fear as I told Mr Andersen that the end of this appalling war seems still a long way off. We cannot be satisfied with anything but an honourable and lasting peace.

The world will not stand a repetition of such an outrage to humanity and civilization.

The allies are every week in a better position to carry on the war than they were at its beginning, while it is fair to assume that our enemies are weakening.[10]

* Crown Princess of Sweden.

The three Hesse sisters, the Tsarina, Grand Duchess Serge of Russia and Princess Louis of Battenberg, were cut off from their brother Ernest, Grand Duke of Hesse, and another sister Irene, Princess Henry of Prussia. On the outbreak of war, Princess Louis and Princess Henry had had the foresight to exchange their personal maids before travel became impossible. Princess Louis' maid was German, her sister's English. On returning to her native country, the latter servant reported that Prince Henry 'lived on board his flagship,' though he was at home fairly often.

Throughout the war, King George received regular letters from foreign heads of state. His correspondence from King Albert of the Belgians was usually limited to formal expressions of gratitude for British solidarity during the conflict. 'Your visit here in days of difficulty and trial was a great comfort to us,' King Albert wrote (7 January 1915), 'and I will always remember with gratitude the great honour you bestowed on us in bringing me the Ordre [sic] of the Garter.'[11]

His sense of history was gratified by an offer from King George to appoint him Colonel-in-Chief of the 5th Dragoon Guards, named after Princess Charlotte of Wales;* 'it was an exceedingly amiable attention of yours to select a Regiment of which my grandfather had been Colonel-in-Chief',[12] he wrote on 7 August 1915.

King George's replies to his brother monarchs were generally drafted by the Foreign Office. In the spring of 1915 a cypher telegram to Sir George Buchanan for Tsar Nicholas II (20 April) discussed the imminent participation of another ally in Europe on the side of the entente:

> I am most anxious however that the co-operation of Italy should be obtained with the very least possible delay, and I feel convinced that you are equally with me desirous that no means should be neglected which will tend to shorten the war and secure the definite victory of the Allies. The co-operation of Italy would almost certainly lead other countries at present neutral to adhere to our common cause, and a combination would thus be formed which our common enemies would find it extremely difficult if not impossible to resist for any length of time. I therefore earnestly hope that you will agree with me that it is of paramount importance to secure the adhesion of Italy, and much as I should have liked to have seen full effect given to certain considerations put forward by you, I much fear that unless an agreement is speedily concluded with her we will run the risk of losing altogether a most valuable ally.
>
> I am disappointed at learning that Italy cannot certainly promise to enter the field till one month after date of signature of Alliance, though she may do so earlier, but I think it would be deplorable for us definitely to refuse all Italian co-operation and break off negotiations on this point. When once Italy has signed the Alliance co-operation in one month at latest will be better than none at all and the effect upon attitude of other neutrals will be most favourable to us.[13]

---

* Princess Charlotte, daughter of the Prince Regent, later King George IV, had been the first wife of Prince Leopold of Saxe-Coburg Saalfeld, but died in childbirth in 1817. He was elected King Leopold I of the Belgians in 1830; King Albert was a grandson through his second marriage.

UNCONQUERABLE.

The Kaiser. "SO, YOU SEE—YOU'VE LOST EVERYTHING."
The King of the Belgians. "NOT MY SOUL."

'Unconquerable', from a Punch *cartoon by Bernard Partridge, 21 October 1914*

Within a week, negotiations had been concluded, and Italy entered the war on the Allies' side. For this the King was grateful to the Tsar (26 April):

> You will have heard that the signature took place today of the instruments confirming the adhesion of Italy to our common cause. The moral effect of this, when the time comes to make it known, will be most favourable. I cannot sufficiently thank you for the great assistance which you have afforded in bringing these delicate negotiations to a successful issue, and I highly appreciate and am most grateful for all that you have done in the matter. I take this opportunity of expressing to you my great admiration for the splendid achievements of your valiant troops, and I look forward with full confidence to a complete victory over our enemies.[14]

One of the King's duties, and one with which other senior members of the family could assist, was to show solidarity with foreign monarchs and their representatives. The King's second son Prince Albert had served as a midshipman in the Royal Navy at the outbreak of war, but his spell at sea was interrupted by recurring gastric trouble. While on sick-leave ashore, it was decided that he could begin to relieve the King of some of his minor duties. In April 1916 he was asked to welcome Prince Alexander, Regent of Serbia, on his arrival at Charing Cross for a visit to England in the interests of his country which had suffered so greatly at the hands of the central powers. 'I am still

Alexander, Regent of Serbia, and Prince Albert, driving to Buckingham Palace on a visit by the former to London, April 1916

leading the quiet life with a Serbian Prince thrown in last week', Albert wrote to his equerry, Dr Louis Greig. 'Pretty stiff time with him, as he can't talk English.'[15] Both Princes conversed in French.

Meanwhile King George was obliged to turn his attention to the personal dilemmas of King Ferdinand and Queen Marie of Roumania.

King Carol of Roumania, Ferdinand's childless uncle, was a member of the Catholic branch of the Hohenzollern family. Thus his loyalties had always been inclined towards Germany, though the ministers shared Crown Princess Marie's enthusiasm for the entente. During his reign, there was little likelihood of Roumania changing her allegiance or neutrality, but after his death in October 1914 the situation changed. The weak-willed King Ferdinand, who had brothers fighting in the German Army, believed in the invincibility of the German military machine. Moreover, Roumania was almost completely surrounded by the central powers. The only entente ally with whom she shared a border, Russia, was too heavily engaged elsewhere with her grossly inadequate forces to be of any practical assistance.

With the accession of King Ferdinand, seven of Queen Victoria's grandchildren occupied European thrones as reigning sovereigns or consorts for nearly two and a half years, from October 1914 to March 1917, namely King George V of Great Britain, the German Emperor, Empress Alexandra of Russia, Queen Maud of Norway, Queen Sophie of the Hellenes, Queen Marie of Roumania, and Queen Ena of Spain.

Carol I, King of Roumania

The Roumanian ministers had placed King Carol under some pressure to declare war on Austria-Hungary, with the ultimate aim of liberating Roumanians who lived in Transylvania and pave the way for a new Greater Roumania with Transylvania within her borders. Yet Queen Marie longed to join in on the side of the entente. Her favourite sister, Grand Duchess Cyril of Russia, had been continually urging her to exercise her influence in this direction since her husband's accession to the throne. It made no difference to them that their cousin, Emperor William, 'wildly elated by recent victories, was sending snorting telegrams which passed *en clair* through our country. One, to his sister, Queen Sophie of Greece, contained loud threats against any who would dare oppose his victorious armies and his Deutscher Gott.'[16]

'This terrible war has taught one to weigh one's words and be as careful as possible even when one's heart is bursting with the longing to say what one really thinks', Queen Marie wrote to King George V (13 March 1915). 'We are all going through anxious times, and how much suffering there is everywhere. Being neutral I get news from all sides, and each of course is dead sure of victory, tries to persuade us, that defeat for them is impossible. We had to sit still and watch, whilst conflicting passions raged over our little country, promises and threats being dangled over our heads.'[17]

'No German success or victory shakes Roumania's allegiance,' she told him two months later, 'nor can make her believe that any but the Entente can win.'[18] At the behest of the Roumanian Prime Minister, Ion Bratianu, she stated the terms of their country's allegiance to the entente, namely recognition of her claims to Transylvania; to the Banat, a region south-west of Transylvania known for its rich mineral deposits and fertile plains; and to Bukovina, a mountainous territory of natural forests north-west of Moldavia. All of these lands had belonged to Roumania until wrested from her by the Austro-Hungarian empire. A similar letter to Tsar Nicholas II brought a reply in which he declared that he and his ministers were 'deeply amazed by your country's *enormous* demands'.

Writing to the Tsar (15 February 1916), King George confessed to feeling 'rather uncomfortable' about the Roumanians:

I admit that they are in a very awkward position but I trust they will remain neutral in spite of all threats from Germany, until you can assemble sufficient troops to help them. These Zeppelin raids are making the people here very bitter against the Germans, they murder women and children and have done no harm to any workshop or military establishment; they show that they are simply brutes and barbarians. I trust Sweden will remain quiet; we shall be very careful to treat them with a delicate hand. I wish again to say that the people of this Empire are more determined than ever to fight this war out to a finish and until they have vanquished the enemy, and I am sure the people in Russia have the same sentiments. And with God's help we shall do it.[19]

Before long, there was a new but hardly unexpected threat to the Anglo-Russian alliance; as the King reported to the Tsar (23 August):

Information has reached me from more than one source, including one undoubtedly well disposed neutral source, that German agents in Russia have recently been making great efforts to sow division between your country and mine by exciting distrust and spreading false reports of the intentions of my Government. In particular, I hear it is repeated and in some quarters believed in Russia that England means to oppose the possession or retention of Constantinople by Russia. No suspicion of this sort can be entertained by your Government which knows that the agreement of March 1915 was made by my Government with the concurrence of the leaders of the Opposition, who were specially called into Council for the purpose and who are now members of the Government. But I am distressed to think that any doubts should exist anywhere in Russia as to British good faith and permanent intentions. I and my Government consider the possession of Constantinople and other territory, as stipulated in the agreements made by us with Russia and France during this war, to be one of the cardinal and permanent conditions of peace, when the war has been carried to a successful end. I earnestly hope that, if in this or any other matters between us, you think it desirable you will at any time instruct your ministers to enter into the frankest explanations with my Government or will yourself communicate direct with me. You know, my dear Nicky, how devoted I am to you and I can assure you that my Government regards your Country with equally strong feelings of friendship and we are determined to stand by the promises we have made as your Allies. So do not allow your people to be misled by the evil workings of our enemies.[20]

By now the entente powers were ready to pay their potential allies almost any price in the way of territorial rewards. On 27 August, King Ferdinand of Roumania declared war on the central powers. 'I always knew that it would end like that', wrote Queen Marie to King George (11 September 1916):

Ferdinand, King of Roumania

Marie, Queen of Roumania

Indeed I was confident that it would not end otherwise, but the struggles were hard and poor Nando has made a tremendous sacrifice – the greatest that can be asked of a King and a man, to go against his own brothers, again [*sic*] the country he was born in, that he loved . . . we are separated from England by the whole of Europe, yet we feel that England can be our great support and it is England that we trust. I never imagined that it would be the lot of our generation, we who were children together, to see this great war and in a way to have to remodel the face of Europe.[21]

At first the war went badly for Roumania. An advance to liberate their brothers in Transylvania was checked almost at once. The Russians were slow to come to their aid, and they faced invasions on two fronts – Germans and Austro-Hungarians from the north and west, and Bulgarians from the south. The Roumanian Army fell back in confusion, and in December 1916 German troops entered Bucharest in triumph. By the time Russia came to her aid, the German advance had been halted and the front line stabilized, but it was only a temporary respite before the revolution took Russia out of the war altogether.

Of equal concern to the King was the problem of Greek neutrality and the conflict between King Constantine and his Prime Minister, Eleutherios Venizelos. As a son of Queen Alexandra's brother, the assassinated King George, and husband of the former Princess Sophie of Prussia, sister of the German Emperor, he had close family ties with the main monarchs on both sides, and no quarrel with either.

The generally accepted view, chiefly as a result of French propaganda, was that King Constantine was pro-German. It has lasted to this day, although the British military attaché and principal British naval officer in Athens during the war – who were undoubtedly in a better position to know – maintained that his sympathies lay solidly with Britain and the allied powers. However, the conflict did not directly concern Greece, and the country had been left exhausted and depleted by the Balkan wars. He shared the view of the military command that to consolidate her gains, she needed a long period of peace.

Venizelos shared the view of many of his countrymen that their tasks begun in the Balkan wars were not yet completed. Persecuted Greek minorities in Asia Minor were still anxious for liberation from Turkish oppression. Only by joining the entente powers, and sharing in the fruits of what they regarded as inevitable allied victory, could Greece safeguard her newly-won territories and achieve the ultimate dream of total national integration. Greece would realize her dream of a new Byzantium by joining the war against Germany's ally Turkey and capturing Constantinople from the Turks.

The situation was complicated by two factors. King Constantine distrusted Venizelos, whom he suspected of wishing to foment internal revolution and establish a republic with himself as President; and General Sarrail, French Commander-in-Chief of the allied forces at Salonika, was a 'political' soldier of the left, claiming to have evidence that showed the Greek General Staff were in communication with Berlin.

An incident two years before had given grounds for suspicion, particularly among the French, that King Constantine was an ally of Germany. During a tour of Europe in the summer of 1913, a few months after his accession to the throne, he had visited Germany and attended army manoeuvres. The day before they were due to begin, he was guest of honour at a dinner at which the German Emperor proposed the health of his brother-in-law in most fulsome terms, praising his military skill and emphasizing that he had been a pupil at the German military academy. Taken completely by surprise, the flattered King made an impromptu speech of thanks in which he acknowledged his debt to Germany, as well as that of many of his staff officers to their training at Berlin. The observance of such courtesies between brother sovereigns was only to be expected. But a photograph was widely circulated of King Constantine in German Field-Marshal's uniform, complete with spiked helmet, following manoeuvres with the Emperor and the German high command. The Berlin press published it alongside a draft of his speech, with the emphasis of the wording altered slightly by the wily Emperor. To this, the King had made no objection at the time.

In France the reaction was one of dismay. Even in Britain some people expressed regret that the nephew of Queen Alexandra should be seen to be 'flirting' with the Emperor. When chided by his secretary for having agreed to the draft, the King answered sadly, 'How was I supposed to know that the thing would be telegraphed all over Europe?' In vain did he point out that King George V was also a German Field-Marshal, and the Emperor a British one.

Almost from the outbreak of war, the Emperor had repeatedly telegraphed King Constantine, urging him to come in on the side of the central powers, and not to throw in his lot with the 'Serbian assassins'. He took no notice of his refusals, until the exasperated King announced his intention of sending back his German decorations and Field-Marshal's baton.

The incident was used against him to devastating effect in 1915, when the Chief of the General Staff, Colonel John Metaxas, resigned in protest after refusing to join the British attack on the Dardanelles, and was supported by the King, and at this Venizelos also resigned. The King had refused to participate in what he and his staff all too accurately foresaw as the tragic, costly blunder of the Dardanelles expedition, as the risk of success was too remote to justify the lives of his subjects. However, as a gesture of goodwill to the Allies, he gave them the plans drawn up by the Greek General Staff for Constantinople by land instead of by sea, where the city's defences were obviously impregnable.

Yet against allied propaganda, this counted for nothing. The country was soon divided between Venizelos' supporters, encouraged by France and Britain, who wanted Greece to join the war, and the King and most of the military, who were intent on neutrality.

Even more damaging to King Constantine was his wife's nationality. Despite her German birth, Queen Sophie was just as pro-British as her mother, the late Empress Frederick, had been. She had stood with her youngest sisters beside their mother when she had been ostracized in the early days of her widowhood, and had always disliked her ostentatious eldest brother, who banned her from returning to Germany for three years early in her married life, as she had announced her intention of entering the Greek Orthodox Church without asking his permission. To Queen Sophie, 'beloved England' was a second home.

Nevertheless, she was a convenient target for allied propaganda. It was said that she had a private cable installed at the palace by which she could communicate with German submarines, and that her husband's severe attack of pleurisy in 1915 was not illness, but a wound left after she stabbed him in the chest with a dagger, because he refused to enter the war on the side of Germany.

King Constantine had had a faithful British supporter in Lord Kitchener, 'a soldier and an idealist like himself'. Both men had met in Athens in 1915 and instantly liked and trusted each other. Afterwards, Kitchener reported that he had spoken to him as one soldier to another. 'He is in the right. When we want the Greeks we can have them on our side.'[22]

Had Kitchener not been lost at sea that summer, and had there been another point of view raised to counter that of Lloyd George, then Minister of War and an ardent admirer of Venizelos, King Constantine's fate might have been a happier one.

In August 1916, on the entry of Roumania into the war, Venizelos and his party leaders established a provisional government at Salonika. Sir Edward Grey was distressed at the anti-Greek propaganda prevalent in Britain and France. He shared King George's view that, as the country had entered war in defence of Belgian neutrality, it was unethical for them to impose their will on another small neutral state, particularly as Britain would be unable to protect Greece if matters were to go badly.

At the instigation of France, the Allies had taken peremptory action which seemed inconsistent with international law. They seized control of the Greek postal and telegraph systems, demanded the dismissal of enemy agents, and ordered proceedings to be taken against Greek subjects accused of being accomplices in acts of corruption and espionage.

A constant thorn in the side of King Constantine was the writer Compton Mackenzie, who had been sent to Greece to work in counter-espionage during the war. The King was infuriated by the way in which this Briton had hurled himself into Greek domestic politics. While the other Allies and the Germans took sides in the rift between him and Venizelos, they did so as foreigners serving their own countries' purposes. Mackenzie joined in as 'a supernumerary Greek', devoting himself ruthlessly to the purpose of British interests, combined with those of a Greater Greece whose territory would include the coastline of Turkey, and become the controlling power of the Eastern Mediterranean. Mackenzie and Venizelos were two of a kind, and in 1916 the King sent his brother, Prince Andrew, to Paris and London to ask their governments if they would control their respective intelligence establishments. The Prince convinced King George V that the Z Bureau, Mackenzie's organization, was plotting to destabilize and overthrow King Constantine. Under pressure from his sovereign to withdraw him, Lord Denman was sent out to see the situation for himself, but he returned with a recommendation that Mackenzie should be left where he was, in view of his highly effective work in having created the secret service organization in Greece.[23]

Nevertheless, King George V remained uneasy. 'Are we justified in interfering to this extent in the internal Government of a neutral and friendly country, even though we be one of the guarantors of its Constitution?' he asked

Grey in September. 'I cannot help feeling that in this Greek question we have allowed France too much to dictate a policy, and that as a Republic she may be somewhat intolerant of, if not anxious to abolish, the monarchy in Greece. But this I am sure is *not* the policy of my Government.'[24]

He expressed his misgivings in detail to Tsar Nicholas (1 October 1916):

> The situation in Greece is most difficult to understand, as a revolution has broken out headed by M. Venizelos, and Tino seems to do nothing and one is afraid that unless he declares war on Bulgaria he will have to abdicate, which is the last thing that you and I want. With regard to your answer to my telegram of last month, I can assure you that both I and my Government are most desirous that the recognition by the Allies, that Russia is fully entitled to the possession of Constantinople and the Straits, should be published as soon as possible in their respective capitals. But the French Government is against this being done at the present moment lest it might strengthen the Turkish Alliance, and encourage the Turks to fight to the bitter end. I know you will also appreciate the necessity for regarding the sentiment of my eighty million Moslem subjects.
>
> We must choose the right time, as far as they are concerned, to make the announcement, in order to reduce as much as possible the chance of any serious rising amongst them. Therefore my Government would also prefer to wait until the final victory of the Allies is evident to the whole world, and merely a question of time, before publicly stating the conclusion to which we have all agreed.[25]

King Constantine's position was undermined further in November 1916, when Venizelos formally declared war on the central powers. Admiral Dartiges de Fournet led a Franco-British squadron to Greece and presented King Constantine (still refusing to abandon his neutrality) with an ultimatum, demanding compliance with certain drastic conditions, including the surrender by the Greek Army of much of their equipment and material. The King refused to agree to these conditions, and on 1 December the Admiral disembarked detachments of French and British marines to advance on Athens. To their surprise, they met spirited resistance from troops who were loyal to the King, and were driven back after a short battle in which there were some casualties.

On 6 December King Constantine addressed a telegram to King George V, justifying his actions by pointing out that the allied landing had been repulsed as it was known to be part of a Venizelist conspiracy. Whatever King George's personal feelings, he was obliged to support the allied cause. The allied powers, he replied, had confined their demands upon Greece to the observance of a benevolent neutrality, but they had received 'indubitable proof of action on the part of the Greek Government, both damaging to their naval and military interests and of direct assistance to the enemy's forces'. Demands in conjunction with the allied powers would 'include reparation for the unprovoked attack made by your troops and guarantees for the future'.[26]

Despite her pro-German sympathies, as well as those of her King and Queen, Sweden was never brought into either armed camp. The country's aristocracy and its military, professional and business classes were strongly influenced by

Swedish porcelain plate with portraits (clockwise from top) of King Gustav V of Sweden, King Haakon VII of Norway, and King Christian X of Denmark, marking the Malmo Peace Conference of 1914 at which they affirmed Scandinavian neutrality during the Great War

Germany, and German was the principal foreign language then taught in Sweden. There were strong demands for Sweden to declare openly on the side of the central powers, but the government prudently decided not to commit the country to war.

Yet it was inevitable that she would somehow become involved, albeit indirectly. The government asserted its right to trade with belligerent countries, an arrangement which favoured Germany in particular. As far as Britain was concerned, the blockade was an important weapon in her fight against Germany, and the Allies therefore stopped a large percentage of Scandinavian trade, which affected exports to Germany and also caused an acute shortage of food in Sweden by the summer of 1916. King Gustav V was thus moved to write to King George V (16 July 1916):

> I should like to communicate with you directly in a matter which is of very great importance to us here.
>
> I am alluding to the considerable difficulties in our foreign commercial relations since the beginning of this terrible war and I am sorry to say, that these difficulties are increasing more and more.

As of course you will know, as well as I do, there are frequent differences of opinion between our two governments about the import into this country of raw materials and other goods which for various reasons are of vital importance to us.

I should like to point out to you that certain measures taken by the British authorities regarding our trade seems – according to our views – not to be consistent with our rights and interests. This is most especially the case with the measures extending to the import of goods for government use. I am sorry to say that all this friction is constantly producing a considerable amount of irritation amongst our people.

I need not assure you that I am most anxious to maintain and to develop the good and friendly relations not only between our two governments, but also between our peoples. I therefore most earnestly beg of you as a friend kindly to use your influence to bring about some change in the present course of affairs to which I have alluded.

I hope you will not misunderstand my good intentions in writing to you, but I thought that it might be a good thing that you should be informed by me directly as to my views in this important matter . . .[27]

King George was grateful for the frank approach, replying (1 August 1916):

I am very sorry to hear that controversy should, as you say, have arisen as to goods consigned to Swedish Government Departments. It is certainly not my wish that the Swedish Government should be hampered in any way by the want of any article necessary for its activities. On the other hand you would not wish, I am sure, that goods consigned to your Government should, directly or indirectly reach my enemies. I hope it may be possible to arrive at some agreement by which both these objects may be attained. Indeed, it would be an excellent thing if some general agreement could be made which would secure to Sweden and her people the free importation of enough goods of all kinds to satisfy their own needs, and would at the same time prevent any such goods going to my enemies.

Some inconvenience must, I am afraid, be caused even to neutral countries by this terrible war, but you may rest assured that the measures taken by my Government with a view to bringing the war to as early a conclusion as possible will be enforced with the utmost consideration for Sweden and other neutral countries consistently with my belligerent rights, and my Government will be always ready to cooperate with yours for that object.

There is nothing which I desire more fervently than the closest and most friendly relations between Sweden and Great Britain.[28]

The situation was shortly to be exacerbated by unrestricted submarine warfare and the entry of the United States on the Allies' side. Not until May 1918 was an agreement reached with Britain and the United States, that permitted Sweden to import produce again from the west, and only on condition that exports to Germany were limited, and that a large part of Sweden's merchant fleet was to be put at the Allies' disposal.

8 'This wonderful moment of England's great victory'

In March 1917 the royal family in Britain received news which, although depressing, was scarcely unexpected. On learning in January of the murder of Rasputin, Queen Alexandra had written to King George V of the death of 'the wretched Russian monk', which was 'only regretted by poor dear Alicky who might have ruined the whole future of Russia through his influence'. Alicky, she continued, 'thinks herself like their Empress Catherine'.[1]

If she, and those among the Romanovs – in other words, nearly all of them apart from the Tsar and Tsarina themselves – who despised and feared the disastrous influence Rasputin had had on imperial policy since the outbreak of war, thought that his murder would save the tottering imperial throne, they were mistaken. Ten weeks later, revolution broke out in Petrograd. Rioting in the streets escalated, workers went on strike, and large numbers of previously loyal troops gradually renounced their allegiance to the Tsar. Seeing power slipping from its grasp, the Duma committee warned that the time for imperial

Alexis, Tsarevich of Russia, from a beaker commemorating his review of Cossack troops at the Front, 1916

*Grand Duke Michael, who was nominated
by Tsar Nicholas II as his successor*

concessions had gone. There was no alternative but for the Tsar to abdicate in favour of his son Alexis, with the next in succession, the Tsar's brother Grand Duke Michael as Regent.

Nicholas drew up a form of abdication, but it was made clear to him that His Imperial Majesty Tsar Alexis II, a sickly child of twelve to whom the slightest physical accident would probably prove fatal, would be henceforth separated from his parents. With a heavy heart, Nicholas decided to renounce the succession for himself and his son, nominating Michael as Tsar instead.* Astonished by the abrupt turn of events, and advised that a new torrent of revolution in Russia would probably be released if a new Tsar took the throne against the will of the people, Michael declined the poisoned chalice. With this the Romanovs ceased to reign, and a provisional government took power.

Republican France and the United States† regarded the news as a triumph for democracy and cause for celebration, and Liberal and Labour members at

---

* Grand Duke Michael was morganatically married to Countess Natalia Brassova, a match that had incensed the Tsar, Tsarina and Dowager Tsarina, chiefly as she had already been divorced from two previous husbands. He was shot by the Bolsheviks in 1918.

† Diplomatic relations with Germany had been broken off in February 1917, although the United States did not formally declare war for another two months.

Westminster rejoiced at what they saw as the downfall of a tyrant. At least one of the Tsar's cousins in Russia had no sympathy with him. 'He calmly and deliberately abdicated at this first demand of this same new government', Grand Duchess Cyril wrote to her sister Queen Marie of Roumania (10 March), her exasperation and bitterness exacerbated by anxiety for her family and the fact that she was expecting another child:

> Where is the logic? The absolute truth is that of the sixty millions of his subjects not one would or did stand for him so he never even tried to apply to them but this is not the way he and Alix put it now. Everyone says what a fearful punishment but I say it is not a punishment, it is a pure logical result of their acts. Just as if they had taken a match and put a fire to their own garments.[2]

Lloyd George, who had succeeded Asquith as Prime Minister three months earlier, addressed a telegram to the head of the new regime, applauding the adoption by Russia of 'responsible government', and describing the revolution as 'the greatest service that the Russian people have yet made to the cause for which the Allies are fighting'. These apparently republican sentiments irked King George V, until it was tactfully pointed out to him that the British monarchy was likewise founded on revolution.

Queen Mary's reaction, on paper at least, was characteristically restrained. Two days after they heard of the Tsar's abdication, she noted that 'Minny', Grand Duchess George Michaelovitch,* came to tea with them and 'we discussed the surprising events in Russia'.

'Events of last week have deeply distressed me', King George telegraphed to the Tsar (19 March). 'My thoughts are constantly with you and I shall always remain your true and devoted friend as you know I have been in the past.'[3]

King Manuel of Portugal had now settled at Fulwell Park, Twickenham. In September 1913 he was happily married to Princess Augusta Victoria, a niece of King Ferdinand of Roumania. As the son of a French Princess himself, on the outbreak of war he had offered to serve in the British Army in the defence of France. For political reasons, this was thought inexpedient. The Prince of Wales had initially been refused permission to serve in France, as it would have been embarrassing for the British heir to the throne to be captured by the Germans. When he refused to accept no for an answer, the War Office reluctantly allowed him to go to France, but he was always kept well away from the line of battle. Though the former King of Portugal, now a republic and a neutral state, would be less of a prize as a German hostage, the eventuality would still have been an unwelcome one for the British government. He therefore devoted himself during the conflict to helping nurse and look after wounded servicemen at home.

As a former monarch who had undergone similar experiences to Tsar Nicholas, he wrote a letter of condolence to King George (18 March 1917):

> I want to tell you what my thoughts are with you during these terrible events in Russia! I know unhappily by my own experience what a revolution is & I can

---

* Marie, Princess of Greece and Denmark, sister of King Constantine.

understand it better than anybody else. I feel very much upset & sorry: upset by what a revolution means, sorry because I am very fond of poor Nicky & I cannot forget how kind he was to me when I was in Russia.[4]

Within a few days of the Tsar's abdication, Paul Milyukov, Foreign Minister of the provisional government, suggested that the imperial family should come to England. Sir George Buchanan, British Ambassador in Russia, reported it to the Foreign Office in London. Before there was time to consider, a second telegram came from Moscow, conveying Milyukov's urgent demand (as opposed to an inquiry) for the former Tsar to be given asylum in England. While the British government would be pleased if he could leave Russia safely, ministers wondered whether France, Switzerland, or Denmark, would not be a more suitable destination.

This provoked a more urgent request from Petrograd. Buchanan reported that Milyukov was anxious to get the ex-Emperor out of Russia as soon as possible for reasons of his own security, 'the extremists having excited opinion against His Majesty'. Buchanan almost begged the Foreign Office that, 'in spite of the obvious objections, I may be authorized without delay to offer His Majesty asylum in England and at the same time assure the Russian Government that he will remain there during the war'.[5]

Accordingly Lord Stamfordham, the King's private secretary, was invited by Lloyd George, Andrew Bonar Law, Leader of the House of Commons, and Hardinge, Permanent Under-Secretary at the Foreign Office, to discuss the former Russian sovereign's future. While the three men agreed that the proposal that they should receive him in the country 'could not be refused', Stamfordham raised the problem of how he and the family would support themselves in exile. To a suggestion that the King should place a house at their disposal, he replied that only Balmoral was available, but it would be a most unsuitable residence at that time of year. It was decided that Buchanan, in formally offering asylum to the Tsar, should ask the Russian government to provide enough funds for him to live in suitable dignity.

Buchanan's message that Britain was prepared to receive the family evoked no immediate response from the Russian government, who were now apprehensive of the extremists' anger in the event of any attempt to remove him to safety. Milyukov did not reject the British offer for which he had pleaded urgently, yet made no effort to accept it. It was a fatal delay, allowing revenge-seeking Russians to consolidate their strength, and giving King George time to have second thoughts about helping his cousin.

The first sign of royal doubt came in a letter from Stamfordham to Balfour, Foreign Secretary, on 30 March, eight days after the meeting at Downing Street. Notwithstanding the King's strong personal friendship for the Emperor, reported his secretary, he wondered not only about the dangers of the voyage, but also 'on general grounds of expediency, whether it is advisable that the Imperial Family should take up their residence in this country'.[6]

To this, Balfour answered that 'unless the position changes', they doubted whether it was possible to withdraw the invitation already sent. Within a week, however, the King was aware of how much resentment the proposal had aroused. Labour members of Parliament angrily condemned the idea, and it was assumed that the King had originally issued the invitation. Could not Sir George Buchanan, suggested Stamfordham, approach the Russian government with a view to making other plans for the future residence of the deposed Tsar and his family?

King George V was increasingly anxious that the presence of his cousins in Britain would compromise the position of the Queen and himself. He had had similar abuse after receiving members of the supposedly pro-German Greek royal family only a few months earlier, but such criticism was nothing compared to the indignation which this new proposal regarding the Romanovs had provoked before they had even left Russia, let alone set foot on British soil. He feared not merely for his popularity, but for his throne. Even if the government accepted responsibility, public opinion would believe that they were doing so simply to screen the King; and the government was looking towards a close understanding with Russia's new rulers and their continuance as military allies. Notwithstanding Milyukov's initial requests, to have the exiled Romanovs in Great Britain, they feared, would prejudice good relations between the countries. The extreme Left in Russia, perhaps in an unholy alliance with German agents, would be certain to stir up public opinion against Britain.

That the Romanovs might find a safe haven in France was still entertained. Buchanan was hopeful of sounding out the French government on the question, if only on the grounds that the British public had welcomed the Russian revolution so cordially that they were thus so indisposed against the old regime that the presence of the Emperor might provoke demonstrations that would cause serious embarrassment.[7]

Sir Francis Bertie knew that they would not be welcome in France. The Tsarina, he maintained, had done all she could to bring about an understanding with Germany, and was regarded as 'a criminal or a criminal lunatic', and her husband as 'a criminal from his weakness and submission to her promptings'.

King George V was evidently, therefore, responsible for depriving the imperial family of their best, if not their only, means of escape from Russia. He had persuaded his government to withdraw their original offer of asylum. Whether his decision made much difference is questionable. The kindly Milyukov may have lacked the strength to defy the Russian Left, who sought revenge on the old regime by allowing them out of the country; and the Tsar's children were suffering from measles, which would have made their ever protective parents even less prepared than usual to let them be moved.

Superficially it may be seen as a cowardly decision on the part of the King. It has, however, to be viewed in the context of its time. In 1917 Britain was exhausted by war and vociferous, albeit unrepresentative, elements suggested that the spectre of republicanism was not altogether dead. How, asked angry letters delivered to 10 Downing Street, could a sovereign with Hanoverian ancestors and a Queen descended from the house of Teck have sympathies with any nation other than Germany, and was it surprising that the war was lasting so long with a pro-German monarch on the throne?

Britain had seemed an unlikely theatre of revolution, but after three years of war with no end apparently in sight, and with mutterings from the likes of

H.G. Wells about 'an alien and uninspiring court', it looked like tempting providence for a constitutional monarch to identify himself so blatantly with Russian imperial autocracy. Although in a more peaceful age King Edward VII had not needed to conceal his anger when socialist Members of Parliament had criticized his visit to the Tsar at Reval, his son thought it prudent to tread more carefully. In 1917 the instinct for self-preservation, and maintenance of the British monarchy, was paramount.

In order to help restore public confidence that summer, the King was prevailed upon to sweep away all the German names of the royal family. No longer did the house of Saxe-Coburg Gotha reign, but instead the unimpeachably English-sounding house of Windsor. The Battenbergs were Anglicized to Mountbattens, the Duke of Teck was henceforth the Duke of Cambridge, and his younger brother Prince Alexander of Teck became Earl of Athlone.

Overseas, the gesture was regarded with ridicule. The German Emperor said that he looked forward to attending a performance of Shakespeare's *The merry wives of Saxe-Coburg Gotha*. At home, however, the move succeeded in diluting the argument that the monarch and his family were Germans through and through. Some might find the court uninspiring, but it was no longer alien.

Elsewhere in Europe, opinion was hardening against Germany. From Stockholm, the Crown Princess of Sweden wrote to Queen Mary (22 May 1917):

> The sinking of 3 Swedish ships with cereals & other much needed things on board when on their way from England has done more to produce an increased anti-German feeling than anything else that has happened lately! It is curious to note how when a person or a nation are made to feel a thing in a personal way, they respond at once! Owing to the shortage of so many foodstuffs here, especially all cereals, potatoes sugar tea coffee milk & eggs these ships were being looked forward to with such great expectations & their non arrival has caused both great gloom & wave of fury & anger against the Germans. As one pro German paper remarked sadly, nothing could have done more towards promoting an *anti* German feeling.
>
> There is a good deal of unrest in the country, partly owing to the shortage of food & partly owing to the Russian revolution. The Socialist party mean to have several more or less fundamental laws changed & I fear my father in law will have anything but a pleasant time!
>
> My mother in law too has contrived to make herself more & more unpopular & that falls back on him, people even go as far as comparing her to poor Alicky & say she is just as reactionary! I'm awfully sorry about it yet at the same time, I can't help agreeing with a lot of what these same people say.
>
> I'm afraid my pen has run away with me but if you won't quote me it doesn't matter so much![8]

Even so, King George V still had to proceed cautiously, particularly where unpopular foreign monarchs were concerned. Although he had deprecated the

COMFORT IN EXILE.

IMPERIAL BROTHER-IN-LAW. "AFTER ALL, MY DEAR TINO, YOU ARE SOMETHING BETTER THAN A KING; YOU ARE A FIELD-MARSHAL IN MY ARMY! YOU SHALL PRESENTLY HAVE A COMMAND ON THE WESTERN FRONT."

TINO (*without enthusiasm*). "THANK YOU VERY MUCH."

'Comfort in Exile', from a Punch *cartoon by Bernard Partridge, 20 June 1917*

attitude of the entente powers towards Greece, pointing out that a 'kindly' instead of a 'bullying' attitude might have induced the Balkan country to join them, it was to no avail. Neutral Greece had suffered nothing at German hands, but she had been persecuted shamefully by the Allies, particularly France, who had spared no effort to undermine the position of King Constantine and Queen Sophie. They had bombed Athens and blockaded the country. At length the King and Queen were almost ready to throw in their lot with the central powers, a move with which many of their long-suffering subjects concurred.

In June 1917 a French warship, carrying Senator Charles Jonnart, High Commissioner of the Protecting Powers of Greece, dropped anchor off Athens. The Greek Prime Minister was presented with an ultimatum, demanding the abdication of King Constantine and the nomination of a successor from among his sons, provided it was not Crown Prince George, who was regarded as too closely identified with his parents' 'pro-German' views. Broken in spirit and health, and determined that no more blood should be shed for his sake, the King accepted without a second thought. He and Queen Sophie agreed to leave the country, although without signing any act of abdication. Their second son, now King Alexander, was left to reign in his stead.

King Alexander proclaimed that he would 'carry out his father's sacred mandate', *Punch* observed dryly. 'But when it was pointed out to him that, if this was really his desire, an opportunity of following in his father's footsteps would doubtless be granted him, he tried again.'[9]

As for his parents, it was suggested that the Isle of Wight might be an appropriate place of exile, but King George V let it be known that he did not approve. In view of the Greek monarchy's unpopularity among the British public, to permit them to do so would have inflamed opinion at home. Instead they settled in Switzerland.

Greece was now politically reunited, and Venizelos, reinstalled as Prime Minister, declared war on the central powers. At the same time it was revealed that King Alexander had fallen in love with Aspasia Manos, daughter of one of his father's equerries. Despite his parents' disapproval, he was determined to marry her.

His resolve was hardened by a curious episode. Britain was anxious to extend the hand of friendship to Greece, now that she was officially an ally. In March 1918 the Duke of Connaught arrived in Athens to invest King Alexander with the Insignia of the Knight Grand Cross of the Order of the Bath, on behalf of King George V. After completing his mission, the Duke asked him for a private audience the next day. Alexander had been told that the real purpose of this mission was to propose a marriage between him and King George's only daughter, Princess Mary, now aged almost twenty-one. He spent a sleepless night worrying about it, aware that such a proposal would be difficult to refuse without giving offence.

Much to his relief, all the Duke wanted to do was to meet Mlle Manos, about whom he had heard so much. The King cheerfully arranged an informal meeting, and the elderly Duke, whose wife had died the previous year, was greatly charmed by her. Before his departure, he told the King with a mischievous twinkle in his eye that, if only he had been a little younger, he would have proposed to her himself.

By the summer and autumn of 1917, after revolution had taken Russia out of the war, King Ferdinand, Queen Marie, and the Roumanian government were based at the town of Jassy. So were the headquarters of their army, ravaged by an epidemic of typhus during the severe winter of 1916–17. Foreign ministers in Great Britain, France, Italy and the United States cabled from there to their respective countries, asking their governments to put pressure on Russia to hold the front and, in case exodus proved inevitable, to guarantee King Ferdinand's position as head of his country wherever he might be forced to flee. While the Allies equivocated, Russian troops seized all means of transport that might have made a Roumanian royal flight feasible.

The only word from western Europe was 'a very warm telegram' from King George to Queen Marie, advising her that she and her children were welcome in England at any time. Unlike her dethroned cousins in Russia and Greece, she and King Ferdinand were still popular in Britain. 'At first the telegram made me very happy,' she noted, 'but on riper reflection I understood that it was a bad sign; they recognize that we are in danger and that our position is untenable.'[10]

By the fourth winter of the war, King George V was as tired and war-weary as many of his subjects. Lloyd George had told him in conversation during October that the Russians and Italians were 'out of the battle', the French evidently had little fight left in them, and little assistance could be expected from the United States. The brunt of any future fighting would therefore fall on Britain. He insisted that they should obtain from their Allies a firm statement as to whether or not they would be ready to resume a serious offensive the following year, otherwise Britain would be left dangerously weakened, her ranks thinned through sustained fighting. The state of Europe gave the King and Queen little cause for optimism as they left for a much-needed rest at Sandringham over Christmas 1917.

'I fear we will all suffer this winter in many ways, but do pray for better & happier times in the spring', Queen Maud of Norway wrote from Christiania to Queen Mary (28 December), 'there is so much one longs to talk about but daren't write, it is all very hard being separated so long, I am dying to see you all again'.[11]

King Haakon likewise did his best to offer words of comfort during what was a critical time for them all, in a Christmas Day letter to his sister-in-law:

You could not have given me a nicer present as those pictures will for always remind me of what your brave people have done both at sea and on shore for the good cause for which they are fighting. It is rather disheartening I see how your antagonists seem to gain by using every dirty trick one can think of and they seem quite to have forgotten the word shame during these years. The affairs in Russia seem to be as bad as possible but I do not believe that it can last, although it may last long enough for that country to be out of reckoning for the rest of the time the war lasts and I fear you will before long feel that the Germans and Austrians have got a lot of war material free to use against your poor people. One can not but wonder how it will all end and if it will not end by all the lower classes refusing to continue the war. The Germans and now also the Russian Socialists are hard at

King George V and Queen Mary, with King Albert and Queen Elisabeth of the Belgians

work even here in the neutral countries and as we are in for very hard and strong restrictions I suppose even we may have interior troubles as I fear people will not understand that we who are neutral have to put up with that sort of thing as well as everybody else.[12]

On both sides, sovereigns were aware that time was running out. At the same time Emperor Charles of Austria-Hungary, who had succeeded his octogenarian great-uncle Francis Joseph on the Habsburg throne in November 1916, was warning Emperor William that if the monarchs themselves could not conclude peace themselves during the next few months, the people would go over their heads and a revolutionary flood would sweep away everything for which their families and soldiers were fighting and dying.

The Russians' rejection of peace terms at the treaty of Brest-Litovsk in March 1918 rejuvenated the German Army and triggered a new offensive. That same month the beleaguered Roumanians were forced to sign the humiliating treaty of Bucharest, conceding substantial amounts of territory and reparations to the central powers, and allied missions had to leave the country at once. Queen Marie sent a despairing letter to King George; 'cut off, betrayed, encircled by enemies, we have had to give up, in spite of the high spirit of our troops . . . rather would I have died with our army to the last man, than confess myself beaten, for have I not English blood in my veins?'[13]

Much later she received a telegram from King George, expressing his sympathy and intense admiration 'of the heroic efforts made by the gallant Roumanian Army against the overwhelming forces which encircled it. You may be confident that we and our Allies will do our utmost to redress the grievous wrongs Roumania has suffered in the great cause for which we went to war.'[14]

*Porcelain mug with portraits of Emperor
Charles and Empress Zita of Austria,
c. 1917*

Meanwhile the final offensive had begun on 21 March 1918, and within two or three days, it looked possible that General Ludendorff's army might succeed in separating the French and British Armies. On 28 March King George crossed over to France, as it was felt that his presence with the troops would assist in restoring confidence. He visited as many units as possible, driving over three hundred miles in three days. Yet he returned in a mood of grave anxiety. A letter from King Manuel (29 March), recovering at the Imperial Hotel, Torquay, after a nervous breakdown, awaited him:

> I feel I must write you a few lines to tell you that our thoughts are with you in this terrible moment. I want you to know that our prayers have been, more than ever, with your wonderful troops; may God bless them & give them a rapid victory!
> I only wished I could be of any use to you! You know dear Georgie that my modest services are always & entirely at your disposal & I can assure you that I would be only too glad if they could be used. I have done all I can in the special Orthopaedics Hospitals & I have the consolation of knowing that I have done my duty. But I would like to do more in a moment of anxiety, for you whom I love & for this Country which I admire so much & which I consider my second country![15]

Though King George had been anxious for the ex-Tsar's safety and feared that if imprisoned in Russia he might not come out alive, he probably believed that the Bolsheviks' anger would be satisfied by the execution of their former ruler at most. That they would show such flagrant disregard for international opinion by butchering the whole family was a possibility hardly envisaged by any but the most pessimistic. In July 1918 the King was informed that 'dear Nicky' had been shot, but there were no further details.

Not for another month was he to be informed that his crippled wife, daughters and son had been executed in their last prison, a house at Ekaterinburg, along with most of their remaining servants. 'It's too horrible and shows what fiends these Bolshevists are',[16] he noted in his diary. According to the Prince of Wales, his father ever after blamed 'those politicians' for his cousin's fate; 'If it had been one of their kind, they would have acted fast enough. But just because the poor man was an Emperor – '.[17] Lord Esher, who likewise loyally blamed the British government, remarked to Lord Stamfordham that if the country had been led by the Duke of Wellington or Lord Beaconsfield, the Romanovs would have lomg since been granted safety at Claremont, where King Louis-Philippe of France and his family had fled after being deposed in the revolution of 1848.

By this time, the end of the conflict was in sight. On 4 August, the fourth anniversary of Britain's declaration of war, King Manuel wrote to King George from the Imperial Hotel, Harrogate:

> We just returned now from church where we have been praying God, to protect the British Army & Navy, to bless their King & to give us soon the complete victory!

I feel it is a duty for me to write you a few lines with our heartfelt wishes in this anniversary. It is a great consolation & hope that it falls in a moment when so good news are coming from the front. Let us have faith that more & more good news will follow & that soon will [sic] shall see a glorious end to this terrible war!

You know too well my dear Georgie that my ambition would be to be fighting & that my services could be more useful either at the front here in England my adopted country.[18]

The former King had never wavered in his support for the British cause. Although his wife was of German birth, and had felt the pang of divided loyalties, she had unequivocally taken the British side as well. At a time when King George V had many other, more pressing duties on his mind, they were eternally grateful to him for aiding negotiations with the Portuguese ministers regarding his property in Portugal; 'the question is getting every day more important for us owing to our financial difficulties. All what I have is in Portugal & as you can well imagine Mimi has not received a penny from what belongs to her, since the beginning of the war! You can then understand our difficulties & the importance that the resolution of the question of my property has for me.'[19]

On 14 September the allied forces launched their offensive along the southern Macedonian frontier. Within days they had broken through the Bulgarian front. The Bulgarian troops retreated, and on 29 September Bulgarian peace delegates agreed to the cessation of all hostilities with the Allies. King Ferdinand shrewdly abdicated in favour of his eldest son, 24-year-old Crown Prince Boris.

As Queen Marie of Roumania expressed it, 'for the first time we really see light ahead'. The deadlock had been broken at last. French troops had entered Sofia, the Allies were advancing into Serbia and Albania, and the German front was crumbling everywhere.

One afternoon a French aeroplane flying up from Salonika dropped a message for the Queen. Written on a tiny scrap of paper, it promised her that Roumania would not be forgotten. In other words, territorial promises made to the country when she joined the entente powers would be remembered in victory.

Too late, Emperor Charles of Austria renounced the German alliance, and signed an armistice with Britain and France on 4 November. Yet he was powerless against the demands of revolutionary crowds in Vienna, and within a few days he signed a document of abdication agreed jointly by members of the last imperial Cabinet and socialist ministers of the new republic.

That same week, over the border in Germany, Emperor William met his generals for the last time. It followed several days of revolution, which had begun with a naval mutiny at Kiel, and spread to agitators and Social Democrats in Berlin. The Emperor was warned that the troops were deserting, and in effect he no longer had an army. Faced with the inevitable, he abdicated as well. Haunted by the news of what had happened to his cousins at Ekaterinburg in July, he was relieved when arrangements were quickly made for him to be sent to exile and safety in neutral Holland.

In this hour of triumph, King George could not resist a note of condemnation. While acknowledging that Emperor William had done great things for his country, 'his ambition was so great that he wished to dominate the world and created his military machine for that object. No man can dominate the world, it has been tried before, and now he has utterly ruined his country and himself. I look upon him as the greatest criminal known for having plunged the world into this ghastly war which has lasted over 4 years and 3 months with all its misery.'[20]

In celebration, a delighted Queen Ena wrote to King George from Madrid (17 November 1918):

> Up to now I have never liked to bother you with letters, knowing how overwhelmed you must have been during these last terrible years, which have now, thank God, come to an end. Though far away from you all, my heart & thoughts have constantly been in England. You can understand how trying my position has often been among the many conflicting interests of a neutral court & how hard to disguise one's true feelings, as the news was good or bad for the Allies. But now in this wonderful moment of England's great victory, when your feelings of pride & relief must be almost too big for words, I wish by one short line to tell you how truly I rejoice with you in this supreme hour & what great pride I feel at having been born an Englishwoman with English traditions. The excitement here has been intense & the Allied Flags are displayed in most of the streets.[21]

Queen Ena's godmother, Empress Eugenie, was similarly elated at the victory, and the subsequent return to France of Alsace-Lorraine. She felt that France's defeat at the hands of Bismarck had been avenged; 'it allows me to die with my head held high'. Even during the darkest hours of war, she had refused to condemn the man whom most Britons held responsible.

Princess Marie Louise, daughter of Queen Victoria's third daughter Princess Christian, recalled discussing with the Empress the part played by Emperor William in the events that had led to war. She remarked that if the Emperor was really responsible for the war and the misery it had brought, then his own country as well as Europe would be justified in getting rid of him. The Empress gently reproved her, saying that nobody who had experienced a revolution would wish even their worst enemy to undergo all the horrors that it entailed; 'I do not wish that William II should fall a victim to the anger and disillusionment of his people.'[22]

Now aged ninety-two, the exiled Empress' spirit was as indomitable as ever. During the war she had converted a wing of Farnborough Hill into a hospital for officers, financed entirely by herself, and took a considerable interest in her patients' welfare. King George V awarded her the Grand Cross of the British Empire for services to the war effort, and sent the Prince of Wales and Prince Albert to Farnborough to invest her with the decoration. In reply, she wrote how much she appreciated this token of friendship, which she owed 'much more to the kindness of Your Majesty than to any merit of my own'.[23]

9 'Strength and fidelity'

On 22 November 1918 King Albert of the Belgians re-entered Brussels in triumph. Beside him rode Queen Elisabeth, followed by their sons Prince Leopold and Prince Charles; among the horsemen who followed them were Prince Albert, and Queen Mary's brother, Earl of Athlone. It was an indication of the role that the British monarchy, a survivor amid the crowns which had fallen into what the Russian Bolshevik leader Lenin dismissed as 'the dustbin of history', would assume in Europe during the years ahead. Only hindsight would reveal how appropriate it was that the second son of King George V, and not the Prince of Wales, would have the highest profile in Europe of any member of his family during the next few years.

At Christmas 1918 Prince Albert found himself attached to the staff of General Salmond, at Spa, Belgium. At the end of the year he visited General Currie, Commander-in-Chief of the Canadian forces, quartered in the Schaumburg Palace at Bonn. It was the home of Princess Victoria of Prussia, whom he met for the first time.

The widowed Princess professed ignorance of all German atrocities committed during the war, and appeared unable to understand the deep sense of resentment entertained by the Allies. She seemed to have very little idea of the family's feelings towards Germany, he wrote to his parents. All the atrocities and the treatment of prisoners were a revelation to her, as she had been kept shielded from the real state of affairs. She asked after the family, Prince Albert wrote to his father, and hoped that they would all be friends again shortly. 'I told her politely I did not think it was possible for a great many years!!! She told everybody there that her brother did not want the war or any Zeppelin raids or U boats, but that of course was only a ruse to become friendly with us . . .'. To this, the King replied the sooner she knew the real feeling of bitterness which existed in Britain against Germany the better.[1]

Yet King George V was not a man to kick a fallen enemy. He was furious when told that the wife of a British Minister to Holland had jeered at the ex-Emperor as he arrived from Germany to begin his exile. A few months later, her husband was prematurely retired from the Diplomatic Service. Likewise, Lloyd George's proposal to have the former warlord extradited from Holland and put on trial for war crimes incensed him, especially as he only learned about it from the newspapers. To his relief, the Dutch government refused all requests for extradition.

The King neither met nor corresponded with his cousin again. The Emperor was hurt at not receiving a word of condolence from his English cousins after the Empress died in 1921, her spirit completely broken by the humiliation of her husband's defeat and abdication.

Prince Albert, second son of King George V, c. 1918

Other former monarchs also felt the icy blast of royal displeasure from Windsor. While attending an Ornithological Congress at Oxford, Tsar Ferdinand of Bulgaria's delight at being paid all possible honours was marred by disgust at an order from King George V that none of the family were to receive him. His voice grated with anger as he told Hector Bolitho how the King had been 'very unkind to my person. I cannot forgive that.'[2]

Shortly before the Armistice in November 1918, Asquith remarked to the King that the war had brought 'a slump in Emperors' which neither of them could have foreseen at the start of the conflict. Tsar Nicholas had been murdered; Emperor Charles of Austria-Hungary was a fugitive; and Emperor William was on the verge of abdication. As the King admitted, it was not a good time for monarchies. All the minor German kings, princes and grand dukes had lost their titles, although some of them were permitted to remain in Germany as long as they undertook not to engage in any political activity. Two other grandsons of Queen Victoria, Prince Henry of Prussia and Ernest, Grand Duke of Hesse and the Rhine, shared this privilege. After the treaty of Brest-Litovsk in March, the King had suggested that the German empire should be dismantled after the war, and the kings, princes, grand dukes and dukes restored to the positions of prestigious independence which they had enjoyed before Bismarck's wars had united Germany under Prussia half a century earlier. His belief in the efficacy of monarchy had already been illustrated by his conviction that India's problems would be best solved by a strengthening of the rule of the hereditary princes.

During the war the King and his family had been unable to meet their Scandinavian relations, and in Norway Queen Maud felt dreadfully isolated, deprived of the comfort of staying at her beloved Appleton every year. She wrote to Queen Mary (30 November 1918) of being 'wild with excitement at the idea of *at last* coming home and seeing you all again! It seems all like a *dream*, to me, everything has changed so quickly from the *awful* war into peace.'[3]

Queen Ena wrote (1 October 1919) in similar terms: 'You can't think how we are both looking forward to seeing you again after all these long sad years that we have not met.'[4]

Queen Marie of Roumania was equally ecstatic. Once enemy forces of occupation were withdrawn from Roumania, she and King George were able to correspond more freely again. 'Nothing shook me, neither threats, nor misery, nor humiliation nor isolation', she wrote (25 November 1918). 'At the darkest hours when no news reached us I clung firmly to my belief in your strength and fidelity.'[5]

By the beginning of 1919 the thrones of Britain, Belgium, Holland, Italy, Greece, Spain, the Scandinavian countries and the Balkans still remained. Yet of these, the Greek crown was doomed; the Spanish crown was soon to disappear, albeit temporarily; while the Kings of Italy and the Balkan countries recognized that their days were numbered, and would be swept away within thirty years or so.

Not even the British throne could be regarded as completely safe in peacetime. On Armistice night, cheering crowds had surged around Buckingham Palace, calling King George and Queen Mary to show themselves on the palace balcony time after time. On five successive days they drove in an open carriage through the streets of the capital; 'the demonstrations of the people are indeed touching', noted the King.

Yet republicanism was rarely far below the surface. At a meeting called in the Albert Hall organized by the Communists to celebrate the third anniversary of the Soviet Socialist Republics, the name of the King evoked a wave of hissing. With post-war unemployment ever rising, the King remained anxious about discontent, protest marches, and subsequent action by police and troops; as Stamfordham warned the Prime Minister, 'riot begets revolt and possibly revolution'.

From Madrid, Queen Ena looked with alarm on every sign of post-war industrial confrontation in her native country. 'I am sure you must all be anxious about the coal-strike & I do hope that this fearful catastrophe may still be avoided', she wrote to Queen Mary (26 September 1920). 'Really what hateful times we are living in!'[6]

Soon after the cessation of hostilities, Queen Marie found herself called upon to assume a role on the European stage of which she could once have only dreamed. Roumania's official representatives to the peace conference in Paris after the armistice acquitted themselves poorly, thus jeopardizing the country's plans for post-war expansion. The French Minister in Roumania, Count de Saint Aulaire, accordingly suggested that it might help matters if the Queen came to Paris in order to exercise her charm on President Clemenceau.

She was delighted to be chosen. The Roumanian ministers decided that, as the British government was thought to be the most outspoken anti-Roumanian power at the conference, it would be as well if she could visit England and speak to her cousin, King George V. She had good reason to be anxious, as her letter to the King (11 January 1919) revealed:

> Communications are still so bad that it is almost impossible to be well-informed from far, but lately disquieting rumours have reached us that we are not to be treated as allies at the peace discussions and that as we were obliged because of Russia's treason and because of our tragic situation to conclude a peace that according to every foreign officer then in the land, was absolutely inevitable, our treaty of alliance is not to be respected.
>
> Personally, I have always had faith in our Allies, absolute, unshakable faith, even when most about me doubted – I would laugh in their faces and tell them that they did not know England if they could imagine that she would go back on her word because our misfortunes had made us helpless. We only gave way when all was lost, when those far-off could not come to our assistance, when Russia was starving us out, cutting us off from all means of receiving the promised ammunition – we had ammunition for a few weeks and one knows what that means in modern war! That was in January and we were told that our Allies could make no efforts till towards Autumn![7]

As an effort to remind him, and the rest of Roumania's allies, of their obligations, it evidently succeeded. King George V felt obliged to tell the representatives of the other powers that they could hardly go back on promises made to the small Balkan nation, which had rendered such sacrifices at a critical juncture during the conflict.

The Queen asked to be allowed to take her daughters with her, offering the excuse that life in post-war Bucharest was too disorganized to leave them at home. Her main reason for doing so was to prepare the two older girls for the royal marriage market. In particular her elder daughter, Princess Elisabeth, was extremely fat, and her mother hoped that 'more normal, more severe, more European surroundings would be able to open her eyes'.

Arriving in Paris in the first week of March 1919, Queen Marie made an impact little short of that created by King Edward VII nearly sixteen years earlier. Almost at once she charmed the sceptical if not once-hostile Clemenceau and Lloyd George into seeing matters from the Roumanian point of view. Shortly before leaving for England, she granted an interview to a correspondent of *The Times* in which she declared her intention and hope 'to arouse the interest of your people in my people'. On the day of her arrival in London, 12 March, the paper carried a timely editorial headed 'The resurrection of Roumania', paying tribute to the suffering, bravery and commonsense of the people, and their representative in Europe, 'the Queen of an Allied State, who has done her full woman's part in sharing the sorrows and the sufferings of her adopted country'.

The Queen found it quite emotionally affecting to be met at the station by King George and Queen Mary. Arriving at Buckingham Palace in time for late supper, she met the Prince of Wales for the first time. With his 'child's face' and 'hair the colour of ripe corn', she found him 'the most attractive boy' she had ever seen.

Despite her welcome at the palace, she realized how far she had strayed from English ways; 'I was a royal guest and had to be very careful not to overstep any of the established conventions . . . I felt that my relatives were watching me, a little anxious as to what surprises I might bring into their well ordered existence.' 'Try not to be shocked at me', she appealed to the King. 'Forgive me if I am different from what you think a Queen ought to be.' In Roumania she was so used to being surrounded by corrupt public servants that she had long accepted it as part of her role to take on some of the mundane functions of government herself. In a country where her cousins could trust the government and civil service to run matters, it was all so different. At Buckingham Palace, she found everything 'so restricted and one is always afraid of upsetting their conventionalities'.

She knew that her hard-working schedule was inclined to create havoc. Rather upsetting to British routine were her breakfast-parties starting at 9 a.m., at which she argued her country's needs to busy statesmen brought to the palace by her friends, including Waldorf Astor, whose recent succession to the peerage had brought his wife Nancy to Westminster as the first woman to take her seat in the House of Commons. Aware of the servants' disapproval, she called them together to explain the urgency of her case. Though they gave way on the surface, she sensed that they deplored her unconventional ways as much as the King and Queen did.

Boldly Queen Marie took on representatives of the government and business.

She soon had the British press on her side. The *Daily Mirror* called her an 'Irresistible Ambassador', while the *Illustrated London News* published a full-page cover picture of her in Red Cross uniform, reading to a dying soldier. The caption, which referred to Roumania's wartime ordeal, referred to her close family ties with the King. Lord Curzon, acting Secretary of State for Foreign Affairs, gave an official dinner in her honour so that she could plead Roumania's cause with those who were in a position to help. Curzon himself was too ceremonious to inspire any feelings of warmth, but Winston Churchill, Secretary for War and Air, was more sympathetic. They remembered each other from childhood days, when Winston had played with Princess Marie of Edinburgh, her sisters and brother, while they lived at Clarence House.

The Queen had arranged for Bratianu to follow her to England, so she could present him to the King, 'to wipe out any ill feeling that may be between him & the English'. She acted as interpreter at their meeting, knowing that the King would be far more receptive to what her Prime Minister had to say if his words were communicated through her.

Between receptions and official functions, Queen Marie made time to see old friends, among them the Astors. She found Waldorf Astor 'advanced', and regarded herself as an 'advanced Queen'. Both regretted 'that the court shuts itself off so much in the same old circle'. She found a similarly kindred spirit in the Prince of Wales, who shared her impatience with his parents' conventional and old-fashioned ways. She accompanied Queen Mary on visits round the hospitals. and could not but feel a twinge of envy when she compared the well-ordered hospitals with the impoverished institutions in Roumania.

Never really comfortable with the staid, reserved Queen Mary, she preferred the company of the ageing Queen Mother, Alexandra, whom she had so loved and revered in childhood. Although 'Aunt Alix' had regarded Marie and her sisters as 'much too German' as girls, and been glad that she had not married the future King George V after all, she clung to Marie as a link with imperial Russia and her favourite sister, the Dowager Tsarina. Queen Alexandra showed her letters from her sister, still in the Crimea. Although she and a few surviving members of the imperial family were guarded by a volunteer detachment of Russian officers, it was no longer safe for them to stay in the country.

Queen Marie was still greatly concerned about her mother, the Dowager Duchess of Coburg, who had been left almost penniless by Russia's collapse and now lived in Zurich. When they talked about family matters, related Queen Marie, 'our eyes were full of tears'.

Fortunately, rescue for the Dowager Tsarina was at hand. The French evacuation of Odessa had brought Bolshevik forces within striking distance of the Crimea, and a British warship was sent urgently to Yalta with orders to fetch the Tsarina. Queen Alexandra despatched a passionate letter to her sister, begging her to leave while yet there was time. She agreed to do so, on condition that the relatives and friends who were with her in the Crimea could also be taken on board. They included her daughter Grand Duchess Xenia and her children, and the former imperial army Commander-in-Chief, Grand Duke Nicholas, and his wife Grand Duchess Anastasia, sister of Queen Eleanor of Italy. Not until she was certain that none of her family had been left behind did the fiercely protective matriarch permit the Captain to sail.

At Malta the party transhipped from HMS *Marlborough* to HMS *Lord Nelson*. On the voyage to England, the ship's officers were surprised to find the Tsarina 'great fun' despite everything that she had been through. While loath to leave Russia and all its memories – some happy, some bitter – behind her for the last time, she was evidently in high spirits at the thought of seeing her family in Europe again. One evening she sent for the Captain and demanded that there should be dancing on the quarter deck. In vain did he point out that wartime regulations were still being observed, and that all the officers were already in bed or on watch. She brushed his objections aside, insisted that the officers be gathered together, and the Marine band summoned to play dance music while she personally supervised the impromptu party.

On 9 May *Lord Nelson* arrived at Portsmouth. Despite the emotion of the occasion, the sisters were careful to observe full ceremonial while still being observed in public. The Empress stood slightly apart from the exiles on the quarter deck, with her daughter and grandsons, while Queen Alexandra was piped on board. Each had her daughter by her side, as they moved forward to greet each other, the confused, ageing Queen very calm while the Tsarina was unable to hide her excitement. Presentations were made, first to the Tsarina's Russian friends, then to the ship's officers, before the sisters who had been parted for so long could go off and talk in private as they boarded the train for London.

Their cousin Grand Duchess Marie,* who had recently come to live in London, noted that their arrival in the capital had been 'shrouded in mystery, and every effort was made to avoid publicity'. The welcoming party of Russian exiles, of which she was one, were only advised at the last minute about the time of the train's arrival. 'On our way to the platform we were stopped at every corner by officers of the police, to whom we were obliged to give our names, and got through with great difficulty. We emerged on the platform just as the train was coming in. The scene we were looking upon was reminiscent of receptions in former days, and yet how different! The brilliance and bustle were gone, and the feeling of welcome, even if only official, was somehow lacking.' Absence of publicity had ensured that the occasion was as private a family matter as possible.

Though King George, Queen Mary and several members of the family were present with a group of household officials in attendance, there were no crowds; the station was comparatively quiet. Grand Duchess Marie was struck by how calm and contained the smiling Dowager Tsarina appeared to be. 'Did she make comparisons between her present arrival and those of the past? Did she notice the emptiness of the station, the uneasiness around her; did she perceive the mixed feelings with which she was received? Whether she did or not, nothing of what was going on escaped us; the impressions we brought away were painful.'[8]

---

* Daughter of Grand Duke Paul, youngest son of Tsar Alexander II. Her brother Grand Duke Dmitri had been banished for his part in the murder of Rasputin.

Queen Alexandra, c. 1920

As they arrived in London, Grand Duchess Xenia's servants took one look at King George V and were convinced that he was the Tsar. Relieved that their prayers that he had been moved to safety after all had been answered, they prostrated themselves in front of him, and only with difficulty were they persuaded that he was not their 'Holy Father' after all.

That the two elderly widowed sisters obviously enjoyed being together again, after all they had been through, is borne out by glimpses left of them by younger observers. Although the years were taking their toll of Queen Alexandra in particular, in a sense it was almost like a second childhood for them. For a while 'Minnie' lived with her sister at Marlborough House, and they alternately amused and exasperated each other – as well as anybody else within earshot – by grumbling in voices loud enough for the other to hear, about having to live in such comparative poverty after almost a lifetime of regal splendour and no need to have to worry about money. They attended the wedding of the Queen's lady-in-waiting, Zoia, daughter of Baron and Baroness de Stoeckl, and came to inspect the trousseau, 'like children, holding out a garment and exclaiming: "We would never have been allowed to wear such thin things."'[9]

On another occasion, the sisters were expected to attend a state banquet, but kept the distinguished company waiting as they had become so engrossed in a game of billiards that they had forgotten the time.

In July 1919 Nathalia, Countess Brassova, widow of Grand Duke Michael, and her eight-year-old son George, were summoned to meet the Dowager Tsarina in London. Queen Alexandra and her embittered spinster daughter Princess Victoria, from whom she was now rarely parted, were 'very charming' to her, but the Dowager Tsarina was rather distant. 'She was rather nice to me,' the Countess wrote afterwards, 'but I feel that she does not like me and will never forgive me that I married her son.'[10] The audience lasted for an hour, but she was relieved to leave her unbending mother-in-law in order to have lunch with Grand Duchess Xenia, who was then living in a flat in Draycott Place.

According to Grand Duchess Marie, it was not the most comfortable of homes, 'smothered by a large family of boys and numerous female servants who had followed her out of Russia. Smiling, always perfectly enchanting and a little bewildered, [Xenia] moved about the house in search of a little privacy.'[11] Her husband, Grand Duke Alexander, had moved to France, leaving her with the family of six sons and one daughter. Although they had separated for good, they never divorced.

After lengthy negotiations between the Foreign Office and the Bolshevik government, the latter agreed to return a large consignment of the Dowager Tsarina's possessions from the Anitchkov Palace to London. During the worst days of the revolution, the palace had been guarded, and it was known that most if not all of her valuables had survived.

On their arrival in November 1919, King George asked Sir Frederick Ponsonby to receive them from the Captain of a British cruiser and store them at Buckingham Palace. Fifteen packing cases were carried up to the Throne Room while Ponsonby witnessed everything being opened by several workmen, with an Inspector from Buckingham Palace and M Nabokov, an official from the imperial Russian Embassy who had survived the revolution, in attendance. They contained 'nothing but absolutely worthless trash', including pokers, shovels, tongs, harness and saddlery, much of which had perished. A case labelled 'Books from the Empress's library' was full of old Russian railway guides, children's stories and novels, instead of the books in fine bindings which she had collected over the years and was looking forward to seeing again.

Ponsonby took the precaution of drawing up statements that the cases were untouched, and listing the contents briefly, in order that the Bolsheviks could not charge him or anyone else at the palace with having stolen any pictures, trinkets or articles of value. Nabokov was about to slip furtively from the Throne Room when he was called back to sign the document. It seemed inconceivable, Ponsonby considered, that the Soviet government 'should have taken so much trouble with the farce, but no doubt they made great capital over their goodness in letting the Empress have all her valuable things'.[12]

The Dowager Tsarina was at Sandringham when the bruised, grimy packing cases were returned, as it had not been thought necessary to bring her to London to check them. When she was told the truth, she seemed stunned at first, scarcely able to believe it; then she smiled philosophically, saying that it was just what she had expected from all she had heard of the Bolsheviks' behaviour. Never again did she mention the packing cases. Such items as had any value were sold for her, but they fetched very little, and strenuous efforts were made to get some diplomatic redress, but in vain.

Like her mother, Grand Duchess Xenia had had unlimited wealth while living in Russia, and understood nothing about money. Peter Bark, who had been Russian Finance Minister until the revolution, offered his services and was accepted. He found that she was simply penniless, having 'sold' all her jewels to a man she met one day who disappeared without paying her. She had a house in Paris which Bark sold without difficulty, but she was so unbusinesslike in her personal affairs that he found it impossible to check on her liabilities.

After she moved from Draycott Place, the King lent her Frogmore Cottage,* and generously settled on her the gift of £2,400 a year. A clerk was engaged to look after her accounts, and hand her the balance after her staff's salaries and wages had been paid. However, she almost starved herself, and never spent a penny on her clothes, so she could give more to her sons.

In exile, she always shunned pomp and ceremony. 'The Russian revolution took almost everything from me,' she explained, 'but the Bolsheviks left me with one privilege – to be a private person.'[13] A skilled artist in watercolours, she painted flower pictures which were often given to friends or sold for charity. As a patron of the Russian Benevolent Society, she never ceased to take an interest in the fate of other, less fortunate, refugees from her old country.

Though the Dowager Duchess of Coburg had rebuked her two eldest daughters for their pro-allied stance during the war, feeling herself obliged to champion

---

* She lived there until 1937, when King George VI granted her a grace-and-favour residence at Wilderness House, Hampton Court, where she stayed until her death in 1960.

the cause of Germany and the central powers, she was eternally grateful for the moral support and financial assistance King George and Queen Mary had given her in her last days. Humiliated at having to sell most of her magnificent jewels in order to survive, she was too proud to consult anybody, and consequently sold them for about a quarter of their value. Aged and broken in spirit by her experiences, she died on 25 October 1920, aged sixty-seven. It was said that she expired after receiving a letter addressed simply to 'Frau Coburg'.

Queen Marie of Roumania saw her mother's passing as a blessed release, as she told King George V (29 November):

> Her death was a terrible, cruel shock to us all, we were in no wise prepared for it, I had been with her hardly two months before. She was certainly, thin weak & very changed, but nothing made us imagine that her end could be so near.
>
> Her life had become too sad and all about her too had changed. She was breaking her heart over it, she could bear no more. The death of Uncle Paul after all those other dreadful deaths was what was just too much for her – after that news, according to those with her, she was never the same again, she became suddenly old and broken down – her usual splendid health forsaking her all at once.
>
> She had seen everything crumble, Russia with all her family and her fortune, then Germany – everything she had believed in, it was too much; mourn her as we do, none of us are cruel enough to wish her back into this sad world where she has suffered over much.[14]

One of the Dowager Duchess's last wishes was that Queen Mary should receive one of her jewels, a chain with sapphires and a brooch to match. She had insisted that it should be a Russian jewel, according to Queen Marie of Roumania; 'Bee* will bring it to dear May, and ask her to think of my sad old Mama sometimes when she wears it.'[15]

---

* The Infanta of Orleans, the Dowager Duchess's youngest daughter.

10 'Don't let England forget'

Queen Alexandra continued to take a close, even protective interest in the troubled affairs of the Greek monarchy, the maintenance of which she regarded as a sacred family trust. King Constantine had been recalled to his throne in 1920 by an overwhelming vote in a referendum, shortly after his son King Alexander had died in agony, following complications after being bitten by a pet monkey which he was trying to separate from his dog. However, he had not been forgiven for his supposedly treacherous neutral stance during the war. The French government refused to recognize him as sovereign, and encouraged the other European powers to do likewise.

'Promise me to do all you can for Greece & poor excellent *honest* Tino who has been so infamously treated by the world & France', the Queen wrote to King George V (27 February 1921). 'Don't let England forget that we put my excellent brother on the Greek throne and the only cause of dear *honest* Tino's present awkward position is simply and solely his having married poor dear Sophie the sister of that ass William.'[1]

The Greek royal family in exile, Switzerland, c. 1918. Left to right, sitting: Prince George; Queen Sophie; King Constantine, with Princess Katherine on his knee. Left to right, standing: Princess Helen; Prince Paul; Prince Irene

Britain's cold-shouldering of the King resulted in a petty but embarrassing incident at the wedding of his daughter Helen to Carol, Crown Prince of Roumania, the following month. A large royal party was out walking one day when they saw the new British Minister, Lord Granville. Observing diplomatic instructions to the letter, Granville had not paid an official call on the King. An informal meeting of this nature, however, was surely a different matter, and as he was an old friend of King Constantine and Queen Sophie, they were ready to welcome him. But he pointedly took no notice of them. He greeted Queen Marie of Roumania warmly, and without the slightest sign of recognition towards the others, he turned and walked away, leaving them shocked and dismayed.

Queen Alexandra continued to press their cause, though she was hardly an influential champion. Seven months later (5 October), she was still entreating her son to do 'all you can in your power for the sake of Uncle Willy – as *Papa* would have done – We put him there and it is *our duty* to help his Son to remain there. His horrid Minister V[enizelos] was the cause of his having to leave his dear Country.'[2]

In vain did the King reply that he was unable to act against the policies of the Allies (9 October 1921):

> With regard to poor Tino. Rightly or wrongly the Allies considered that he was pro-German & that he was working against them & they made him abdicate & put his 2nd son Alexander on the throne & he went to reside in Switzerland. Feeling in this country was very bitter against him in all classes & still continues. His poor son then died & he returned to his country at the wish of the overwhelming majority of his people. The Allies still refused to recognise him as the King. Then came the war between Greece & Turkey which the Allies did all they could to prevent. At first the Greeks were successful, but they unfortunately failed to take Ankara or to defeat the Turkish Army & have had to retire where they will remain during the winter, both armies pretty well exhausted. Whether either side will ask for the mediation of the Allies remains to be seen. In the meantime Greece has no more money & unless she makes peace & disbands her army she will be bankrupt. A short time ago we sounded France as to whether she would be inclined to recognise Tino, but Briand refused absolutely so there the matter stands. The only way to help Tino in his difficult position would be to recognise him, but that at the present moment is impossible. I am not prepared now, on account of the strong feeling (which may be quite unjust) which certainly exists in this country against him to do anything, in fact no one would even listen to me if I did. Under the circumstances there is nothing to be done but to wait & see what happens in the next few weeks. I hope I have made myself clear, I am sorry for him, very sorry.[3]

Trying to talk to her about it was equally fruitless, as he complained to Queen Mary afterwards that it was impossible to make 'Motherdear' hear, much less understand. Yet she refused to give up; a month later (2 November), she had returned to the fray, insisting that '*England* must never forget they put my brother on the Greek throne & we are in consequence *bound* to support his successors.'[4] Queen Victoria and King Edward VII might have taken a firmer stand; but King George recognized that the influence of the British crown had diminished since the era of his father and grandmother.

Earlier that year, Beverley Nichols, a young English journalist, had been asked to go to Athens under the special protection of the Greek royal family. Here he would be given access to secret archives, as a result of which he would be expected to write a book containing 'sensational information' that would restore the prestige of King Constantine, after years of calumny, and persuade the French and British governments to recognize him. 'King Tino' was popularly regarded as an arch-traitor, 'a sort of miniature Kaiser, who by his treachery and his double dealing had imperilled our cause throughout the whole of the Near East'.[5]

Nichols got on very well with the Greek royal family, and was convinced at once that the legend of 'Tino's' perfidy was false, owing more to ruthless propaganda by agents and wartime hysteria than to any reasoned argument. He had several private meetings with the King, and fully accepted his version of events, especially regarding his reservations in taking part in the débâcle of the Dardanelles and the subsequent allied failure at Gallipoli.

As for Queen Sophie, Nichols would never forget his first sight of her; 'for she had the saddest face of any woman I have ever seen. Standing there, dressed entirely in black, a bowl of lilies by her side, her face rose from the shadows like one who has known every suffering.'[6] She told him that her greatest wish was to return to England, and that her most fervent dream was that her daughters should marry Englishmen.

Nichols abandoned his idea of writing a book, ostensibly as there was no story. Yet he was impressed by their magnanimity towards Britain, their lack of ostentation, their apparently cheerful acceptance of reduced financial circumstances, and the pride that prevented them from accepting help from the King's wealthy American sister-in-law, Mrs Leeds, wife of Prince Christopher.

However, time was running out for the hapless King and Queen. A disastrous military campaign against Turkey in the summer of 1922 led to further demands for King Constantine's abdication, and this last blow broke him completely. Leaving the throne to his eldest son, now King George II, he and Queen Sophie retired to exile in Sicily. He had virtually lost the will to live, and in January 1923 he collapsed and died, clutching a leather pouch containing a handful of Greek soil.

During the autumn of 1922, the new government in Athens court-martialled several individuals whom it held personally responsible for the military disaster. Five former political leaders and a senior army commander were sentenced to death and executed. A wave of revulsion swept throughout Europe at this savage reprisal, and Britain severed diplomatic relations with Greece. King Constantine's younger brother, Prince Andrew (husband of the eldest daughter of Prince and Princess Louis of Battenberg), had been a Lieutenant-General in command of an army corps in Asia Minor. He had been arrested, and would probably have shared the fate of the others had it not been for the timely intervention of the Foreign Office in London. Commander Gerald Talbot, a former naval attaché in Greece, with an almost unrivalled knowledge of the country's political relations, was sent out from Switzerland to negotiate on behalf of the Prince's release. Encouraged by certain officials in London, including Harold Nicolson (who was commissioned, many years later, to write an official biography of King George V), he reached an understanding with the revolutionary government that the Prince could be smuggled out of prison only on condition that they were not seen to be submitting to British naval pressure.

Prince Andrew was accordingly released from his cell under cover of darkness, reunited with his wife, and they were conveyed to Corfu on board a Royal Navy cutter to be met by their five children.* They sailed for England, later settling at St Cloud, near Paris.

For many years it was asserted that King George had initiated the rescue operation by telephoning the Admiralty and ordering the Royal Navy to save his cousin; and that 'the power of royalty, the despatch of a gunboat, could still influence events in foreign lands in 1922'.[7] It was left to Kenneth Rose's researches among Foreign Office papers to reveal that the King had kept strictly within his constitutional limits on this issue. He did no more than express encouragement through the customary channels to the Foreign Office, and certainly did not initiate the exercise. However, he showed his appreciation of Talbot's dedication to duty by appointing him a Knight Commander of the Royal Victorian Order.

Though the Habsburgs were never part of the family in the way that the Romanovs were, King George V still felt morally obliged to assist the dethroned Emperor Charles and his family to the limits of his constitutional propriety.

After signing the document of abdication by which he renounced his imperial power but not his crown, Emperor Charles and his family left Vienna and settled in his hunting-lodge at Eckartsau, north-east of Vienna, his own private property and not a state dwelling. However, pressure had been placed on him almost immediately to depart from Austrian soil. The Empress Zita's brother, Prince Sixtus of Bourbon-Parma, feared that, if the revolutionary government of the new republic was to fall into the hands of the extreme left, there might be a repetition of events at Ekaterinburg in 1918 which had so shocked the world. President Poincaré informed Prince Sixtus that there was little he could do personally, and suggested that he should consult King George. As he knew, the murder of the Romanovs was very much on the King's conscience. The King and Queen Mary agreed that something had to be done. The need for military protection above all was urgent, and France would lend Britain diplomatic support.

A British officer from the Royal Army Medical Corps, Colonel Summerhayes, was attached to the imperial family for their protection. However, the War Office at Whitehall considered that in sending one of their representatives, they ran the risk of being politically implicated with possibly detrimental results for British relations with the Republic of Austria, and replaced him with Lieutenant-Colonel Edward Strutt, a Catholic with a distinguished war record and a fluent command of German.

To Strutt, the Emperor confided that he relied implicitly on King George, whom he considered more trustworthy than any other crowned head in Europe.

---

* The youngest, Prince Philip, a son of seventeen months, is now the Duke of Edinburgh.

He told Strutt that escutcheons of distinguished British people still hung in the Stefanskirche, and was curious to know whether His Majesty had still retained the Austrian banners at St George's Chapel, Windsor.

At thirty-one, the Emperor was young enough to nurse hopes of resuming his position as head of state, and anxious to warn his fellow-monarchs, including King George and King Alfonso of Spain, that Bolshevism could still devour all constituent states of the old Austro-Hungarian empire unless they took swift action to prevent it. He suggested the despatch of entente troops to the Danube to keep radical unrest under control; delivery of food supplies to prevent famine, and therefore unrest; and entente support for a confederation to be reformed from the nations of the old empire under Habsburg leadership.

Fortuitously, King Alfonso received the letter just after a communist coup in Budapest, and he passed it to King George. Although the latter was concerned at the dangers, he could do no more than acknowledge it and say that a translation of the Emperor's letter had been passed to the Prime Minister for discussion at the forthcoming peace conference. Much as the entente powers feared the threat of a possible Bolshevik takeover, they had scant enthusiasm for the idea of a revived Habsburg confederation.

The threat of Bolshevik domination had been mentioned from another quarter. King George's cousin, Grand Duchess Cyril of Russia, whose husband had been one of the few Grand Dukes to leave the disintegrating empire in safety, wrote to him (29 January 1919) from their exile in Borgo, Finland, to

Emperor Charles and Empress Zita of Austria-Hungary and their seven elder children, in exile, Hertenstein, October 1921. Children, left to right: Archdukes Charles Louis and Felix; Archduchess Charlotte, on her mother's arms; Archduke Rudolf; Archduchess Adelaide; Archdukes Robert and Otto

seek British help for White Russian forces in the Russian civil war, 'to destroy the source itself from which this contamination of bolshevism spreads over the world'.[8] King George could do no more than write back sympathetically, insisting that he was exerting his 'utmost endeavours', but he was quite well aware of the threat.

Meanwhile, Strutt was advised in March 1919 that it was 'highly advisable to get the Emperor out of Austria and into Switzerland at once', adding that the British government could not guarantee them a safe journey. The Emperor and Empress agreed to go, on condition that Strutt would understand that their departure from Austrian soil was in no sense an act of abdication. Before they left, he signed a document known to posterity as the 'Feldkirch manifesto', in which he demonstrated that he was undertaking an act of voluntary self-banishment, and declaring the new republican government 'null and void' for him and his family.

Soon after settling in Switzerland, the Emperor wrote to King George V, thanking him for his generosity and concern.

Two years later the Emperor made two abortive attempts to regain his Hungarian throne. After the second, the French Prime Minister, Aristide Briand, formally disassociated himself from the former sovereign whom his country had secretly supported for so long. He called upon the Hungarian government to proclaim the deposition of King Charles and hand him over to the British naval Danube flotilla presently in Budapest. From there, he would be conducted to the Black Sea and put on board a British cruiser.

A suggestion was made that Malta might become a temporary home for Charles and his family, but this was ruled out as the Prince of Wales was due to visit the island shortly. To have the Habsburgs in residence would be inconvenient and politically insensitive. The peace conference contemplated having them interned in a British possession, but the majority present 'were opposed to Great Britain being his gaoler', and in November 1921 the Emperor and his family were conveyed to Madeira. By this time the Emperor's health was deteriorating, and he died at the early age of thirty-four on 1 April 1922.

Though Queen Alexandra and the Dowager Tsarina had been overjoyed at their reunion, their life together at Marlborough House was far from happy. The passage of time revealed how much they had grown apart. 'In reality they were just two old women with weary and furrowed souls and very little now in common but their age', commented Grand Duchess Marie.

> For over fifty years they had led entirely different lives with different, sometimes even conflicting interests, and had developed different points of view. Their meetings in the past had been frequent perhaps, but short and full of social diversions; then too they were free to come and go as they pleased, now they were tied together. The Empress found the Queen's deafness trying, the Queen was irritated by the incursion of the Empress's attendants into her well-ordered household. Discreetly and pathetically one complained of the other, each one commenting upon the changes in her sister's disposition. They missed their former perfect understanding and could not make out what had come between them although their affection was as deep as ever.[9]

It was irritating for the more sprightly, still mentally active Minnie to hear her sister talking to a guest, addressing him or her by the name of somebody who had been dead for fifty years. Such lapses on Alix's part made Minnie pity her, but in doing so she became apologetic and somewhat superior in her attitude to her. At the same time, she was jealous of Alix's vast collection of souvenirs and knick-knacks, collected over the years, while she herself had nothing but the jewels she had managed to bring out of Russia. It was irksome that her elder sister could generously make presents to their visitors while she had nothing to give, and a savage if unintentional reminder of how dependent she had become on the hospitality and goodwill of her more fortunate British relations.

Before long, Queen Alexandra was too tired to cope with life in London any more. Henceforth she would retire for good to Sandringham. The Dowager Tsarina did not appreciate the thought of living as a recluse in the Norfolk countryside. After the blows dealt to her spirit by the Russian revolution, she had recovered her old zest, and wanted her own establishment.

The rest of the family decided that they would assist her financially to return to her native Denmark, and Queen Alexandra – who was still quite lucid at times – accepted that it was for the best if they parted company. With King George V and Princess Victoria, she agreed that they would pay her an allowance of £10,000 a year, although such was the precarious state of his mother's and sister's finances that the King soon found himself meeting the full cost. Ponsonby was asked to become her Comptroller, but he declined the position, knowing that it would be impossible for him to restrain her from giving freely to Russian beggars who would doubtless come seeking her sympathy.

The sisters' old home at Hvidore had initially been allotted to her younger daughter, Grand Duchess Olga. Her loveless marriage to Prince Peter of Oldenburg had been annulled in 1916, and she was now happily married to Nicholas Koulikovsky. With their two young sons, they had escaped to safety from Russia a few months after the Dowager Tsarina. The latter settled at first in a wing of the Amalienborg Palace, and King Christian X was persuaded to contribute to his aunt's expenses, but he made no secret at his irritation in having to help support her, and he was angered by her extravagance. Matters came to a head one evening when he sent her a message asking her to turn off some of the unnecessary lighting that blazed away at his expense. In her fury, she immediately ordered her servants to turn on every light in her apartments and leave it burning all night. After that, it was decided that she too must make her home at Hvidore.

After the Armistice, King George V was keen to delegate some of the ceremonial duties of British royalty to his sons. It was necessary for the monarchy to have a high profile as it adapted to changing times if it was to survive, while stopping short of embracing the unconventional quite as wholeheartedly as Queen Marie of Roumania did; and an accident in which the King had been thrown from his horse in France in October 1915 had left his never very robust constitution permanently weakened.

Christian X, King of Denmark

While the Prince of Wales undertook a series of gruelling tours throughout the British empire, it fell to the King's second son, Prince Albert, created Duke of York in 1920, to represent him as a royal ambassador at several of the surviving European courts. In February 1921 the King sent him to Brussels to present the Distinguished Flying Cross to King Albert, and to confer decorations on several Belgian subjects in recognition of their wartime services to Britain. It was the Duke's first experience of a state visit, and he acquitted himself very creditably. The British Ambassador informed Lord Stamfordham that the Duke had spoken most pleasantly to the Belgians 'whom I had the honour of introducing to him, and many of them told me afterwards how pleased they had been to have the opportunity of meeting His Royal Highness'.[10] Making fluent conversation with strangers, and in a foreign tongue, had been something of an ordeal for the Duke, by nature shy and retiring, and afflicted with a severe stammer.

The following year, Queen Marie invited King George to be chief sponsor, or 'Koom', at the wedding of her daughter Marie to Alexander, King of the Serbs, Croats and Slovenes, and to send one of his sons to represent him at the ceremony in Belgrade. Before the war, tradition had dictated that the Koom at the weddings of Kings of Serbia was the Tsar of Russia; and it was a stark reminder of the grim fate which had overtaken the Tsar, as well as King Alexander I of Serbia, at whose wedding he had undertaken the same duty.

The King consulted the Foreign Office, who replied that there was no political objection; on the contrary, there would be 'some advantage to Great

Britain standing forth as the foremost supporter of a monarchical regime where this is not running counter to nationalist sentiment'.[11] He therefore accepted the invitation, and sent the Duke of York to deputize for him at the marriage on 8 June 1922.

There was, however, a threat to his security which the Foreign Office took rather lightly. At about the time the invitation was accepted, a report was received from the Secret Intelligence Service's representative in Austria of a plot, involving Hungarian, Croatian and Bulgarian Macedonian revolutionaries, to assassinate King Alexander during the wedding festivities. As neither King George nor the Prince of Wales were involved, the Foreign Office took a rather relaxed view of the threat until within two or three days of the wedding. The Assistant Commissioner of the Metropolitan Police, Scotland Yard, had received confidential information 'from a trustworthy source' that the Bulgarian-Macedonian Committee had recommended a certain Marian Kilfanski, who was in league with Serbian communists, to seditious groups in Serbia, as a suitable man for assassinating the King. As the Duke of York would be very close to him throughout the ceremonies, he would obviously be in some danger as well.

Fortunately, memories of the near-catastrophe at Madrid in May 1906, and the assassination at Sarajevo eight years later, loomed large in the authorities' minds, and they took their security duties as seriously as circumstances permitted. Another British observer reported to the Foreign Office that the small crowds on the wedding day were probably due to a heavy police presence and massive security precautions.

As representative of the 'Koom', the principal figure in the ceremony after the bridal couple, the Duke was received in great state and rode in the procession immediately before the bridegroom's carriage. The Irish horse from the Serbian royal stables which he was lent to ride proved rather restive, and his expert horsemanship in keeping the animal under control delighted onlookers as much as his observance of the custom of scattering handfuls of silver coins to the children, in answer to the traditional cry of 'O Koom, your purse is burning.'

While at Belgrade, the Duke of York made the acquaintance of several relations for the first time. He had already met King Alexander in London in 1916, while he was Regent for his elderly father King Peter (who had died in 1921), and was on friendly terms with the King's cousin, the cultivated Anglophile Prince Paul of Serbia, and several members of the Greek royal family, among them Prince George, later King George II. Most of the others, however, had been strangers to him until now.

Four months later, the Duke was back in the Balkans. Queen Marie and King Ferdinand had decided to celebrate the creation of Greater Roumania with a Coronation. As a result of the Peace Settlement of 1919, Roumania had received large tracts of former Austro-Hungarian territory. King George V wanted to evade the invitation on the grounds of expense, but the Foreign Office was so keen for him to be represented that it offered to pay if the Duke of York could go.

On 12 October 1922 the Duke arrived at the Roumanian royal castle at Sinaia, to join a party including Queen Marie's youngest sister, the Infanta Beatrice of Spain, and her husband, the Infante Alfonso, Prince Paul of Serbia, and the Queen's daughter, the newly-married Queen Marie of Yugoslavia. After a weary overnight train journey to Alba Julia, Transylvania, where the Coronation was to take place in a huge purpose-built church, the Duke endured an even more demanding day, with ritual in the cathedral followed by a mock-medieval ceremony on a dais outside, stage-managed by the Queen. There was a tinsel quality about the occasion; the crown was a Paris-made copy of a sixteenth-century original, and the Queen's jewels were by Cartier.

As it was a tedious business, Lord Stamfordham was pleased to tell the King how excellently his son had done. Feeling that King George had not realized 'what an unqualified success the Duke of York was in Rumania', he pointed out that the Duke's private secretary, Colonel Waterhouse, remarked on how admirably in every way His Royal Highness had done, 'and that when once he got away "on his own" he was a different being, never failing to "rise to the occasion"', proving himself easily the most important of the foreign visitors at the Coronation.[12]

The Balkan countries were now evidently regarded by the Foreign Office as the Duke of York's 'sphere'. Soon after his marriage to Lady Elizabeth Bowes-Lyon in April the following year, King George V was asked to send a member of his family to represent him at a double function at Belgrade in October – the christening of King Alexander's son, Crown Prince Peter, followed by the wedding of his uncle, Prince Paul of Serbia, the following day. Mildly irritated by Queen Marie's repeated requests for support, the King was prepared to decline the invitation, but the Foreign Office decided otherwise.

The Duke and Duchess of York were preparing for a family holiday at Holwick Hall, a property of the Strathmore family, in County Durham. Aware that they had been suggested as godparents to the baby Prince, the Duke was relieved when his father did not insist that he should go, and exasperated when the Foreign Secretary, Lord Curzon, suddenly changed his mind. The King telegraphed rather apologetically from Balmoral on 23 September, asking his son if he and the Duchess could leave for Belgrade almost at once. 'Curzon should be drowned for giving me such short notice', was the Duke's reaction.

Leaving London for Belgrade on 18 October, the Duke and Duchess made their first trip abroad as a married couple to the splendour of Balkan royal pageantry. 'We were quite a large family party & how we all lived in the Palace is a mystery', the Duke wrote to his father. 'We were not too comfortable & there was no hot water!!'[13]

Rather to his surprise, in accordance with custom, at the christening the Duke of York received a set of hand-embroidered underwear from the child's parents, in exchange for the traditional Koom's gift of a gold coin. The Duke was given charge of the baby, which he had to carry on a cushion, for most of the service. When the elderly Patriarch of the Serbian Orthodox Church had to take hold of the Prince for total immersion, he lost control and dropped him completely in the font. The Duke had to retrieve him hastily and hand him back, screaming fiercely, to the shaking clergyman.

To his father, he wrote: 'You can imagine what I felt like carrying the baby on a cushion. It screamed most of the time which drowned the singing & the service altogether. It was made as short as possible, which was lucky & the chapel was of course over-heated as they were frightened of the baby catching cold.'[14]

The Duke and Duchess of York

Royal group at the christening of Crown Prince Peter of Yugoslavia, October 1923. Left to right: King Alexander; Queen Elisabeth of the Hellenes; Queen Marie of Roumania (seated, holding her baby grandson); King Ferdinand of Roumania; the Duchess and Duke of York

The Duke was to take his responsibilities to this young godson very seriously in the years ahead. In due course King Peter of Yugoslavia, as he was to become, would be grateful for the steadfast support of the man destined to become King George VI of Great Britain.

On the next day, the marriage of Prince Paul of Serbia and Princess Olga of Greece was solemnized by the Patriarch. After the ceremony, the royal relations watched the bride carry out the traditional Serbian wedding custom of stepping over a strip of cloth, symbolizing the moat of her husband's house, scattering corn, and kissing a baby boy, in this case the newly-christened Crown Prince Peter. 'Cousin Missy as usual was in great form', the Duke wrote back to his father, noting also that the widowed Queen Sophie of Greece had 'aged a great deal, poor lady, after all she has been through'. Apart from the bride and groom, the Duchess of York had met none of the Balkan royalty before, but she was a great success. 'They were all enchanted with Elizabeth, especially Cousin Missy. She was wonderful with all of them & they were all strangers except two Paul & Olga.'[15]

After meeting the Duchess of York for the first time, Queen Marie of Roumania thought her 'one of the dearest, sweetest, most gentle . . . and most agreeable women I have ever met'.

Four months earlier, Crown Prince Gustav Adolf of Sweden had come to London for the summer season. It was three years since the Crown Princess had died suddenly, following complications from an inflammation of the eyes and erysipelas, leaving him with five young children. Because of his close relationship with the royal family, he was invited to Ascot, and to various weekend parties. It was noticed that he appeared very fond of Louise Mountbatten, younger sister of Princess Andrew of Greece, and George, Marquis of Milford Haven.

At the age of thirty-three, the tall, angular and rather plain Louise had virtually given up thoughts of marriage. She never regretted having turned down the chance of becoming the last Queen of Portugal, and was reputed to have told friends and family that she would never marry a King or a widower. Although attracted to Crown Prince Gustav Adolf from the start, she dreaded the consequences, and hated the thought of leaving England. However, within a few weeks she accepted his proposal, and on 3 November 1923 they were married at the Chapel Royal, St James's.

Early the following summer, Queen Marie of Roumania returned to England, this time with King Ferdinand, as official guests of state. On her previous visit in 1919, she had been free to move around virtually as she pleased. This time, their days were filled with presentations and receptions, including laying the traditional wreath on the tomb of the unknown soldier, and the Lord Mayor's banquet, and attending the Wembley Empire Exhibition. There was a traditional state dinner for one hundred and fifty guests at Buckingham Palace, and a reciprocal dinner and concert later at the Roumanian Embassy. Queen Marie was concerned that the music might be 'one degree too classical' for her rather philistine cousin, and she hastily arranged to have the programme shortened.

At a court ball given in honour of King Ferdinand and Queen Marie, the latter was filled with sympathy for Queen Mary, and all that she evidently had to put up with in her marriage. It was customary for all members of royalty to sit on a dais, and King George insisted that nobody could step down except to dance. Although Queen Marie had given up dancing since the death of her infant son, Prince Mircea, in 1917, she tried once or twice to leave so she could speak to friends. Every time she was brought a stern message from the King by a gentleman-in-waiting that if she wished to speak to someone, he or she could be brought up to where she was sitting.

Frustrated at such excessive formality, Queen Marie revised her opinion of Queen Mary, whom she had previously found too unnatural and stiff. She now saw the real reason; 'May does not dare budge. George is a real tyrant & stickler at form like his father, but without his father's renowned ease of manner.'[16]

She was still much impressed by the Prince of Wales, who looked extraordinarily youthful for his thirty years, although she perceived something of the rebellious spirit inside; 'later if he goes it too hard, his eyes will get tired, the bloom will fade, but for the moment he is "le Prince Charmant" . . . '.

Queen Marie herself did not attract unanimous praise. The American-born diarist 'Chips' Channon was scathing about her Moroccan caftan, embroidered

King George V and Queen Mary, with King Ferdinand and Queen Marie of Roumania, 1924

in silver and made for the occasion. He thought she looked 'ridiculous' in a 'green sea-foam crêpe-de-chine saut-de-lit [dressing gown] spotted with goldfish she had painted on herself. Her double chins were kept in place by strands of pearls attached to an exotic headdress.' At nearly fifty years of age, the Queen was no longer the slim young woman of earlier days, and her more picturesque gowns may have looked conventional enough in the Balkans, but at the court of St James and Buckingham Palace she appeared oddly out of place. She was magnanimous enough to admit that Queen Mary, who refrained from dressing in anything but the most conventional clothes in order not to offend the King's sense of propriety, had 'magnificent and monumental' style.

After the Dowager Tsarina's return to Denmark, she and Queen Alexandra never saw each other again. Such vague plans as the Queen may have had for visiting her younger sister were frustrated by old age, for she was too frail to travel abroad. Her last years were clouded by increasing deafness, failing eyesight, and above all by the unhappy turn of events in Greece. On 19 November 1925, after declining for several months, she suffered a massive heart attack at Sandringham and died the following day.

Queen Sophie had always had fond memories of her aunt, and valued her support. She wrote the King a heartfelt note of condolence (23 November):

Queen Alexandra's funeral procession, London, 27 November 1925. Includes, left to right: King George V; Prince of Wales; King Haakon VII of Norway; King Christian X of Denmark; King Albert of the Belgians; Crown Prince Olav of Norway; Crown Prince Carol of Roumania; Albert, Duke of York

Your adorable mother – had always been so sweet & kind to me – ever since my childhood – this I shall never forget! I loved & admired her from all my heart. She leaves a terrible blank behind her – I know the pain – of that awful silence!!! Now she is happy and at peace – with her & our beloved ones -- after having been loved – like few others. I trust she did not suffer.[17]

Because of severe weather, the Dowager Tsarina was dissuaded from crossing the North Sea to attend her sister's funeral. The remaining crowned heads of Europe attended, or sent representatives to, the last rites. Yet the modest procession which followed her coffin on a mournful winter's day was in stark contrast to the splendid cavalcade of royal and imperial power on the day her husband had been buried some fifteen years earlier.

11 'Such touching loyalty'

Sir Frederick Ponsonby's removal of the Empress Frederick's correspondence from Friedrichshof in February 1901* was destined to have controversial consequences some twenty-seven years later.

In September 1888, at the height of her persecution by the ruling clique at Berlin, the Empress had requested the temporary return of correspondence with her mother from the Royal Archives at Windsor. She planned to edit and publish it within her lifetime as a vindication of her husband and herself, and drafted a memorandum to this effect. Her work was cut short by illness, and when she realized she would not live long enough to finish the task, it was to her trusted godson Ponsonby, on his last visit to Friedrichshof, that she had turned in order to make sure the papers went back to England.

Ever since that evening in February 1901, he had understood that she intended the letters to be published. By 1927 a stream of biographies and reminiscences – including those of Chancellor Bismarck, two volumes of the former Emperor William's memoirs, and most of all a biography of the Emperor by Emil Ludwig, based on official German state documents – virtually forced his hand. While Ludwig's book was hardly flattering towards the Emperor William, it painted an even more damning portrait of his mother, who it stated had 'cherished in her heart a secret grudge against her misshapen son', 'regarded her husband's blood as less illustrious than her father's', and had so mistrusted German doctors that, when Crown Prince Frederick William was seriously ill in 1887, insisted on summoning a British doctor to manage the case. German medical circles had been too proud to admit that Dr (later Sir) Morell Mackenzie was the foremost European laryngologist of his day; and that they were saving face by summoning a doctor from abroad, since if the Crown Prince should die, they would be exonerated from all blame.

Irritated at this distorted portrait of the Empress, Ponsonby was determined that the truth should be suppressed no longer.

When he asked King George V as to whether publication would meet with court approval or not, the sovereign said he was opposed to the idea in principle. He recommended that Ponsonby should consult the Empress's surviving brother and sisters, the Duke of Connaught, Princess Louise, Duchess of Argyll, and Princess Beatrice. Only the latter had her doubts. A shy, retiring woman, who had naturally sympathized with her unhappy eldest sister, she regarded all family correspondence as strictly private, and she shrank from the idea of old

---

* See above, p. 3.

wounds being opened up in public. The more ebullient Duke and Duchess, however, agreed wholeheartedly with Ponsonby's idea. At this, the King withdrew his qualified opposition and said he neither approved nor disapproved; Ponsonby must act as he thought was best.

Examining the correspondence carefully, he found that there were sixty volumes, each containing around four hundred pages. After reading through them carefully for nearly a year, he invoked the aid of his confidential typist. On the recommendation of the publisher, Sir Frederick Macmillan, he also engaged Sidney Markham, who had completed the official two-volume biography of King Edward VII which Sir Sidney Lee had left unfinished on his death. Markham assisted him in finding corroborative material from published works, and assisted him with the running commentary between the selections of letters. The result, *Letters of the Empress Frederick*, was published in October 1928.

The book received enthusiastic reviews in the press, and sold very well. Because of its references to Emperor William, it attracted considerable news coverage.

The royal family were oddly divided on the subject. While the King expressed cautious interest at first, he was easily swayed by his sister Princess Victoria, a sharp-tongued spinster only too ready to find fault with everything. She called it 'one of the most dreadful books ever published', and he then joined in the criticism, although with less conviction. Queen Mary told Ponsonby that, while he was justified in publishing the letters, he should have been more selective. Princess Beatrice did not read the book, but only the extracts in the papers, and said she too thought it was 'dreadful'.

Among Ponsonby's supporters were the Duchess of Argyll, who wrote him 'a charming letter of approval', and the Duke of Connaught, who wrote at great length to say that he was undoubtedly right in publishing the letters. The Emperor had already offered his version of events, and Emil Ludwig's biography 'would form history unless contradicted'. He, too, had always believed that his sister meant the letters to be published. So had the Empress's two youngest surviving daughters, Queen Sophie of the Hellenes and Princess Frederick Charles, Landgrave of Hesse. They thanked him for carrying out their mother's wishes, the Landgravine signing herself, 'Yours gratefully and sincerely, Margaret'.

Ponsonby had been courteous – and rash – enough to inform the German Emperor in advance. Not surprisingly, he was determined to prevent publication, and informed Ponsonby in writing that, as the letters belonged to him as his mother's heir, he had no right to publish; and that it was his duty to return them to him as it was too soon for their publication. The clandestine removal of the correspondence, he insisted, was theft, and if necessary he would place the matter in the hands of a lawyer versed in international publication law.

Knowing better than to argue with the Emperor, Ponsonby merely acknowledged the receipt of this message. Herr von Kleist, the Minister in charge of all matters relating to the royal family in Berlin, replied on the legal position, saying that in giving him her letters the Empress had not handed over the copyright, which still remained the property of the Emperor. He then appealed to Ponsonby to withdraw the book on the grounds that publication would be detrimental to the royal family.

Sir Frederick Macmillan next consulted with a lawyer, who ruled that the ink and paper belonged to the person to whom the letters were addressed, but the copyright belonged to the person who wrote the letters. This went some way towards validating the Emperor's claim that he owned the copyright. However, this had belonged to the Empress at the time, and as it was arguable that she had conferred on Ponsonby the deed of gift when she asked him to take them back to England, the Emperor would have to prove that the copyright had not been transferred at the same time.

Ponsonby replied to Herr Kleist that his right to publish the letters was undeniable, and on sentimental grounds he maintained that, as he was selected by the Empress as a person in whom she could trust implicitly to carry out her dying wishes, he could not betray that trust. The Emperor next employed an eminent KC with instructions to bring an injunction against Ponsonby, but as he could not prove that there was no deed of gift, his efforts were in vain.

After the book's appearance, Emil Ludwig wrote an article in the *Observer*, in which he took back his views on the character of the Empress as expressed in his book, and admitted that he would have made substantial changes in his text if the book had been available earlier. He asked why it had not been published sooner. Ponsonby's reply was published in *The Times*.* He admitted that he had hesitated to publish them at first, but he had been virtually forced into doing so by the Emperor's and Ludwig's own books. He also gave an account of the Emperor's efforts to prevent publication, asked why he had never made any attempt to defend his mother, and why nobody in Germany had stood up for her when slanderous attacks were made on her memory.[1]

Having failed to prevent the book from appearing, the Emperor conceded defeat and purchased the German publication rights on condition that he would be allowed to write the preface. In doing so he performed a masterly act of self-vindication, his preface presenting a creditable if not fully understanding insight into his mother's character:

> She had always been prone to speak hastily and put down words on paper without thinking. She now saw everything in the worst possible light and read coldness and indifference into a silence really caused by inability to help. Such was her temperament that she had to lash out in all directions. She surpassed most of her contemporaries in intelligence and good intentions, yet was the most wretched and unfortunate woman ever to wear a crown.[2]

The Empress's former Lord Chamberlain, Count Reischach, regretted that Ponsonby had seen fit to publish the letters. 'In the eyes of many Germans he has done the Empress harm', he wrote to Lord Stamfordham (12 July 1929). 'I don't think so; but they were not intended for publication – one can write

---

* He had been asked for an answer by the *Observer*, but was in bed with influenza at the time and unable to meet the editor's deadline.

everything to a Mother. How wise are the Queen's answers: she was not so exceptional as her daughter, nor so cultured, but she had much more understanding of life.'³ While not inclined to disagree, Stamfordham replied (21 July) that 'on the other hand perhaps it gave Germans, who had never understood her, a better idea of the Empress'.⁴ That Emil Ludwig had found it necessary to re-evaluate his opinions was surely proof enough.

The death of Queen Alexandra in November 1925 had left the Dowager Tsarina in a state of shock. When she recovered from the grief of losing her favourite sister, it was said by those close to her that she had the air of someone who had lost her way in a wilderness. Aged and enfeebled, her zest for life was gone. In October 1928 she fell into a coma. Grand Duchess Xenia came from England to be with her and Olga at Hvidore, and the sisters kept a vigil for three days and nights while she passed from unconsciousness into her final sleep. Like her elder sister, she died within a few weeks of what would have been her eighty-first birthday.

A couple of days after the state funeral at Roskilde Cathedral, King Christian X called on Grand Duchess Olga to ask if her mother's jewellery was still at Hvidore. Astonished that he should raise the issue at such a sensitive time, she told him that she did not know for certain. She thought the box of jewels was on its way to London.

Grand Duchesses Olga and Xenia of Russia at Hvidore, in mourning for their mother, 1928

What had happened was that Sir Frederick Ponsonby, on the instructions of King George V, had sent Sir Peter Bark to go and meet the Grand Duchesses at Copenhagen. They were convinced that the jewels should be kept in a bank-safe in London until the sisters had decided what should be done with them. Evidently King Christian was not to be trusted. However, Xenia took it on herself to arrange matters, and dealt with Bark herself. Olga, who was given to understand that the matter could not concern her closely as she had married a commoner, was not informed until the box was on its way across the North Sea. Not surprisingly, she was greatly upset at this high-handed treatment, and the matter caused a rift between the sisters which was never healed. The jewels were sold in London the following year, with proceeds being divided between them.[5]

During the last years of King George's reign, the inter-monarchical contacts with his European counterparts were few and far between. On the whole, they were restricted to ceremonial occasions, family weddings, funerals, and the like.

With his aversion to travel and increasingly poor health, the King was glad not to be obliged to maintain the kind of programme which his father had carried out. He could delegate such duties as there were to his sons, while well aware that Britain's economic problems in the 1920s necessitated restricting the acceptance of such invitations on the grounds of expense.

Queen Ena of Spain was a regular visitor to Britain. Her marriage to King Alfonso, while not quite so explosive as the bomb attack which had nearly claimed their lives on their wedding day, had not been a success. They had had six children; while both daughters were healthy enough, two of their four sons suffered from the hereditary taint of haemophilia. The King was bitterly disappointed, claiming angrily in private that he had not been warned of the risks inherent in marrying a granddaughter of Queen Victoria. A restless, mercurial man by nature, he sought feminine company elsewhere, and within a few years, theirs was little more than a marriage in name.

One cross which Queen Ena found particularly hard to bear was the cruel behaviour of her cousin, the Infanta of Orleans. The former Princess Beatrice of Edinburgh had theoretically been a candidate for King Alfonso's hand when he visited England in 1905. Four years later she married the King's cousin and namesake, the Infante Alfonso, and settled in Madrid. A lively, flirtatious woman with a streak of jealousy and selfishness, very different in character from Queen Ena, she had never forgiven her cousin for winning the King instead of her. As King Alfonso and his wife drifted further apart, he too regretted not having married the Princess who would have almost certainly produced healthy children.* While it is doubtful whether the Infanta became King Alfonso's lover, she certainly enjoyed his confidence, and although she

---

* All of the Duke and Duchess of Edinburgh's daughters gave birth to children, and none were haemophiliacs. One of Queen Ena's three brothers, Prince Leopold, suffered from haemophilia, and died at the age of thirty-three.

pretended to be the Queen's trusted friend, she was instrumental in helping the King's cronies to obtain mistresses for him. Although the Queen Mother's relations with her daughter-in-law were distant, she was so disgusted at the Infanta's behaviour and intrigue that she ordered her to leave the country.

While Queen Ena did her best to identify herself with her husband's country on public occasions, in private she never hid her preference for all things English. English ideas on hygiene, diet and an early bed for her children held sway in the nursery, much to the irritation of her mother-in-law, and Christmas was always celebrated in the English manner with a decorated tree, dinner and plum pudding sent out by her mother, Princess Beatrice. In many of her letters to Queen Mary, she thanked her for sending bull's-eyes from Balmoral – although, to her chagrin, the rest of the family often helped themselves first.

She was particularly proud of her eldest son, named Alfonso after his father. 'I think you would approve of him,' she wrote to King George V (17 November 1918), 'as he looks absolutely English & English characteristics come out in him more & more.'[6]

As the years passed, she increasingly sought solace in visits to her mother's country, which always remained 'home'. She would be met by the Spanish Ambassador at Dover, and at Victoria Station by a member of the royal family, often King George V himself. In London she spent her time shopping, visiting friends, going to the theatre, and giving luncheon parties at Claridge's. Sometimes King Alfonso came too, but he generally returned to Spain first, leaving her to stay with Princess Beatrice at Kensington Palace, 'far nicer for me than remaining alone at the hotel'. It was always with regret that she took leave of her elderly mother, exchanging the comparative freedom and security of her native land for the formality and uncertainties of life in Spain, where she found the heat 'fearful', and regularly suffered from hay fever.

In January 1931 she had a telephone call from London to tell her that Princess Beatrice was seriously ill. She had broken her arm in a fall at Kensington Palace and then developed bronchial trouble. It was doubtful whether she would survive for more than a few days. Queen Ena came to England as soon as she could. Her mother recovered, but it was a slow and painful convalescence, and she had to spend several weeks by her bedside, and did not return to Spain until February.

While she was away, the political situation in Spain took a turn for the worse. In 1923 King Alfonso had suspended parliamentary government and appointed General Primo de Rivera to head a military dictatorship. On his death in 1930 another dictator was appointed, with the task of preparing Spain for immediate elections. Although Queen Ena was given an emotional welcome as she returned to Spain, it was an illusion. Convinced that the election results would be favourable, King Alfonso went to England for a short holiday in March. The elections, on 12 April, gave the Monarchist parties a majority, but the Republicans polled far better than they had expected. Demonstrations of crowds, calling '*Viva la Republica!*' and waving red flags, convinced the King that he could not allow a state of civil war to develop. He declared that he would leave Spain for a while, without formally abdicating. None the less, his departure from the kingdom was regarded as an act of abdication. He spent his last years in exile; separated from Queen Ena, he died in Rome in 1941.

The early 1930s were sad years for several members of European royalty. 'Post-war Europe is a very different place from the easy-going Old World,' the Canadian commentator Thomas Guerin observed in 1929, 'where Kings ruled by Divine Right and men spent their adolescence doing service in the army. Most of the Sovereigns are gone, and the trappings of the military caste have been put away in mothballs while their owners grow old hoping for another war. Crowns are melted down or placed in museums while waiting for a better day . . . '.[7]

In March 1924 the National Assembly in Greece had passed a resolution abolishing the monarchy and declaring the country a republic, a measure ratified by plebiscite the following year, and with the banishment of the royal family, King George II went into exile. His mother, 'poor misjudged Queen Sophie', as the Infanta Eulalia called her, had already settled in Florence.

Always a reserved character, embittered by her experiences, Queen Sophie had inherited much of her mother's personality. Those who did not know her well were inclined to have scant sympathy for her. In particular, she had little in common with her flamboyant cousin, Queen Marie of Roumania, who found her impossibly defeatist. Queen Sophie distrusted the hothouse atmosphere of the Roumanian court and the decadence of Bucharest, and had tried to caution her daughter Helen against marrying the wayward Prince Carol. It gave her no pleasure to see the marriage fall apart almost at once. Yet other members of the British colony in Florence soon found good reason to revise the unfavourable opinions they had previously formed of her. Like Beverley Nichols, they realized that she was not the scheming virago of wartime propaganda.

Despite the Allies' bullying of her husband's country, Queen Sophie never lost her affection for England. From Florence, she wrote to King George V (15 March 1928):

> You were kind enough to say to my son Georgie last year that you had no objection to my crossing to England, if I kept away from town and remained quietly in a small place. I wanted so much to ask you this once more. As I am most anxious to put my youngest daughter Katharine into school in England for the summer months at Broadstairs – and would so much like to join her there a little later, before going to Roumania. I am so homesick and dying to see dear England again. I have absolutely nothing to do with politics – have not seen William since 14 years and hardly ever hear from him – so hope I can give no offence by living quietly – and out of the world in a small place if my means permit.
>
> I am too old and sad and tired to go out in society. Journeys are so expensive and life in England especially so, I could only afford a very simple lodging. If you prefer my not seeing you I would not like to put you to any inconvenience. Else if you could meet me quietly somewhere, it would be a great joy for me to see you dears again after so many long and sad years.[8]

When King George V fell seriously ill in November 1928, the family braced themselves for the worst. For some days he hovered between life and death, and his convalescence lasted several months. With relief Queen Sophie wrote to him the following spring (17 May 1929):

I am so delighted you are well again, able to return to Windsor that I cannot refrain from sending you a line. We did pray so hard for you – God heard our prayers so I went also to the thanksgiving service – thought so much of you having followed you daily – in all your well known agonies. My Tino darling had it twice – also had *12* doctors round him. Men are rather difficult to nurse!! but still we got him through. It was the greatest joy – to see your picture in the papers again to see you up about & about [*sic*]. It all brought you, if possible, still nearer to your people who showed such touching loyalty. It was splendid.[9]

Her delight was tempered by disappointment that she was unable to visit England that summer, 'for the simple reason – I cannot afford it. I shall go to the Tyrol where the heat gets unbearable.' That January she had travelled to Doorn to visit the German Emperor William on his seventieth birthday, hoping that as fellow-exiles they could recapture the old brother-sister feelings of childhood. But he greeted her politely yet distantly, and during their conversation he never once alluded to her past sorrows or asked her about her plans for the future. They were like two strangers meeting for the first time, and she returned to Frankfurt hurt and embittered.

Three months later, on 20 April, their brother Prince Henry died after a bout of bronchitis, aggravated by pneumonia. Since the German revolution he and his family had been permitted to live peacefully on their estate at Hemmelmark, near Kiel, on condition that he undertook 'not to interfere with the government'. *The Times* noted with indulgence in his obituary that it was 'not perhaps fanciful to detect in him certain English attributes of moderation, good humour, and plain sense, while the Hohenzollern strain predominated in his elder brother'.[10] In his earnest desire for Britain and Germany to be as one up to the outbreak of the Great War, he had indeed been his parents' son. Among the first messages of condolence received by his widow was one from King George V.

Queen Sophie did not live long enough to see the restoration of the Greek monarchy. Entering hospital in Frankfurt for an operation late in 1931, it was discovered that she had cancer. She died peacefully, surrounded by her children, on 13 January 1932.

By this time another unhappy exile was nearing the end of his days. King Manuel of Portugal, claimed Prince Christopher of Greece, had grown prematurely old and saddened; failure to regain his throne had been a bitter disappointment to him.[11] His marriage had been happy, though childless. He sought solace in religion, and visited Rome regularly, staying at Prince and Princess Christopher's villa. Whenever he was there, a constant procession of cardinals and other dignitaries from the Vatican was often to be seen calling upon him.

He loved music, and was a gifted amateur pianist, although he never fulfilled his cherished ambition of conducting an orchestra. In exile he had ample time to devote himself to his collection of sixteenth-century Portuguese incunabula. Some of his happiest hours were spent in research at the British Museum library, working on a three-volume bibliography, *Early Portuguese Books, 1489–1600*. The first volume was published in 1929.

Throughout these years, King Manuel and his wife had been living at Fulwell Park largely on goodwill, while involved in lengthy negotiations with the republican Portuguese government for the release and return of his private property and of revenues from the family estates in his former kingdom, after the sums advanced to the Privy Purse and to his mother by the Treasury during his father's reign had been refunded. With King George V's encouragement, the Foreign Office did all it could to assist the exiled King, and the British Minister (and subsequently Ambassador) in Lisbon was frequently requested to intercede on his behalf. King George was kept informed of the negotiations, though his role was limited to encouragement of the Foreign Office's efforts, rather than in direct intervention.

King Manuel was abroad during the summer of 1931, largely for health reasons, and he was staying in Paris to visit an exhibition of Portuguese art, when the good news for which he had waited so long came through. To King George V he wrote (10 August):

> I have just received the good news that the Portuguese government has finally & favourably settled the question of Alter by publishing a new decree by which all my rights are recognised. There is no doubt that the resolution taken by the Portuguese government is, to *a very great extent*, due to your intervention, and I am more greatful [*sic*] than I can say to you & to May! I beg you both to accept my heartfelt thanks. Once more you have saved us![12]

Unhappily, he did not live long to enjoy the fruits of the work done on his behalf. On 1 July 1932, a few days after the publication of the second volume of his bibliography, he attended the tennis tournament at Wimbledon, returning to Fulwell Park in apparently good health. The following morning he complained of a sore throat, and visited his laryngologist in London. Returning to Twickenham, he retired to bed at one o'clock, where he was seized with an attack of breathlessness some forty minutes later. By two o'clock he was dead. He was forty-two years of age. Among the first messages of condolence to arrive was one from the King and Queen.

Queen Maud of Norway must have counted herself one of the most fortunate of contemporary European royalty. Norway was a democratic socialist state, in which republican elements had learnt to accept their new monarchy with good grace if not enthusiasm. King Haakon was the most unassuming, easily approachable of men, while Queen Maud had none of the luxury-loving characteristics of her father, or the obsession with clothes of her mother. Their unassuming demeanour and lack of extravagance immediately disarmed criticism from all but those who were most hostile to the concept of twentieth-century monarchy.

Queen Maud was frequently unwell in winter, suffering from neuralgia and intense headaches. She generally escaped the worst of the cold damp Norwegian weather by visiting England, spending six to eight weeks in her house at Appleton on the Sandringham estate in autumn. After returning to Norway for

Norwegian royal family group on Crown Prince Olav's engagement to Princess Martha of Sweden (both on right), 1928. King Haakon VII and Queen Maud are on the left

Christmas, she came back to Norfolk early in the new year. She travelled with a modest entourage, usually consisting of only a lady-in-waiting and a secretary. Much of this time in her old haunts was spent visiting her brother and sisters.

King George used to tease her unmercifully yet kindly. When told one day that she kept a special handkerchief for her spaniel, he asked her, 'Where are its galoshes?' and told her not to forget its cough drops. When at home in Norway, she kept up a lively correspondence with King George and Queen Mary, and she was the most indulgent of grandmothers when Crown Prince Olav, who had married Princess Martha of Sweden in 1929, produced a family.

After King Ferdinand of Roumania died in 1927, Queen Marie turned increasingly to her writing. Not only did it give her something with which to occupy herself during widowhood, but it also provided solace from the persecution she received at the hands of her bullying son King Carol. He was the product of a flawed upbringing, largely as a result of his grandparents' persistent interference. During his childhood his mother had been overruled at every turn, and by the time she was in a position to assert herself, the damage to her spoilt and over-indulged eldest son had been done. After his marriage to Princess Helen had broken up, he resumed his affair with a Jewish adventuress, Magda Lupescu – a move which obliged him to renounce his rights to the throne and go into exile. King Ferdinand was thus succeeded in 1927 by his five-year-old grandson Michael; but in 1930 Carol was invited back by the Roumanian government as King. Jealous of Queen Marie's reputation at home and abroad, he dismissed several of the officials in her household, forbade her to see a number of close friends, and ordered her to break off all personal relations with the cruelly-wronged Princess Helen ('Sitta'), who would have been Queen Consort but for their divorce. Security around Queen Marie was tightened, and all her private conversations were reported to the King.

As one of the few survivors of her own generation, and as a link with happier childhood days, Queen Marie found King George V a trusted confidant, especially when she wanted to ask small favours for her family. She wrote to him (23 July 1932) when her younger daughter Ileana was expecting her first child:

. . . and remembering the happy days when she was under your roof in 1919, and how kind you and May were to her then, she has asked me to write and beg you to be God-father to their child, be it a boy or a girl.

I have never written to you lately, as my life has been very difficult & very sad, so sad that it does not bear putting down in writing. I know echos have [*sic*] reached you. If ever we are to meet again in this world, I shall tell you everything, it would be a relief to let my heavy heart overflow, but written words are too weighty and I as mother can only be dumb.

I did all I could; I see everything; I thought that patience, affection might change the situation; I have struggled for over two years, swallowing every unkindness, every setback, but all in vain, there is some dark force against which all my good will shatters.

I am never allowed to lift my voice, not even to cry out 'take care!' all mother's rights are denied me, even the right of being loved.

It is all so dark, so incomprehensible that sometimes I feel that I am dreaming a night-mare from which I cannot awake.

Ileana was not allowed to have her child in my home so I came here to her. A wee little house, almost a cottage, but very pretty & excellent air – I shall do everything I can for her, but of course it is not as though she had been under my roof.

Send us a kindly word of acceptance, it will greatly cheer us up. Lately I have been living in a world which I no more understand & which has become very lonely; Ileana married, Sitta gone, Nicky banished, but I struggle on, I look beaten, but am I really beaten? I was always a good fighter you remember. But fight against one's flesh & blood?[13]

King George was deeply moved by this *cri de coeur*. It was with regret that he had to decline her invitation, but he could still offer her some words of comfort (27 July 1932):

I am greatly touched by you and Ileana wishing me to be Godfather to her baby when it is born. I suppose that the baby will of course be a Roman Catholic, and if so I fear it would be impossible for me to be a Godfather. Being a Protestant our rule is very strict, neither my father nor I have ever done so and therefore I regret that I shall not be able to accept your proposal. Otherwise I am sure you both know that I should have liked to have done so to show my affection for you both.

What a terribly sad letter yours is. In reading it the tears came into my eyes, as I fully realise all the misery you have gone through during the last two years. I have seen Sitta and George,* and they have both told me of the many cruel insults and unkindnesses which have been heaped upon you; even this last cruel act, that Ileana was forbidden to enter the country to have her baby in your house is cruel and disgraceful. I do hope that some day soon we may meet and then you will be able to pour your heart out to me and tell me all that you have gone through, as you know how deeply I sympathise with you in the impossible position in which you have been placed. I cannot help thinking that he (King Carol) is mad, certainly his actions lead one to think so and one wonders what he will do next.[14]

In the spring of 1934 Queen Marie was invited to London for the publication by Cassell of the first volume of her autobiography, *The story of my life*. By the time she arrived almost everybody she knew was reading or had read it, and she was overwhelmed by its generous critical reception.

Staying in London, she divided her time between publicity appearances, and parties with the Astors and other old friends. In Scotland she visited the royal family, and writing to an American friend she described herself and her hosts, talking about King George's 'especial affection' for her. 'I stimulate him,' she remarked, 'an uncrushable vitality makes the blood course more quickly through his veins. May feels it also. She likes being with me, and then I am never heavy on her hands. I know so perfectly how to look after myself and be happy over everything, finding interests everywhere . . . '. Wryly she commented on the difference between herself and her cousins; they were

---

* Helen's brother, King George II of the Hellenes, who was then living in London.

'scrupulously polite, but their demonstrations of pleasure or affection are always restrained and decorous. You can think, as contrast, impulsive, uncalculating, unconventional *me*. I am always astonished that they really like me, but they do!'[15]

In Scotland she also visited the Duke of York and his family. She was enchanted by the Princesses, who sang and acted out nursery rhymes for her. Princess Elizabeth was 'a quite perfect child, friendly, polite, unselfconscious, amiable & intelligent and into the bargain pretty'; while her sister Margaret was 'a replica in small and is also a delicious child'.

Also visiting England that year were the Duke and Duchess of Brunswick, whose wedding in Berlin in May 1913 had seen the last great reunion of so many members of the European imperial and royal families in their final flowering. Their daughter Frederica attended boarding school at North Foreland Lodge, near Broadstairs, Kent, and on coming to see her, the Duke and Duchess were invited to visit the King and Queen and their family at the same time.

They were introduced to the Duke and Duchess of York and their daughters, and at Kensington Palace they met 'the old aunts', Princess Louise, Duchess of Argyll, and her younger sister, Princess Beatrice. Though the latter had aged quickly, Louise at eighty-six was 'still unbelievably fresh and lively'. Though she rarely received guests, Louise made an exception for the Duchess of Brunswick, and took her on a guided tour of the palace. With great pride, the octogenarian Duchess showed her the room where 'my mother was entrusted with the Crown of England'.[16]

Shortly after they returned home, the Duke and Duchess of Brunswick were astonished to receive a message from Hitler, conveyed by his close adviser Herr von Ribbentrop. It amounted to a virtual demand that they should make arrangements for a marriage between Princess Frederica and Edward, Prince of Wales. Without hesitation they refused to give it a second thought. The difference in ages between them – twenty-three years – made such an idea look absurd, and they were determined that their children should be allowed to choose for themselves.* To the Duchess, it seemed almost incredible that her daughter should be suggested as a wife for the same Prince to whom she had been linked by similar rumours some twenty years earlier.

The idea demonstrated the German government's intention of capitalizing on the Prince of Wales' widely-known Nazi sympathies. A few months earlier Count Mensdorff, the former Austrian Ambassador in London, who was extremely well-informed about British affairs, had been astonished at how sympathetic he was towards the Nazi party, seeing them as the only bulwark in Europe against communism. At about the same time he told Prince Louis Ferdinand of Prussia, son of the former Crown Prince, that Germany's internal affairs were its own business, dictators were 'very popular these days', and that 'we might want one in England before long'.[17]

---

* Princess Frederica later married Prince Paul of the Hellenes, youngest son of King Constantine and Queen Sophie.

The Prince of Wales, 1932

Prince George, youngest surviving son of King George V

He represented a broad-based consensus of opinion in Britain and other European countries that National Socialism had achieved much in improving housing and living conditions for the working class, and reductions in unemployment, and thought that the future of the continent lay between an enfeebled, degenerate France and a newly resurgent Germany. Stories of Nazi brutality were dismissed as exaggeration or propaganda based on communist scare tactics. Needless to say, the German government attached great importance to his attitude, and successive ambassadors were instructed to cultivate him. The Prince of Wales' views were shared by, among others, Crown Prince Olav of Norway, who wrote to him in December 1935 that the only hope for a secure Europe was a close relationship between England and Germany.

King George V distrusted Nazi Germany and regarded its leaders with distaste. In 1932 he had forbidden the Prince of Wales to attend the wedding of the Crown Prince of Sweden to Princess Sibylla of Saxe-Coburg because her father, the English-born and Eton-educated Duke of Saxe-Coburg, was a fervent supporter of Hitler.

Although the relationship between the British and Greek monarchies had been soured by the Great War, their families were united when King George's youngest surviving son, also named George, announced his engagement to Princess Marina of Greece. The couple had first met in 1923, and though the Prince was immediately taken with her, she returned home before anything

Family group on Prince George's engagement, August 1934. From left: Princess Nicholas of the Hellenes; King George V; Princess Marina; Prince George; Queen Mary; Prince Nicholas of the Hellenes

could come of it. When they met again ten years later, on another visit to England, it was evident that they had eyes for nobody but each other. In August 1934 Marina's brother-in-law, Prince Paul of Yugoslavia,* acted as matchmaker by inviting Prince George to come and stay at Bohinj, his summer home in the Slovenian mountains, when the Princess was also there.

The Greek royal family had been held in low public esteem in Britain during the war, but the match was a popular one. Princess Marina had known the tribulations of living in exile with her family, and had no fortune to her name. There was undoubtedly much sympathy for her among the public, who were pleasantly surprised to find how attractive she was. Prince George told Prince Paul gleefully that, when crowds gathered to welcome her at Victoria Station in September, they expected 'a dowdy princess – such as unfortunately my family are'. When she stepped out of the carriage, they could scarcely believe their eyes, and shouted good-naturedly, 'Don't change – don't let them change you!'

At London, on 9 October, Queen Marie visited the Chelsea Flower Show and then stopped at the house of an old friend. While there, the Roumanian Ambassador rang to report that her son-in-law, King Alexander of Yugoslavia, on a visit to France, had been assassinated in Marseilles by a Macedonian terrorist. She travelled immediately to Paris to join her widowed daughter.

---

* Prince Paul of Serbia until 1929, when the Kingdom of Serbs, Croats and Slovenes was named Yugoslavia.

King Alexander's funeral cast a shadow over the wedding arrangements. The Prince and Princess joined other relatives for the obsequies in Belgrade, and there were fears that the wedding, planned for 29 November, might have to be postponed. However, the preparations were already too far advanced to do so. The King's assassination had had the effect of helping to bring everyone closer together, and there was a noticeable reopening of royal friendships which had cooled off during and after the war.

Later in October Prince George was created Duke of Kent, and the wedding was solemnized on 29 November as planned. There were two ceremonies, one at Westminster Abbey, and one according to the rites of the Greek Orthodox Church at the chapel, Buckingham Palace. Among the guests were royalty from Britain, Denmark, Greece, Yugoslavia, and the dethroned imperial houses of Germany and Russia. The latter included Grand Duke and Duchess Cyril and their son Vladimir, who acted as one of the groomsmen for the bridal couple. Aged seventeen at the time, he found there was 'something exceptionally attractive about the old King's manner'. King George was in increasingly poor health by now, but at his son's wedding he appeared to his family in better spirits than he had been for a long time.

The wedding was the first piece of royal pageantry that Britain had witnessed since the Duke of York's wedding in April 1923. It took place at a time when unemployment was at last coming down, and the country was in a mood for celebration. It was also the first royal ceremony to be broadcast by wireless on

King Alexander of Yugoslavia

the BBC, with twelve microphones placed discreetly around Westminster Abbey. It was also notable for the fastest royal procession on record. Shortly beforehand, Scotland Yard had received reports that political fanatics might attempt some form of violence, probably aimed at the life of the bride's brother-in-law, Prince Paul, Regent of Yugoslavia after his cousin's murder, scheduled to travel in the coach with her parents and King George II of the Hellenes. To forestall this, detectives made several visits to buildings on the route of the procession, checking every house, hotel and public building for incendiary devices. A massive police operation watched the crowds and traffic in London on the day itself, while the Head of Special Branch stood a few feet away from Prince Paul, and two bodyguards kept vigil at the door of the Abbey while the ceremony was in progress. To their relief, the day passed off without incident.

Queen Marie of Roumania returned to England in the spring of 1935. The second volume of her memoirs had just been published, and although reviews were less fulsome this time than last, she was invited to preside over the annual banquet of the Royal Literary Fund, the first woman to be thus honoured.

Her visit coincided with King George V's Jubilee celebrations on 6 May. She was so accustomed to the discontented Roumanian peasantry kept at bay by her son's repressive police, that she was astonished at the calm behaviour of the crowds and the good-natured London policemen. As for the King, she found there was 'something comforting, reassuring, touching about the reception the King received . . . No matter that he has no special personality, that she is stiff and sometimes conventional – they were emblems – flags – the kindly father, the benevolent mother.'[18] She also noticed with unease the continued rebellious behaviour of the Prince of Wales, whose affair with Wallis Simpson was already much talked about in society; she noticed that he 'kicks against traditions and restrictions, without realizing that tradition made him, is his raison d'être'. Her difficulties with King Carol made King George and Queen Mary more sympathetic towards her.

Queen Maud of Norway was also in England for the celebrations, and after her return to Norway wrote to Queen Mary on 30 June, 'I *loved* the enthusiasm and devotion which the people have for dear George and you, it is *so* touching – and in no other country I am sure it is like that!'[19]

The often irascible King was deeply moved by his reception. Though such a thought might never have entered the mind of this most modest of monarchs, he could have been forgiven for some measure of self-congratulation. As Winston Churchill observed a few years later, while 'great shocks and disturbances have been fated to most of the empires, monarchies and political organizations of Europe and Asia', the British monarchy stood firm, 'an achievement so remarkable [that] cannot be separated from the personality of the good, wise and truly noble King',[20] who had presided over such an eventful quarter of a century of world history.

Despite anxieties about the behaviour of the Prince of Wales, and grave concern at the behaviour of the dictators in Europe, he had mellowed with age to some extent. To his cousin Ernest, formerly Grand Duke of Hesse and the Rhine, he wrote (16 May) that 'that horrible and unnecessary war has made no difference to my feelings for you'.[21]

King George V and Queen Mary in their Silver Jubilee procession, 6 May 1935

Although she had done away with her monarchy in 1924, Greece was evidently a reluctant republic. In April 1935 the British Minister in Athens, Sir Sydney Waterlow, reported that there was increasing speculation about offering the throne to the Duke of Kent. Waterlow was quick to dismiss the possibility.

Nevertheless, another referendum later that year produced a decisive vote to restore the monarchy. King George II, who had viewed affairs in his home country from the comfort of his residence at Brown's Hotel, Piccadilly, received a deputation in November formally requesting him and his brother, Crown Prince Paul, to return. This strange reversal of fate echoed Queen Marie of Roumania's cynical remark that after people had tried out 'new theories and ideas', then 'they will return again to Monarchy, as a tired and weary wanderer returns to what he knows best and to what has best served him'.[22]

On 14 November, the day that the newly-summoned King and Crown Prince left for Greece, Britain's electors went to the polls. It was the last general election that King George V would witness. To the Prime Minister, Stanley Baldwin (who was returned as leader of the National Government, albeit with a smaller majority), the sovereign appeared to be 'packing up his luggage and getting ready to depart'. His health had deteriorated noticeably over the preceding few weeks. Increasing anxiety over the policy of the dictators in Europe, worry over the Prince of Wales' liaison with Mrs Simpson, and grief at the death of his sister Princess Victoria on 3 December, all took their toll on his declining strength. He and Queen Mary spent Christmas at Sandringham as usual, but by January 1936 he was evidently dying.

Chastened by the news of his cousin's condition, the German Emperor telegraphed a message of sympathy to Queen Mary. Touched at this first contact from him for over twenty years, she sent back a grateful reply, accompanied by a small gift. On 20 January, in the words of the King's physician, Lord Dawson, his life moved 'peacefully to its close'.

The first two Kings of twentieth-century Great Britain had witnessed a remarkable change in the shifting fortunes of European monarchy. In 1901 the Hohenzollern, Habsburg and Romanov empires held sway over a large proportion of Europe, while almost every other nation of significance was a monarchy apart from France, whose latest experiment with republicanism was barely thirty years old.

By 1936 the three empires had long since gone. So had both crowns in the Iberian peninsula, though Spain was technically a monarchy without a King, and remained thus until 1975. The Balkan and Eastern European monarchies would soon go, though Greece had only restored hers the year before. Italy's was likewise destined to survive only for another ten years. Only in the modest constitutional monarchies of the Scandinavian Kingdoms, as well as Netherlands and Belgium, did republicanism never become a potent issue.

Some of their contemporaries held both Kings in far greater veneration than the governments over which they reigned but did not rule. 'I loved Uncle Bertie and Georgie, and so many others, and they have done so much for me', Grand Duchess Olga told her biographer Ian Vorres, shortly before her death in 1960.

'But, of course, it has never been possible to discuss with them the utterly vile politics of successive British Parliaments. They were nearly all anti-Russian – and so often without the least cause.'[23]

Five Kings from the European mainland walked in King George V's funeral procession on 28 January: King Christian X of Denmark; King Haakon VII of Norway; King Carol II of Roumania; King Boris of Bulgaria; and King Leopold III of the Belgians. With them walked the new King of Britain, Edward VIII, and his brothers. Had King Edward not been so preoccupied with Mrs Simpson, for whom he was to relinquish his inheritance within eleven months, perhaps he might have reflected on how secure the throne was which his father had just bequeathed to him. Of the fellow crowned heads who walked behind him, one was destined to die in mysterious circumstances shortly before his country became a republic; two would be forced to abdicate; and the other two would have to witness the occupation of their kingdoms by Nazi Germany, although they would survive the indignity and die in office after peace was declared.

In Great Britain, the monarchy survived the storms of King Edward VIII and his determination to marry a woman with two husbands living. In November 1936, on recognizing the virtual inevitability of his abdication, his horrified heir and brother, the Duke of York, advised his assistant private secretary, Sir Godfrey Thomas, that if he had to take over he would do his best 'to clear up the inevitable mess, if the whole fabric does not crumble under the shock and strain of it all'.[24] Thanks to the sure foundations consolidated – if not laid – by his father and grandfather in a swiftly-changing world, the fabric did not crumble. By the time King George VI died in 1952, there were several former crowned heads throughout Europe who looked upon the still secure crown with a mixture of wonder, envy and admiration.

European Monarchs, 1901–36

GREAT BRITAIN
Edward VII, 1901–10
George V, 1910–36

AUSTRIA-HUNGARY
Francis Joseph, 1848–1916
Charles, 1916–18 *abdicated, died 1922*

BELGIUM
Leopold II, 1865–1909
Albert, 1909–34
Leopold III, 1934–51 *abdicated, died 1983*

BULGARIA
Ferdinand, 1887–1918 (Prince till 1908, then Tsar) *abdicated, died 1948*
Boris III, 1918–43

DENMARK
Christian IX, 1863–1906
Frederick VIII, 1906–12
Christian X, 1912–47

GERMANY
William II, 1888–1918 *abdicated, died 1941*

GREECE
George I, 1863–1913 *assassinated*
Constantine I, 1913–17 *abdicated*
Alexander, 1917–20
Constantine I (restored), 1920–2 *abdicated again, died 1923*
George II, 1922–4 *abdicated when republic declared* (restored) 1935–47

ITALY
Victor Emmanuel III, 1900–46 *abdicated, died 1947*

NETHERLANDS
Wilhelmina, 1890–1948 *abdicated, died 1962*

NORWAY[1]
Haakon VII, 1905–57

PORTUGAL
Carlos, 1889–1908 *assassinated*
Manuel II, 1908–10 *abdicated, died 1932*

ROUMANIA
Carol I, 1881–1914
Ferdinand, 1914–27
Michael, 1927–30
Carol II, 1930–40
Michael (restored), 1940–7 *abdicated*

RUSSIA
Nicholas II, 1894–1917 *abdicated, murdered 1918*

SERBIA/YUGOSLAVIA[2]
Alexander I, 1889–1903 *assassinated*
Peter I, 1903–21
Alexander II, 1921–34 (Regent 1914–21) *assassinated*
Peter II, 1934–45 *abdicated, died 1970*

SPAIN
Alfonso XIII, 1886–1931 *abdicated, died 1941*

SWEDEN
Oscar II, 1872–1907
Gustav V, 1907–50

---

[1] Norway and Sweden united under one King until 1905.
[2] Kingdom of Serbs, Croats and Slovenes proclaimed 1918, named Yugoslavia 1929.

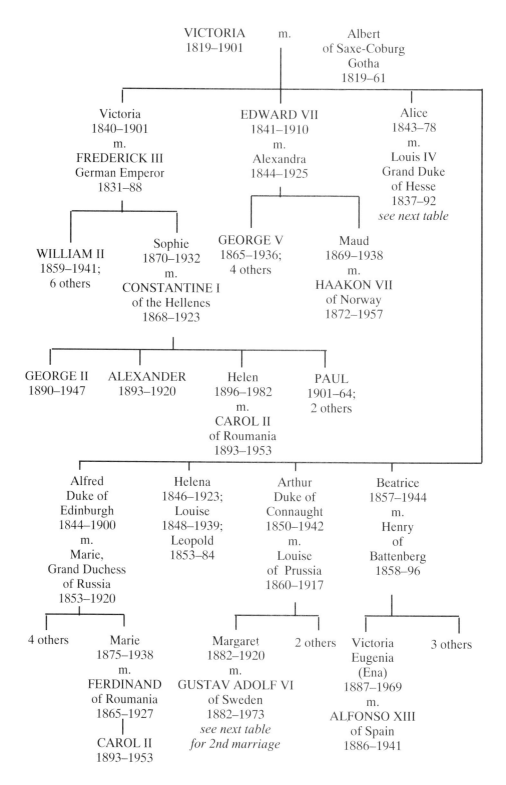

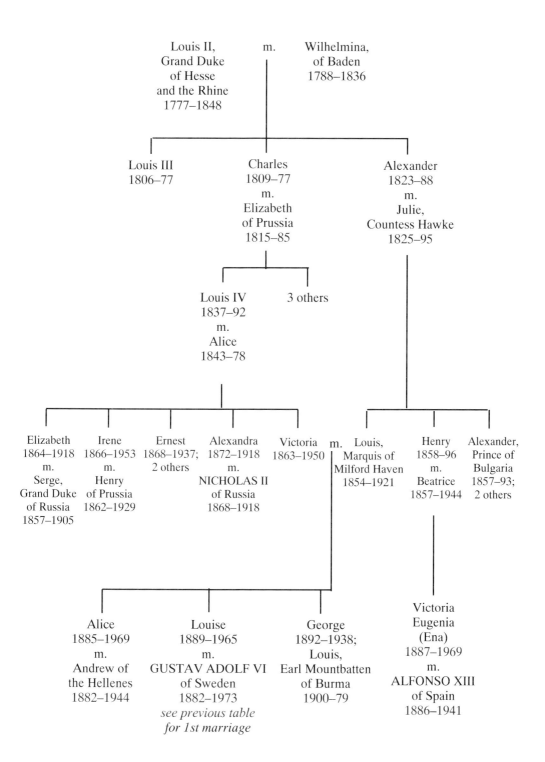

Louis II,
Grand Duke
of Hesse
and the Rhine
1777–1848

m.

Wilhelmina,
of Baden
1788–1836

Louis III
1806–77

Charles
1809–77
m.
Elizabeth
of Prussia
1815–85

Alexander
1823–88
m.
Julie,
Countess Hawke
1825–95

Louis IV
1837–92
m.
Alice
1843–78

3 others

Elizabeth
1864–1918
m.
Serge,
Grand Duke
of Russia
1857–1905

Irene
1866–1953
m.
Henry
of Prussia
1862–1929

Ernest
1868–1937;
2 others

Alexandra
1872–1918
m.
NICHOLAS II
of Russia
1868–1918

Victoria
1863–1950

m.

Louis,
Marquis of
Milford Haven
1854–1921

Henry
1858–96
m.
Beatrice
1857–1944

Alexander,
Prince of
Bulgaria
1857–93;
2 others

Alice
1885–1969
m.
Andrew of
the Hellenes
1882–1944

Louise
1889–1965
m.
GUSTAV ADOLF VI
of Sweden
1882–1973
*see previous table
for 1st marriage*

George
1892–1938;
Louis,
Earl Mountbatten
of Burma
1900–79

Victoria
Eugenia
(Ena)
1887–1969
m.
ALFONSO XIII
of Spain
1886–1941

Reference Notes

Prologue (x–xvi)

1 Bülow, *Memoirs 1897–1903*, 327

Chapter 1 (pp. 1–22)

1 Magnus 272
2 Lee ii 11
3 Reid 196
4 Ponsonby 110
5 RA F23/27
6 RA W42/11
7 RA W42/16
8 Bülow, *Memoirs 1897–1903*, 356
9 Lee ii 279
10 RA X37/37
11 RA X37/44
12 Ponsonby 128
13 RA X37/51
14 RA X37/52
15 Nicolson 77
16 Bülow, *Memoirs 1897–1903*, 549–50
17 RA W42/70
18 Ponsonby 173
19 Legge 81–2
20 Lee ii 270
21 ibid 271

Chapter 2 (pp. 23–40)

1 Van der Kiste, *Windsor and Habsburg*, 118
2 Gore 189
3 Hough 185
4 as above
5 Bolitho 212
6 Buchanan G 62–3
7 Hough 187
8 Lee ii 340

9 Brook-Shepherd, *Uncle of Europe*, 255
10 Lee ii 352
11 ibid 318
12 ibid 319
13 ibid 321
14 Magnus 346
15 Pope-Hennessy 408

Chapter 3 (pp. 41–54)

1 Gilbert 41
2 Pope-Hennessy 406
3 Rose 68
4 Nicolson 95
5 Lee ii 517
6 Pope-Hennessy 400
7 Lee ii 525
8 as above
9 ibid ii 528
10 Brook-Shepherd, *Uncle of Europe*, 256
11 Bülow, *Memoirs 1903–9*, 237–8
12 Magnus 395
13 Lee ii 557
14 ibid 559

Chapter 4 (pp. 55–75)

1 Brook-Shepherd, *Uncle of Europe*, 313
2 Magnus 401
3 Brook-Shepherd, *Uncle of Europe*, 323
4 Vorres 128
5 St Aubyn 362
6 Vorres 128
7 Magnus 400
8 ibid 401

9 Herbert 265

10 Brook-Shepherd, *Uncle of Europe*, 345

11 Windsor, Duke of 67

12 Ziegler, *Mountbatten*, 34

13 Brook-Shepherd, *Uncle of Europe*, 276

14 Lee ii 693

15 RA X37/65

16 Ponsonby 264–5

17 Brook-Shepherd, *Uncle of Europe*, 355–6

18 RA GV AA54/2

19 RA GV AA43/129

20 RA GV AA43/130

21 RA GV AA54/48

22 RA GV AA54/3

23 Blunt 722

24 Leslie 337

Chapter 5 (pp. 76–89)

1 Van der Kiste, *Princess Victoria Melita*, 99

2 Rose 162–3

3 Nicolson 217

4 Vorres 54

5 Nicolson 175

6 RA GV O69/1

7 RA GV AA43/107

8 Christopher of Greece 101

9 RA GV AA43/152

10 Victoria Louise 48

11 Hough 242–3

12 Nicolson 185

13 Crown Prince William 105

14 Nicolson 186

15 RA GV M520A/2A

16 Ponsonby 266

17 Christopher of Greece 97

Chapter 6 (pp. 90–105)

1 Constant 257

2 RA GV AA43/195

3 Pope-Hennessy 480

4 Ponsonby 297–8

5 Rose 166

6 ibid 167

7 RA GV AA43/195

8 Windsor, Duke of 98–9

9 ibid 100

10 Brook-Shepherd, *Victims at Sarajevo*, 209

11 Pope-Hennessy 483

12 William II 243

13 Nicolson 244

14 ibid 245–6

15 Pope-Hennessy 486

16 RA GV Q1549/1

17 RA GV Q1549/5

18 RA GV Q1549/8

19 RA GV Q1549/12

20 RA GV Q1549/15

21 Gore 290

22 Christopher of Greece 122

23 Vorres 131

24 Blucher 14

Chapter 7 (pp. 106–25)

1 Infanta Eulalia 110–11

2 Battiscombe 285

3 Hough 308

4 Battiscombe 284

5 *The Children's Story of the War*, Part 199; *Royalty Digest*, October 1991

6 RA GV CC45/471

7 RA GV CC45/475

8 Churchill 162

9 Battiscombe 288

10 RA GV Q1550/200

11 RA GV Q1550/22

12 RA GV Q1550/23

13 RA GV Q1550/XIX/277

14 RA GV Q1550/XIX/279

15 Wheeler-Bennett 90

16 Marie of Roumania iii 39

17 RA GV Q1550/XVII/125

18 Marie of Roumania iii 26

19 RA GV Q1550/XIX/302

20 RA GV Q1550/XIX/313

21 RA GV Q1550/XVII/135

22 Christopher 110

23 Linklater 156–7
24 Nicolson 282
25 RA GV Q1550/XIX/314
26 Nicolson 283–4
27 RA GV Q1550/88
28 RA GV Q1550/89

Chapter 8 (pp. 126–39)

 1 Battiscombe 290–1
 2 Bucharest Archives
 3 RA GV Q1550/XIX/318
 4 RA GV AA43/264
 5 Buchanan M 247
 6 Nicolson 301
 7 Rose 214
 8 RA GV CC45/531
 9 *Punch* 27.6.1917
10 Marie of Roumania iii 285
11 RA GV CC45/542
12 RA GV CC45/541
13 Marie of Roumania iii 348
14 ibid 349
15 RA GV AA43/278
16 Rose 216
17 Windsor, Duke of 129
18 RA GV AA43/281
19 RA GV AA43/282
20 Rose 229
21 RA GV AA43/288
22 Marie Louise 190
23 Aronson, *Queen Victoria and the Bonapartes*, 236

Chapter 9 (pp. 140–50)

 1 Wheeler-Bennett 120–1
 2 Bolitho 216
 3 Van der Kiste, *Edward VII's Children*, 145
 4 RA GV CC45/575
 5 Nicolson 335
 6 RA GV CC45/587
 7 RA GV Q1550/XVII/184
 8 Grand Duchess Marie 98–100
 9 Stoeckl 179
10 Gray 136–7
11 Grand Duchess Marie 102

12 Ponsonby 336
13 *The Times* 21.4.1960
14 RA GV AA43/314
15 as 14

Chapter 10 (pp. 151–66)

 1 RA GV AA35/32
 2 RA GV AA35/38
 3 RA GV AA38/34
 4 RA GV AA35/39
 5 Nichols 100
 6 ibid 114
 7 Hough 348
 8 Van der Kiste, *Princess Victoria Melita*, 138
 9 Grand Duchess Marie 100–1
10 Wheeler-Bennett 143
11 Bradford 89
12 Wheeler-Bennett 147
13 ibid 193
14 ibid 193–4
15 ibid 194
16 Pakula 329
17 RA GV AA56/92

Chapter 11 (pp. 167–90)

 1 Ponsonby 111–15
 2 Balfour 110
 3 RA GV M2530/1 (translation)
 4 RA GV M2530/2
 5 Vorres 181–3
 6 RA GV AA43/288
 7 Guerin 13
 8 RA GV AA46/185
 9 RA GV AA46/186
10 *The Times* 22.4.1929
11 Christopher of Greece 102
12 RA GV AA43/391
13 RA GV AA43/403
14 RA GV AA43/404
15 Pakula 399–400
16 Victoria Louise 187–8
17 Ziegler, *Edward VIII*, 206
18 Pakula 401
19 Van der Kiste, *Edward VII's Children*, 171

20 Churchill 249–50
21 Rose 229
22 Guerin 204

23 Vorres 237
24 Wheeler-Bennett 283

Bibliography

I MANUSCRIPTS

Royal Archives, Windsor Castle
Bucharest Archives

II BOOKS

Alice, Princess, Countess of Athlone, *For my grandchildren: some reminiscences of Her Royal Highness Princess Alice*. Evans Bros, 1966
Aronson, Theo, *Crowns in conflict: the triumph and the tragedy of European monarchy, 1910–18*. John Murray, 1986
——, *Grandmama of Europe: the crowned descendants of Queen Victoria*. Cassell, 1973
——, *Queen Victoria and the Bonapartes*. Cassell, 1972
Balfour, Michael, *The Kaiser and his times; with an afterword*. Penguin, 1975
Battiscombe, Georgina, *Queen Alexandra*. Constable, 1969
Benson, E.F., *The Kaiser and English relations*. Longman, 1936
Blucher, Evelyn, Princess, *An English wife in Berlin*. Constable, 1920
Blunt, Wilfrid Scawen, *My diaries: being a personal narrative of events, 1888–1914*. Secker, 1919
Bolitho, Hector, *My restless years*. Max Parrish, 1962
Bradford, Sarah, *King George VI*. Weidenfeld & Nicolson, 1989
Brook-Shepherd, Gordon, *Royal Sunset: the dynasties of Europe and the Great War*. Weidenfeld & Nicolson, 1987
——, *Uncle of Europe: the social and diplomatic life of Edward VII*. Collins, 1975
Buchanan, Sir George, *My mission to Russia and other diplomatic memories*, 2 vols. Cassell, 1923
Buchanan, Meriel, *Ambassador's daughter*. Cassell, 1958
Bülow, Bernhard von, *Memoirs*, 4 vols. Putnam, 1931
Christopher of Greece, Prince, *My memoirs*. Right Book Club, 1938
Churchill, Winston, *Great contemporaries*. Odhams, n.e. 1947
Connon, Bryan, *Beverley Nichols: a life*. Constable, 1991
Constant, Stephen, *Foxy Ferdinand, Tsar of Bulgaria*. Sidgwick & Jackson, 1979
Duff, David, *The shy Princess: the life of Her Royal Highness Princess Beatrice*. Evans Bros, 1958
Eulalia, Infanta of Spain, *Court life from within*. Cassell, 1915

Fjellman, Margit, *Louise Mountbatten, Queen of Sweden*. Allen & Unwin, 1968

Gilbert, Martin, *Servant of India: Sir James Dunlop Smith*. Longman, 1966

Gore, John, *King George V, a personal memoir*. John Murray, 1941

Gray, Pauline, *The Grand Duke's woman: the story of the morganatic marriage of Michael Romanoff, the Tsar Nicholas II's brother, and Nathalia Cheremtvskaya*. Macdonald & Jane's, 1976

Guerin, Thomas, *Caps and crowns of Europe*. Carrier, 1929

Herbert, Basil, *King Gustave of Sweden*. Stanley Paul, 1938

Hough, Richard, *Louis and Victoria: the first Mountbattens*. Hutchinson, 1974

Hourmouzios, Stelio, *No ordinary crown: a biography of King Paul of the Hellenes*. Weidenfeld & Nicolson, 1972

King, Stella, *Princess Marina, her life and times*. Cassell, 1969

Lee, Sir Sidney, *King Edward VII*, 2 vols. Macmillan, 1925–7

Legge, Edward, *King Edward in his true colours*. Nash, 1912

Leslie, Anita, *Edwardians in love*. Hutchinson, 1972

Linklater, Andro, *Compton Mackenzie: a life*. Chatto & Windus, 1987

Longford, Elizabeth, *Victoria R.I.* Weidenfeld & Nicolson, 1964

McNaughton, Arnold, *Kings, Queens & Crowns*. Printed privately, 1977

Magnus, Philip, *King Edward the Seventh*. John Murray, 1964

Marie, Grand Duchess of Russia, *A Princess in exile*. Cassell, 1932

Marie, Queen of Roumania, *The story of my life*, 3 vols. Cassell, 1934–5

Marie Louise, Princess, *My memories of six reigns*. Evans Bros, 1956

Massie, Robert K., *Nicholas and Alexandra*. Victor Gollancz, 1968

Muller, Georg Alexander von, *The Kaiser and his court: the Diaries, Note Books and Letters of Admiral Muller, Chief of the Naval Secretariat 1914–1918*. Macdonald, 1961

Nichols, Beverley, *25: being a young man's candid recollections of his elders and betters*. Jonathan Cape, 1926

Nicolson, Harold, *King George V, his life and reign*. Constable, 1952

Noel, Gerard, *Ena: Spain's English Queen*. Constable, 1984

Pakula, Hannah, *The last Romantic: a biography of Queen Marie of Roumania*. Weidenfeld & Nicolson, 1984

Plumb, J.H., & Wheldon, Huw, *Royal heritage: the story of Britain's royal builders and collectors*. BBC, 1977

Ponsonby, Sir Frederick, *Recollections of three reigns*. Eyre & Spottiswoode, 1951

Pope-Hennessy, James, *Queen Mary, 1867–1953*. Allen & Unwin, 1959

Reid, Michaela, *Ask Sir James: Sir James Reid, personal physician to Queen Victoria and physician-in-ordinary to three monarchs*. Hodder & Stoughton, 1987

Rose, Kenneth, *King George V*. Weidenfeld & Nicolson, 1983

St Aubyn, Giles, *Edward VII, Prince and King*. Collins, 1979

Stoeckl, Agnes de, *Not all vanity*. John Murray, 1950

Tisdall, E.E.P., *The Dowager Empress*. Stanley Paul, 1957

Van der Kiste, John, *Edward VII's children*. Alan Sutton, 1989

——, *Princess Victoria Melita, Grand Duchess Cyril of Russia, 1876–1936*. Alan Sutton, 1991

——, *Windsor and Habsburg: the British and Austrian reigning houses 1848–1922.* Alan Sutton, 1987

Victoria Louise of Prussia, Princess, *The Kaiser's daughter: Memoirs of HRH Viktoria Luise, Duchess of Brunswick and Luneburg, Princess of Prussia* (trans. and ed. Robert Vacha). W.H. Allen, 1977

Vorres, Ian, *The last Grand-Duchess: Her Imperial Highness Grand-Duchess Olga Alexandrovna.* Hutchinson, 1964

Wheeler-Bennett, John W., *King George VI, his life and reign.* Macmillan, 1958

Whittle, Tyler, *The last Kaiser: a biography of William II, German Emperor and King of Prussia.* Heinemann, 1977

William, Crown Prince of Germany, *Memoirs of the Crown Prince of Germany.* Thornton Butterworth, 1922

William II, Emperor, *My memoirs, 1878–1918.* Cassell, 1922

Windsor, Duke of, formerly King Edward VIII, *A King's story: memoirs of HRH the Duke of Windsor.* Cassell, 1951

Ziegler, Philip, *Edward VIII: the official biography.* Collins, 1990

——, *Mountbatten: the official biography.* Collins, 1985

III PERIODICALS

Journal of the Commemorative Collectors Society
Punch
Royalty Digest
The Times

Index

Abbreviations: E – King Edward VII; G – King George V; N – Nicholas II, Tsar of Russia; W – William II, German Emperor. Nicknames in brackets and familiar names (e.g. David, for King Edward VIII), are given only if used in text or quoted correspondence. Crowned heads are of Great Britain unless noted otherwise.

* Honorary title only – she married King Manuel after his abdication.